Essays On The
Montemezzi-D'Annunzio
Nave

Italo Montemezzi, 1918
Frontispiece to the score of *La Nave*

Essays On The
Montemezzi-D'Annunzio
Nave

Italo Montemezzi
Ugo Navarra
W. L. Hubbard
Adriano Lualdi
Bruno Barilli
Ildebrando Pizzetti
Guido M. Gatti
Raffaele Mellace

Edited, annotated, and introduced by
David Chandler

Translations by Monica Cuneo
Foreword by Duane D. Printz

First published by Durrant Publishing, 2012
This edition published by Durrant Publishing, 2014

Copyright © 2012–14 David Chandler
All rights reserved

Hardback   ISBN 978-1-905946-37-2
Paperback   ISBN 978-1-905946-38-9

Second Edition 2014

∞ The paper used in this publication meets the minimum requirements of the American National Standard for Information Sciences – Permanence of Paper for Printed Library Materials, ANSI Z39.48–1992. The paper is acid-free and lignin-free.

Printed and bound by Lightning Source
Published by Durrant Publishing
82 Earlham Road, Norwich, NR2 3HA

Dedicated to the memory of
Vera Ryhajlo (1962–2011)

An irreplaceable friend

Make music with your life
a
    jagged
silver tune
cuts every deepday madness
Into jewels   that you wear
                Bob O'Meally

DAVID CHANDLER is a Professor in the English Department at Doshisha University, Kyoto, having obtained his D.Phil at the University of Oxford. His published work is mostly in the field of English literature, but in addition to the present book he has also edited *Alfredo Catalani: Composer of Lucca* (2010), *The First Lives of Alfredo Catalani* (2011) and *Americans on Italo Montemezzi* (2014), and published a number of articles and reviews on musical theatre in various journals.
His website is at: http://www.davidjchandler.co.uk/

MONICA CUNEO is a professional Italian viola player based in Oxford. She studied viola and baroque performance practice at the 'G. Verdi' Conservatory of Music in Milan, and has performed extensively with many symphony and opera house orchestras in different parts of Italy, as well as in chamber groups, and as a soloist. She has developed a parallel career as a translator, and has translated the violist William Primrose's autobiography and three books by the violinist Kato Havas on the prevention and elimination of physical injuries and performance anxiety related to string playing into Italian.
Her website is at: http://www.monicacuneo.com/

RAFFAELE MELLACE is an Associate Professor of Musicology and the History of Music at the University of Genoa, having obtained his PhD in Musicology at the University of Bologna. He has wide-ranging interests in opera, church music, and the relationship between music and literature, and as well as publishing many articles and programme notes he is the author of four books: *Johann Adolf Hasse* (2004), *L'autunno del Metastasio* (2007), *Johann Sebastian Bach. Le cantate* (2012) and *Giuseppe Verdi* (2012).
His website is at: http://www.diras.unige.it/docenti/mellace.php

DUANE D. PRINTZ is the Artistic Director of Teatro Grattacielo, a company she founded in 1994 with a view to reviving the neglected operas of the verismo era. She studied at the Manhattan School of Music and the Accademia di Santa Cecilia in Rome, and has sung in many opera and concert productions in the U.S. and Italy. She has been on the voice faculties of the 92nd Street Y and the H.E.S. Music School in Brooklyn, and has also worked in the world of international finance.
The Teatro Grattacielo website is at: http://www.grattacielo.org/

Contents

Foreword by Duane D. Printz xi
Acknowledgements xv
List of Illustrations xx

General Introduction 1
   Summary of the Montemezzi–D'Annunzio *Nave* 26
   Note on the Texts 30

Part One: Composing and Staging *La Nave* 31
   1. Vincenzo Bucci
      Emporium, October 1918 33
   2. Italo Montemezzi
      Scenario, April 1938 45

Part Two: First Production, Milan 53
   Introduction 55
   1. Unsigned review attributed to **Renato Simoni**
      Corriere della Sera, 4 November 1918 71
   2. Gaetano Cesari
      Il Secolo: Gazzetta di Milano, 4 November 1918 75
   3. Guido Podrecca
      Il Popolo d'Italia, 4 November 1918 83
   4. G. B. Nappi
      La Perseveranza, 5 November 1918 93
   5. Carlo Gatti
      L'Illustrazione Italiana, 10 November 1918 103
   6. Ugo Navarra
      Corriere di Milano, 19 November, 3 December 1918 . . 107
   7. Giacomo Orefice
      Rivista d'Italia, 30 November 1918 125

Part Three: Second Production, Chicago 131
Introduction 133
1. **Karleton Hackett**
   Chicago Evening Post, 19 November 1919 147
2. **Paul T. Gilbert**
   Chicago Evening Post, 19 November 1919 153
3. **Herman Devries**
   Chicago American, 19 November 1919 159
4. **Edward C. Moore**
   Chicago Daily Journal, 19 November 1919 163
5. Unsigned review attributed to **Florence French**
   Musical Leader, 20 November 1919 171
6. Unsigned review attributed to **Jeannette Cox**
   Musical Courier, 20 November 1919 177
7. **William L. Hubbard**
   Chicago Sunday Tribune, 23 November 1919 183
8. **Maurice Rosenfeld**
   Musical America, 29 November 1919 189

Part Four: Third Production, Verona 191
Introduction 193
1. **Giovanni Bertolaso**
   L'Arena, 9 March 1923 197

Part Five: Fourth Production, Rome 203
Introduction 205
1. **Alceo Toni**
   Il Popolo d'Italia, 15 December 1938 225
2. **Adriano Lualdi**
   Il Giornale d'Italia, 16 December 1938 233
3. **Augusto Righetti**
   Il Tevere, 15–16 December 1938 241
4. **Matteo Incagliati**
   Il Messaggero, 15 December 1938 247

5. Bruno Barilli
   Omnibus, 24 December 1938..................253
6. Ildebrando Pizzetti
   La Tribuna, 16 December 1938................257
7. s.s.
   La Stampa, 15 December 1938................265

Part Six: Fifth Production, New York...................271
Introduction 273
1. Peter G. Davis
   MusicalAmerica.com, 5 November 2012..........275
2. Dan Foley
   MusicalCriticism.com, 9 December 2012..........279

Part Seven: Other Criticism, 1924–2008...............285
Introduction 287
1. Guido M. Gatti, extract from
   Musical Quarterly, April 1924..................295
2. Luciano Tomelleri, extract from
   Gabriele D'Annunzio and Music, 1939............301
3. Raffaele Mellace
   Chigiana, 2008...............................309

Foreword to the Second Edition
by Duane D. Printz

HOW MARVELLOUS to have this opportunity to write a Foreword to the second edition of this wonderful book about *La Nave*. The very fact that there *is* a second edition certainly bodes well for our shared aspirations to focus interest on Montemezzi and this neglected period of Italian opera, which we hope will soon be better represented in opera houses around the world.

The first time I heard *La Nave* was with my accompanist, Mark Cogley. I knew immediately that it was a magnificent score even though the piano can hardly give an idea of the full scope of the orchestration. Montemezzi was a brilliant orchestrator and knew every 'colour' in his palette. His control of those musical colours and ability to express so completely those 'musical' pictures are unparalleled: the seabirds chirping, the sunlight glinting on the waves of the lagoon – they are all there! And what a story! The whole range of human emotions is contained in D'Annunzio's play – from love to hatred, lust to murder, religious pomp and grandeur to the basest human emotions, the grotesque to the magnificent. In sum, the entire spectrum of human experience from degradation to renewal and finally to transcendence; and Montemezzi captures it all on every page.

I also knew at that first hearing that *La Nave* would be the most difficult opera I had ever produced because of the large forces required to bring it to life – large cast, large orchestra, and the extremely difficult choruses, sometimes divided into sixteen parts and all male voices which would mean a very large chorus, too. Exactly how difficult the production would prove, though, was something I never imagined in my wildest dreams!

Undaunted, however, we proceeded. I was able to find exactly the singers I was looking for: Tiffany Abban had the perfect voice for Basiliola, a large, luscious dramatic soprano with powerful high notes; Robert Brubaker had the experience and heft to get through the extremely demanding tenor lead; and Daniel Ihn-Kyu Lee was perfect for the Bishop Sergio. By doubling some of the smaller parts and having some of those smaller parts cover other singers, I was able to get the cast down to just under 20 singers. In order to facilitate the choruses, I decided to hire the Dessoff Choirs numbering 96 singers for the large choruses supplemented by a professional group of 18 singers for some of the smaller men's choruses. Then there were the dancers who appear in the 'orgy' scene in the Second Episode. I chose the I Giullari di Piazza who had performed with us in our 2010 production of *I Gioielli della Madonna* to such great effect.

Everything seemed to be moving along swimmingly, but as the date for the rehearsals approached, there were rumblings in the Caribbean! Still, though, it seemed far removed from New York and we began the rehearsals with singers and piano, then added the orchestra. Finally we all realized what we had perhaps not been fully aware of before – this was a magnificent work and we were probably the only people in the world who had heard it! It was so exciting hearing everything finally come together.

A few days later, on the Saturday before the Monday performance, as we went through the dress rehearsal, everyone was somewhat concerned about the approaching storm, now known to us all as Hurricane Sandy, but at that point it still seemed likely that it would turn inland around Virginia and we would escape it. Many members of the orchestra asked me to cancel the performance, but that was not possible. Unless the Rose Theater closed, we would have to go ahead. If we cancelled and they remained open, we would lose our rental fees and would have to rebook another date and pay for it all over again – almost another $25,000.

The next day, Sunday, we had scheduled an evening book-signing party and talk for the first edition of David Chandler's book about *La Nave*. This was at the beautiful home of Elizabeth and Lewis Bryden. As the day progressed, it looked more and more likely that the storm was not turning and was headed directly for New York. As David and I left the party that evening, it was totally surreal: the streets were completely empty, it was foggy, and the air was heavy with moisture giving everything a decidedly dreamlike atmosphere. I raced home to phone the theater again, since they had still not decided whether or not to close the next day.

Finally, around 11:00 p.m. that night the management at the Rose Theater phoned to say they had decided to close. So the next morning, the day of our performance, I began phoning everyone around 8:30 a.m. I would be on the phone until almost 1:00, but I finally got in touch with everybody to cancel our performance. I had several singers who were scheduled to fly out on Tuesday, but, thankfully, the airports were closed at least for a few days so I had a small window of opportunity to rescue the situation. That night, as the storm hit, I stayed up until 2:30 doing the payroll. It still wasn't apparent how dire the situation would become.

The next day, the news was not good, especially in lower Manhattan and the surrounding low areas where the storm surge had destroyed huge swathes of homes and businesses. I began phoning the theater that morning, but the staff had not yet been able to get in to determine if there had been any damage or not. I phoned everyone again to see what their travel plans were and it seemed our only chance to do the opera would be on Wednesday, October 31, the next day, because the airports were going to reopen on Thursday and two of my main singers would be leaving for other engagements. Late that evening, I finally heard from the theater that everything looked ok for Wednesday, so I began phoning everyone yet again and we were on once more.

Late Wednesday afternoon when I arrived at the theater I discovered that they had thrown out all our programs, so our librettos had to serve as the programs, too. The singers, the professional men's chorus and orchestra were all there, but about a third of the Dessoff were unable to get into Manhattan since there was still no public transit available and many of the bridges and tunnels into the city were closed due to flooding.

So, in the end, *La Nave* finally made it to New York City in the midst of a hurricane of epic proportions, but the performance was superb in spite of everything it took to make it happen. And it was all worth it, too, because *La Nave,* for me, stands as the epitome of all the operas we have presented. For its grandeur, both theatrically and musically, it is my most favorite of all. I am so pleased, therefore, that because of Dr. Chandler's scholarly interest in the work, we now have this extended study of *La Nave*'s creation and critical reception, and that we ourselves, everyone connected with Teatro Grattacielo, have become part of that history too.

Teatro Grattacielo
New York City, May 19, 2014

Acknowledgements to the First Edition

MOST BOOKS are collaborative efforts to some extent; this one is more than most. It was conceived and put together at short notice sometime after I learned that Teatro Grattacielo was planning to revive *La Nave*. I was working on a biography of Italo Montemezzi, and the news of the revival was incredibly exciting. I had reached the conclusion that the first two productions of the opera, at La Scala in 1918, and at Chicago in 1919, and the relative failure of the opera compared to its predecessor, *L'Amore dei Tre Re*, represented a decisive turning point in Montemezzi's career – a point of crisis from which, in a certain sense, he never recovered. It thus seemed a good idea to explore the matter of *La Nave*'s critical reception in detail, which is what this book does. I am deeply grateful to all those who have made it possible.

The biggest thanks of all must go to Monica Cuneo, without whom the project would have floundered at an early stage. Not only did she produce a brilliant series of rough translations, as close to the original as possible, which we have then polished up together, she has patiently endured countless emails querying this or that, and taken care of a good deal of correspondence with various Italian libraries and archives. Another major thanks must go to Raffaele Mellace, whose 2008 article on *La Nave* was much the most ambitious and useful piece of research available on the opera. He was enthusiastic about the idea of this book from the beginning, and immediately agreed to prepare a shortened version of his article for inclusion.

Anyone who works in modern higher education knows that a whole generation has grown up believing that 'everything' can be found on the internet. In many ways this is remarkably untrue, as I was regularly reminded in the preparation of this book. In 2012 only one of these reviews could be found online. The rest had to be searched for in libraries and archives, often with considerable difficulty. The British Newspaper Library, surely the best institution of its kind in the world, was able to provide half a dozen. Several of the American reviews were dug out of Chicago libraries by Kris Lipkowski, who also secured a copy of the *Rivista d'Italia* review and has been a brilliant and always enthusiastic research assistant. I am also indebted to Kris for some of the notes in the Chicago section. The only copy of the *Chicago American* review to be found anywhere, it appears, is that preserved in the Harry Ransom Research Center at the University of Texas at Austin; I am grateful to Rick Watson of the Center for arranging for a copy to be made. Stephanie Challener provided a copy of the *Musical America* review from that paper's archive. And I am very grateful to Alain Wolfe of the Chicago Public Library and Richard Schwegel for a copy of the *Musical Courier* review. In the Chicago section of the book I had hoped to include the review of *La Nave* which appeared (presumably) in the December 1919 issue of *Opera News*; no libraries seem to hold that number, unfortunately, but I am nonetheless very grateful to Kris Lipkowski and the various members of the American Music Library Association who tried hard to track one down.

Pulling the American reviews together was challenging, but obtaining the Italian reviews was far more difficult, not least because libraries in Italy often seem designed to deter rather than encourage research, and such standard reference works as Anna Baldazzi's *Bibliografia della Critica Dannunziana nei Periodici Italiani dal 1880 al 1938* (1977) and Laura Granatella's *'Arrestate l'Autore!' D'Annunzio in Scena* (1993) turned out to be alarmingly unreliable. I am, therefore, all the more grateful to friends in Italy, and friends of friends, who despite the obstacles managed to track down what I needed and find a way to get it copied. Maria Jennifer Falcone and Silvia Barbantani were able to get copies of the *Corriere di Milano* and *Omnibus* reviews, as well as others not included in this volume. Simonetta Sargenti obtained the review from *La Perseveranza*, and was able to get a copy of the pamphlet version of Ugo Navarra's review, which turned out to be invaluable, for the newspaper version was often impossible to read. I am grateful to Daniela Greco of the Archivio Storico, Fondazione Arena di Verona, and Laura Rebonato of the Biblioteca Civica di Verona for the review from *L'Arena* and another review not included here. In addition, Daniela was able to obtain a copy of the programme for the 1923 Verona production of *La Nave* courtesy of Ivano Zanoli, to whom thanks are also due. Finally, the president of the Emeroteca-Biblioteca Tucci, Naples, generously went to considerable trouble to provide me with a copy of the review in *Il Messaggero*.

Putting together the images reproduced here was another considerable task. Most of them come from my own collection of opera memorabilia associated with Montemezzi, and in that respect I am grateful above all to eBay, which has made it immeasurably easier to track down the right photo of the right person. From an early stage in the project I was interested in having a picture by Ivan Aivazovsky, my favourite painter of the sea, as a cover, and I am deeply indebted to Jon Goad of Sphinx Fine Art, London, for allowing us to reproduce Aivazovsky's magnificent sketch, *A Strong Wind*, without any fee. Charles Mintzer generously allowed us to reproduce the two superb photographs of Montemezzi and the principals of *La Nave* in Chicago from his collection of Rosa Raisa-related material. The Archivio Storico Ricordi kindly supplied the portrait of Tito Ricordi. Tetsuhito Motoyama went to considerable, and much appreciated, trouble to obtain scans of the Norman Bel Geddes stage designs for *La Nave*.

For advice and help with specific notes and illustrations I am additionally grateful to John Mucci, Alan Mallach, Konrad Dryden, Daniela Greco, Giuseppe Martini, Linda Fairtile, Francesco Izzo, Michael Sharp, John Henderson and Kenichi Akishino. Valerie Langfield, whose knowledge of music is combined with a fine sense of how English prose should be written, heroically read through the introductory sections at the eleventh hour, and suggested many corrections and improvements. Paul Durrant lavished his usual care on the production of the book and patiently watched the project grow and grow.

One of the reasons I have come to prefer writing on opera is that so much research done in my home discipline, English literature, is now blatantly driven by career, research assessment, grant-obtaining, ideological and sometimes commercial imperatives. In the world of opera scholarship, by contrast, a much greater proportion of the research is driven by belief and love, a wish to do something *for* opera rather than for one's career. I have found it a generous and hospitable world, and I am fortunate in particular to know such unfailingly kind and encouraging people as Konrad Dryden, Duane D. Printz and Valerie Langfield. Without Duane's efforts to revive *La Nave*, this book would not have been attempted in the first place, so I am especially grateful to her for that, and for instantly agreeing to write a Foreword. Finally, I owe a lasting debt to Brian Trowell, a great musicologist, who, when I first became interested in the notion of the *Literaturoper* several years ago (an interest initially focused on Holst's Shakespeare opera, *At the Boar's Head*), about which there is still an astonishing lack of writing in English, set me off on the right track.

Second Edition

VERY SOON after the first edition of this book appeared, I began contemplating a second edition. Not only was there now a fifth production of *La Nave* to chronicle, but time constraints had prevented me examining the earlier critical reception quite as much as I would have liked. In particular, I wanted to take a more extended look at the 1938 production, not only for its intrinsic importance, but because I was increasingly recognizing it as an epochal moment in Montemezzi's career. He had lobbied for years for this production, yet by the time it took place he and his wife Katherine must have decided to leave Italy for America. One must assume that he experienced a complex mixture of emotions as he took his bows and read the reviews. There was also the matter of general criticism of the opera, not associated with particular productions, and I have included a sampling of that as well. Altogether, I believe this can be considered the fullest and most up-to-date reception history of any twentieth-century Italian opera now. The format, and the advantages of print-on-demand technology, mean that the book could be further updated if more productions of *La Nave* emerge, as I very much hope they will.

Additional acknowledgements for this second edition must begin with the huge number of people who made the performance of *La Nave* on 31 October 2012 possible. Although I am a little less persuaded of the merits of D'Annunzio's story than Duane, the Teatro Grattacielo production made an overwhelming case for Montemezzi's magnificent musical treatment of the play and convinced me that a book like this is very much worthwhile. I am also very grateful to Peter G. Davis and Dan Foley and their editors for permission to reprint their fine reviews of the New York performance. I am indebted to Jan Brett and the University of Guelph Library for the photograph of Edward Johnson as Marco Gratico, and to Charles Mintzer for the photograph of Rosa Raisa as Basiliola. I am indebted to Katie Papas and the Rush Rhees Library, University of Rochester, for a copy of Alceo Toni's review of *La Nave* in *Il Popolo d'Italia*, and to Vincenzo Frustaci and the Biblioteca Romana e Emeroteca, Rome, for a copy of Augusto Righetti's review in *Il Tevere*.

David Chandler

List of Illustrations

Italo Montemezzi, 1918 . . . . Frontispiece
Cartoon of Montemezzi, 1916 4
La Scala Workshop with 'The Ship' under Construction* 32
Tito Ricordi, c. 1918 37
Mosaic of the Three Magi, Sant'Apollinare Nuovo 40
Mosaic of Empress Theodora, San Vitale 40
Marussig's Costume Designs for the Prologue* 41
Gabriele D'Annunzio, c. 1919 49
La Scala, Early 1900s 54
Marussig's Designs for the Prologue and First Episode* 60
Marussig's Designs for the Second and Third Episodes* 61
Gaetano Cesari (1870–1934) 74
Tullio Serafin, 1919 82
Elena Rakowska, Early 1920s 92
Edward Johnson as Marco Gratico[1] 102
Giacomo Orefice (1865–1922) 126
The Auditorium Theatre, Chicago, 1929 132
Rosa Raisa Advertisement, 1919 137
Bel Geddes' Designs for the Prologue and First Episode† 140
Bel Geddes' Designs for the Second and Third Episodes† 141
Rosa Raisa as Basiliola 152

---

* These illustrations are taken from Vincenzo Bucci's article in *Emporium*, October 1918.
† These illustrations are taken from *Theatre Arts Magazine*, January 1920.
1 © The Edward Johnson Collection, Archival and Special Collections, University of Guelph Library. Reproduced by permission

Cleofonte Campanini, 1913 158
Montemezzi Rehearsing *La Nave*, 1919 162
Melodramatics with Montemezzi, 1919 170
Montemezzi in Chicago with Mary Garden and Rosa Raisa . .176
Maurice Rosenfeld, 1914 188
The Teatro Filarmonico, Verona, Early 1900s 192
Maria Carena, 1924 196
The Teatro Reale, Rome, 1937 204
The First Page of the Teatro Reale Calendar, 1938–39. 210
Building the Ship for the Rome Production 216
Stage Set for the Third Episode[1] 217
Three Music Critics at the Rome Premiere, 1938 232
Carlo Piccinato, 1938. 237
Gina Cigna, 1937. 242
Ildebrando Pizzetti, *c.*1940 258
Pau Civil (1899–1987) 268
The Rose Theater, Time Warner Center 272
The cast and conductor of the New York *Nave* 278
Programme for the New York *Nave*. 281
Montemezzi in 1938 286
Title-page of *Gabriele D'Annunzio e la Musica* (1939) 300
Title-page of the First Edition of D'Annunzio's *Nave* (1908). .308

---

[1] Reproduced from Vittorio Frajese, *Dal Costanzi all'Opera: Cronache, Recensioni e Documenti* (Rome: Edizioni Capitolium, 1977–78).

General Introduction

Montemezzi's *La Nave*: The Propagandistic *Literaturoper*

EDGAR ISTEL, a German musicologist, coined the term *Literaturoper* in 1914 to describe 'the Strauss-Debussy procedure' (*Verfahren Strauß-Debussy*): that is to say, the 'procedure' by which Strauss and Debussy had circumvented the ordinary requirement of an opera composer for a specially prepared libretto by directly setting to music existing spoken plays.[1] The results were two classic and very influential operas: Strauss's *Salome* (1905) and Debussy's *Pelléas et Mélisande* (1902). These operas inspired other composers in many countries similarly to set plays to music, and in the next two decades the *Literaturoper* became something of a fashion, to the extent that it even seemed to pose a threat to the traditional libretto form. By the mid-1920s, the Golden Age of the *Literaturoper* was over, though there have been many subsequent additions to the genre, some very distinguished.

Internationally speaking, the most successful Italian *Literaturoper* was *L'Amore dei Tre Re* (The Love of Three Kings) of 1913, a setting by Italo Montemezzi (1875–1952) of a play by Sem Benelli (1877–1949). Indeed, for many years it was one of the most frequently produced of all *Literaturopern*. In Italy itself, its popularity was surpassed by Riccardo Zandonai's setting of Gabriele D'Annunzio's *Francesca da Rimini* (1914), an opera

---

1 Edgar Istel, *Das Libretto* (Berlin and Leipzig: Schuster and Loeffler, 1914), 44. The term *Literaturoper* did not become widely used and standard until the 1970s; before that time a number of other terms had been used to describe operas that set spoken plays to music. For a useful history of the term, and the theoretical and definitional issues it has raised, see Peter Petersen, 'Der Terminus "Literaturoper" – eine Begriffsbestimmung,' *Archiv für Musikwissenschaft* 56 (1999), 52–70.

which also enjoyed great success internationally, often drawing comparison with *L'Amore dei Tre Re*. These two operas, which appeared within ten months of each other, represent the high water mark of the Italian *Literaturoper*, offering a combination of artistry and popular appeal that no other works in the genre came remotely close to matching. Zandonai perhaps sensed that *Francesca* was a magnificent one-off; having composed it, he immediately reverted to the traditional, specially written libretto. Montemezzi, on the other hand, was encouraged to go on and compose a second *Literaturoper*, choosing as his text *La Nave*, an unmistakably political play by D'Annunzio. The resulting opera, produced immediately after the conclusion of the First World War in 1918, was not a failure in an absolute sense, but it was a failure compared with *L'Amore dei Tre Re*. Discouraged, Montemezzi produced little new music (and no new opera) in the following decade, and consequently lost his place as a leading figure in the operatic world. *La Nave* also marked the end of hopes that the Italian *Literaturoper*, as a distinct form of modern opera, could maintain the sort of widespread popularity that Verdi's or Puccini's operas had enjoyed in the past.

The relative failure of *La Nave* was thus a crucial moment in the history of 1910s Italian opera. Ever since *L'Amore dei Tre Re* had caused a sensation at the Metropolitan Opera House, New York, on 2 January 1914, Montemezzi had been widely regarded as the most promising of the post-Puccini / Mascagni generation of Italian opera composers. Toscanini, who conducted on that memorable night, succinctly summed up the result:

> L'amore dei tre re has been dazzlingly successful with the public and press. Like no other opera of any other modern composer. I'm still incredulous over it.[1]

---

[1] Letter to Ida Polo, 26 January 1914. *The Letters of Arturo Toscanini*, trans. and ed. by Harvey Sachs (London: Faber and Faber, 2002), 86.

The American press was indeed dazzled, with many critics representing Montemezzi as Puccini's successor, and *L'Amore dei Tre Re* as a new kind of Italian opera, closer to the German music drama, exceptionally poetic, and with a unique magic all its own.[1] Some went further: Herman Devries, whose later review of *La Nave* is included in this book, saw in Montemezzi a 'young Wagner': 'the crown of the great Teuton genius seems destined to repose on the brow of a Latin, Montemezzi.'[2] The popular standing of Montemezzi and his opera in America is brilliantly illustrated by Giovanni Viafora's cartoon for *Musical America*'s 'Gallery of Celebrities': 'Effery time he [Montemezzi] hav' three King he draw a fulla house …!' (see illustration overleaf). Even when it became clear that Montemezzi was never going to repeat the success of *L'Amore dei Tre Re*, many Americans continued to treat this opera as one of the greatest of the century, if not indeed of all time.[3] Although the rest of the world was a little less convinced of Montemezzi's genius, *L'Amore dei Tre Re* rapidly established itself in the international repertoire, becoming the most successful Italian opera since *Madama Butterfly* of a decade earlier. The comparative disappointment of *La Nave* and the long silence that followed it thus brought to an end what had seemed an exceptionally promising career.

---

1 For the American response, see *Americans on Italo Montemezzi*, ed. David Chandler (Norwich: Durrant Publishing, 2014), or, failing that, Herbert F. Peyser's 1914 review for *Musical America*, which includes extracts from nine other reviews: 'Success Unequivocal Crowns "L'Amore Dei Tre Re" In Its First American Performance,' *Musical America*, 10 January 1914, 3–5.

2 See below, p. 159.

3 When Donald Jay Grout stated in his classic *Short History of Opera* that '[Montemezzi's] *L'amore dei tre re* is without doubt the greatest Italian tragic opera since Verdi's *Otello*,' he was repeating what was an article of faith for many American critics. See *A Short History of Opera*, 2 vols (New York: Columbia UP, 1947), 2:444–45.

Cartoon of Montemezzi

Musical America, 7 October 1916

The fate of *La Nave* should be of considerable importance to anyone interested in Montemezzi, the Italian *Literaturoper*, or the rapid divorce between new Italian operas and the world of popular entertainment in the period after the First World War. It is a very powerful opera, of great historical significance, and like most of Montemezzi's work it deserves to be better known. This book is essentially a reception history that tries to make available not just the best criticism *La Nave* has received, most of which has been very inaccessible, but also other writing on the opera which may not be good criticism as such but that nevertheless throws valuable light on the contexts in which *La Nave* was judged by audiences, and the sort of responses it has engendered. This general introduction places the opera in the *Literaturoper* tradition, and looks at Montemezzi's reasons for writing it; the subsequent stage history of *La Nave*, and the critical judgments it prompted, are discussed in the introductions to the five sections of the book devoted to the five productions. The final section draws together a selection of other critical writing on the opera, and ends with Raffaele Mellace's concluding essay, which adds a great deal about the compositional process, the opera's departures from the spoken play, and Montemezzi's differences with Tito Ricordi, who shortened D'Annunzio's play for him.

The *Literaturoper* Before Montemezzi

The term *Literaturoper* was coined in Germany, and the vast majority of scholarship concerning this subgenre of opera has been written by German scholars, a negative consequence being that they have devoted most of their attention to German *Literaturopern*, and have often given the impression that it is an essentially German phenomenon. In fact, one can find *Literaturopern* being composed in London as early as the 1750s, when John Christopher Smith (1712–95) experimented with setting shortened versions of Shakespeare's plays to music. But these experiments led nowhere, and the modern history of the *Literaturoper* starts in Russia, with Alexander Dargomïzhsky (1813–69).[1]

In 1848 Dargomïzhsky decided that, instead of obtaining a conventional libretto, he would prepare his own by adapting a shortened version of Pushkin's blank verse drama *Rusalka* and adding some lyrics. His operatic *Rusalka*, first performed in 1856, won considerable praise for its style of 'musical declamation' that had allowed Dargomïzhsky to set long passages of unadapted blank verse.[2] Encouraged by the response, around 1866 Dargomïzhsky went on to set Pushkin's 'Little Tragedy,' *The Stone Guest*, making no changes at all to Pushkin's text apart from the incorporation of two appropriate lyrics where the play calls for singing. The opera, orchestrated by Rimsky-Korsakov, was first performed posthumously in 1872. Dargomïzhsky set Pushkin's words in a lyrical but constantly varied and dramatic style of music that his young admirer César Cui termed 'melodic recitative' and that Richard Taruskin has argued is akin to an art song: 'The extended embodiment of Pushkin's play in Dargomyzhsky's [sic] music ... could perhaps best be described as a gargantuan, kaleidoscopically varied, through-composed "romance."'[3] If one accepts the principles Dargomïzhsky applied to *The Stone Guest*, it is easy to recognize the opera as an extraordinarily inventive

---

[1] The first recognition of the importance of the early Russian *Literaturopern* in German scholarship is found in Jürg Stenzl, 'Heinrich von Kleists *Penthesilea* in der Vertonung von Othmar Schoeck (1923/25),' in *Dichtung und Musik*, ed. Günter Schnitzler (Stuttgart: Klett-Cotta, 1979), 224–45. Despite this early contribution to the modern critical literature on the *Literaturoper*, many critics have gone on writing as though the genre started with Debussy.

[2] For the critical response to *Rusalka*, and the impact this had on Dargomïzhsky's career, see Richard Taruskin, *Opera and Drama in Russia: As Preached and Practiced in the 1860s*, new ed. (Rochester, NY: U of Rochester P, 1993), 252–63.

[3] Ibid. 269.

masterpiece, as well as the first textbook *Literaturoper*; but it is almost entirely lacking in conventional operatic attractions, and has never been a popular work, thus immediately establishing the problem of audience appeal with which the genre has consistently struggled.

Cui and Mussorgsky, both young admirers, indeed disciples of Dargomïzhsky, followed his lead by writing *Literaturopern*. Cui had started work on an opera derived from Heinrich Heine's youthful tragedy, *William Ratcliff*, in 1861; this was originally to have been a fairly conventional opera, with an adapted libretto, but when he fell under Dargomïzhsky's influence Cui began envisaging *Ratcliff* as a *Literaturoper* and he later proudly asserted (not wholly truthfully) that it was composed on the same principles as *The Stone Guest*. Far more original than Cui was Mussorgsky, who in 1868 set several scenes of Gogol's prose comedy *Marriage* to music in a naturalistic idiom that shocked Dargomïzhsky, who felt that so much truth had been at the expense of beauty. Mussorgsky abandoned *Marriage*, having apparently got what he wanted from it, and went on to *Boris Godunov*, which was originally conceived and composed as a *Literaturoper*, though later, after its famous rejection by the selection committee of the Imperial Theatres, reworked along much more traditional lines. It is noteworthy that both Cui and Mussorgsky, having explored the possibilities of the *Literaturoper*, quite quickly forsook the form: this, too, established a recurring feature of the genre. Western Europe became aware of these Russian experiments when Cui published *La musique en Russie* in Paris in 1880. He lavished praise on *The Stone Guest* in particular, which he described as one of the two greatest Russian operas (with Glinka's *Ruslan and Lyudmila*), and the 'clef de voûte de la nouvelle école d'opéra russe' (keystone of the new school of Russian opera).[1]

---

1 *La musique en Russie* (Paris, 1880), 98.

The Russian *Literaturopern* had been driven, in part, by a nationalistic and anti-Italian spirit, so it is rather surprising to find the next example of the form being attempted in Italy. Around 1883 the young Mascagni began work on his own setting of (an Italian translation of) Heine's *William Ratcliff*. His later account, published in 1892, of how he came to write *Guglielmo Ratcliff* emphasized that the opera was inspired simply by a naïve passion for the play:

> I fell in love with it [the published play] and immediately became fixed on the plan of setting *Ratcliff* to music. The verses of Maffei, the translator, seemed beautiful to me, and, judging by what I could remember of my school studies, I deemed them very musical. I declaimed them at night, walking up and down my room, and they inflamed me so much and caused me to love them like a madman …[1]

This account has usually been accepted uncritically. Yet if true it is a stunning coincidence that Mascagni should have chosen for musical setting one of the three plays he could have read about as providing the texts for the Russian *Literaturopern* – Cui had not discussed *Marriage* – and the only one not originally in Russian. In my view, the possibility needs to be seriously entertained that he was aware that Cui had set a shortened version of the play: a possibility only increased by the basic unsuitability of *William Ratcliff* as a source, and Mascagni's immediate reversion to conventional librettos. Cui had been warmly appreciative of his own setting of Heine in *La musique en Russie*, explaining the difficulties involved in setting such a

---

[1] David Stivender, *Mascagni: An Autobiography Compiled, Edited and Translated from Original Sources* (White Plains, NY: Pro/Am Music Resources), 17.

play to music and how he had solved them with recourse to Dargomïzhsky's 'melodic recitative.'

But the question whether Mascagni knowingly imported the idea of the *Literaturoper* from Russia, or whether, as he liked to suggest, he spontaneously developed an Italian equivalent, is less important than the fact that *Guglielmo Ratcliff* failed to establish the form in Italy. Mascagni inevitably struggled with the literary shape of a text almost entirely written in *endecasillabo sciolto*, the Italian equivalent of blank verse, especially as he was a supreme melodist who wanted above all to write the sort of unfettered melodies about to burst out gloriously in *Cavalleria Rusticana*. Despite his attempts to break up lines to create variety, the musical development of the verse is often awkward, and this, with the work's dramatic ineptness, makes it difficult to conclude that the *Literaturoper* form brought Mascagni any benefits beyond saving the cost of commissioning a libretto.[1] *Guglielmo Ratcliff* was put aside for years, then substantially revised in 1893, and finally staged at La Scala on 16 February 1895. The critical reception was mixed, the public less than enthusiastic, and the opera was never to enter the repertoire. *Guglielmo Ratcliff* had no discernible impact on operatic practice in Italy, and Mascagni would not attempt anything remotely comparable for many years. If it registered anywhere, it was in Russia, where, strikingly, Cui and Rimsky-Korsakov now returned to the *Literaturoper* experiment. In 1895 Cui started work on a setting *à la* Dargomïzhsky of Pushkin's *A Feast in Time of Plague*, another of the 'Little Tragedies,' and two years later Rimsky-Korsakov followed him with a comparable setting of Pushkin's *Mozart and Salieri*.

---

1 For a detailed discussion of Mascagni's problems in setting *Guglielmo Ratcliff* see Jürgen Maehder, 'The Origins of Italian *Literaturoper*: *Guglielmo Ratcliff*, *La figlia di Iorio*, *Parisina*, and *Francesca da Rimini*,' in *Reading Opera*, ed. Arthur Groos and Roger Parker (Princeton: Princeton UP, 1988), 92–128, pp. 98–108.

All these earlier attempts at a *Literaturoper* were immediately cast into the shade when Debussy's *Pelléas et Mélisande* received its premiere at the Opéra-Comique, Paris, on 30 April 1902. The question how much Debussy was influenced by Mussorgsky has exercised the pens of many critics; suffice it to say here that he could have read in Cui's *La musique en Russie* of how *Boris Godunov* had originally been attempted as a *Literaturoper*, and this may have had some influence on his decision to set a shortened version of Maurice Maeterlinck's fashionable symbolist prose play without conventional adaptation. *Pelléas* was a much better drama, and much more suitable for musical setting than *William Ratcliff*; it was set in the original language, a language much more familiar to most opera audiences than Russian; and the result was a full-length opera, unlike *The Stone Guest*. These were very considerable advantages even before one starts thinking about the depth of Debussy's mature musical art, the fact that he, unlike Mascagni, was prepared to write a wholly new sort of opera, and the good fortune of having Mary Garden create the role of Mélisande: 'the woman and the artist I had hardly dared hope for,' as Debussy called her.[1] Perhaps the biggest question agitating the operatic world at the turn of the twentieth century was: after Wagner, what? No earlier *Literaturoper* had offered a convincing answer to that question; *Pelléas et Mélisande* did. Then when Richard Strauss, already famous for his symphonic poems, and already being positioned as Wagner's heir, presented *Salome*, his very different *Literaturoper* three years later, it began to look as though the *Literaturoper* was a new evolutionary stage in opera, a successor to the Wagnerian 'music drama,' perhaps even *the* definitive form that modern opera would take. As we have seen, it was the success of *Pelléas et Mélisande* followed by that of *Salome*,

---

[1] Quoted from Michael T. R. B. Turnbull, *Mary Garden* (Aldershot: Scolar Press, 1997), 34.

and the influence exerted by those operas, that led Istel to coin the term *Literaturoper*.

After 1905 examples of *Literaturopern* start cropping up almost everywhere opera was practised as an art form. In the Anglophone world, for example, the young Rutland Boughton, sometime between 1905 and 1911, decided on setting a shortened version of Fiona Macleod's play, *The Immortal Hour*. He abandoned his first draft as 'too like Debussy,'[1] but the opera was completed by 1914, premiered at the first Glastonbury Festival, and later established itself not just as the most popular English language *Literaturoper* but the most successful British opera of the inter-war period. In Italy, the first response to the new trend came from Alberto Franchetti (1860–1942), one of the most internationally-minded Italian composers of the period, who had scored major successes with *Asrael* (1888) and *Germania* (1902). Even before *Salome* appeared, Franchetti decided that he would like to set D'Annunzio's masterful play, *La Figlia di Iorio* (1904); this was initially impossible, because of D'Annunzio's financial demands, but Franchetti's father put up the money, and D'Annunzio himself adapted the text.[2] The resulting opera was odd and rather unsatisfactory. On one hand, Franchetti was in awe of D'Annunzio, and wanted his music 'almost [to] be subordinated' to the latter's poetry;[3] on the other hand, he insisted on far more changes to the text of the play than the Russian composers or Debussy had been prepared to countenance, attempting to make it more like a conventional operatic libretto. D'Annunzio made the changes with gritted teeth, and later revealed his feelings about Franchetti's opera by offering

---

1 Michael Hurd, *Rutland Boughton and the Glastonbury Festivals* (Oxford: Clarendon, 1993), 53.

2 Alan Mallach, *The Autumn of Italian Opera: From Verismo to Modernism, 1890–1915* (Boston: Northeastern UP, 2007), 255.

3 Franchetti quoted by Mallach, ibid.

La Figlia di Iorio, without charge, to Pizzetti, his favourite composer of *Literaturopern*.[1] The sheer novelty of Franchetti's opera, combined with D'Annunzio's huge fame, made it a short-lived success. It was first performed at La Scala on 29 March 1906, where it ran for 12 performances; there were subsequent productions in Genoa, Rome, Turin, Treviso and Buenos Aires. But Franchetti's *Figlia* did not, initially at least, inspire further Italian efforts in the same direction.

L'Amore dei Tre Re

It is more than likely that Montemezzi saw *La Figlia di Iorio* at La Scala. It would be fascinating to know what he thought of it. His own career to this juncture had shown no inclinations towards the *Literaturoper*. His first opera, *Bianca* (unperformed; the score is in private hands), was an apprentice piece which won a modest

---

[1] Mallach quotes snippets of some very negative critical verdicts, ibid. 256, and implies that he agrees with them. Helmut Krausser, in his recent study of Franchetti, gives a more sympathetic verdict, but still a negative one: 'Why the result never really caught anyone's imagination is at once both obvious and yet not at all obvious. For in and of itself, the music is by no means that bad. The first act in particular contains several effective numbers, even if, as a whole, it comes across as a little constrained and lacking in vigour. After that ... Franchetti ploughs on through the opera with all kinds of blasé conventions. It all sounds like a poor imitation of something you've heard before. The decisive shortcoming of the opera is, however, the fact that everything hinges on the female lead role. The piece demands a superb actress who can fully immerse herself in the role of Mila. Mila is a femme fatale, mysterious, inscrutable and yet multifaceted. Franchetti's music does not do justice to this character, and the score never provides that inner gritty tension needed for a rustic murder drama.' *Zwei Ungleiche Rivalen: Puccini und Franchetti* (Munich: Edition Elke Heidenreich bei C. Bertelsmann, 2010), 209; translation by Laura Ball. For Pizzetti's own account of how D'Annunzio later gave *La Figlia di Iorio* to him, see M. J. M., 'Ascetic in Rome: Ildebrando Pizzetti, dean of Italy's composers,' *Opera News*, 18 January 1964, 14–16.

prize awarded by the Milan Conservatory in 1901 for a setting of a one-act libretto by Giuseppe Zuppone Strani (1858–1940). His second, *Giovanni Gallurese*, originally written as a one-act opera for the 1904 Sonzogno competition (in which it failed to place), was composed to a distinctly old-fashioned libretto by the obscure Francesco D'Angelantonio. After failing in the competition, Montemezzi and D'Angelantonio developed their work into a three-act form, and it was put on at the Teatro Vittorio Emanuele, Turin, on 28 January 1905, with great success, running for an impressive sixteen or seventeen performances. *Giovanni Gallurese* greatly impressed the publisher Giulio Ricordi (1840–1912), arguably the most powerful figure in Italian music, who was looking for a young composer who could be groomed as Puccini's heir. Ricordi placed Montemezzi on a monthly stipend and encouraged a collaboration between him and the veteran librettist, Luigi Illica. After some delays, in which it became clear that Montemezzi had too many opinions of his own to get on very well with the crotchety Illica, it was agreed that they would write an opera based on Benjamin Constant's classic novella *Adolphe* (1816). The result was *Héllera*, finally staged at the Teatro Regio, Turin, on 17 March 1909, where it was a failure. Some revisions were made, but it was too late; astonishingly, this was the only staged production *Héllera* ever received. A difficult period in Montemezzi's career followed; Zandonai, eight years his junior, was now the new young hope of Casa Ricordi, in which firm Tito Ricordi (1865–1933), who blatantly favoured the younger composer, was increasingly influential; in 1911 Ricordi cancelled Montemezzi's stipend, believing they would never recoup their investment in him.

Meanwhile, Montemezzi had read of the immense success of Sem Benelli's play *La Cena Delle Beffe* (The Supper of the Jests) at its premiere at the Teatro Argentina, Rome, on 16 April 1909. This play, as poetic as those of D'Annunzio – an obvious influence – but written with much more innate feeling for the theatre, immediately established Benelli as the most promising young dramatist in Italy:

within a year of the first performance it had been played over 400 times there. Montemezzi contacted Benelli soon after the premiere to ask if he could make an opera based on *La Cena*; he learned, to his disappointment, that Benelli had already sold the rights to the thoroughly minor and obscure Tommaso Montefiore (1855–1933). Montemezzi left several accounts of this episode, none of which, unfortunately, makes it clear whether his idea was to set *La Cena* as a *Literaturoper* or to have it adapted along conventional lines. The balance of probability, however, strongly favours the idea that he imagined it being adapted. *Guglielmo Ratcliff* and *La Figlia di Iorio* were the only precedents he could have cited for Italian *Literaturopern*, and neither had made the case for the superiority of 'the Strauss-Debussy procedure'; moreover, the length and dramatic intricacy of *La Cena* would have made it very difficult simply to cut the play down. (When Umberto Giordano later wrote an opera based on *La Cena*, it was adapted, with Benelli's cooperation.) Montemezzi's interest in *La Cena* was doubtless mainly driven by his need to find a new, popular subject after the disappointment of *Héllera*.

At some point in late spring or early summer 1909, Montemezzi and Benelli met in Milan. The results of that meeting can be given in the composer's own words:

> 'I have another idea in my head for a drama,' he [Benelli] told me, 'and I believe it is well suited to the needs of music.'
>
> For two hours we paced the streets of Milan, as Benelli talked of *The Love of Three Kings* and quoted passages which were already simmering in his head. ... At the end of our walk I led the poet to my publishers and a contract was signed immediately.[1]

---

[1] 'Reminiscences of *L'Amore dei Tre Re*,' *Opera News*, 10 February 1941, 16–17, p. 16.

It is easy to understand Casa Ricordi's initial enthusiasm for the project; *La Cena* was the play of the year, and the firm doubtless hoped Benelli would produce another sweeping theatrical success which could be then turned into a popular opera. However, when *L'Amore dei Tre Re* was premiered exactly a year after *La Cena*, on 16 April 1910, again at the Teatro Argentina, it was a failure. *La Cena* had been a clever, fast-moving revenge drama, replete with lots of black humour; Benelli's audience was not prepared for the change to the rather slow-moving, lofty tragedy of *L'Amore dei Tre Re*. When he saw how unsuccessful the spoken play had been, Tito Ricordi attempted to persuade Montemezzi not to go ahead with the contracted opera.[1] Montemezzi, however, was convinced that *L'Amore dei Tre Re* was perfect for his needs, and despite considerable discouragement began composing his first *Literaturoper* in 1910. It is not inconceivable that the original plan, in fact, was to adapt the play into a conventional libretto, but that this had to be abandoned in the face of Ricordi's opposition to the project.

It appears from the account quoted above, and other, comparable accounts, that Benelli wrote most of *L'Amore dei Tre Re* in the knowledge that it would be immediately turned into an opera, and possibly a *Literaturoper*. This may have influenced his construction of the play, which was extraordinarily easy to shorten for Montemezzi's purposes. The action is simple, it develops with ruthless logic, and it is remarkably focused on four characters: the old, blind king Archibaldo (an obvious bass role), his warrior son Manfredo (an obvious baritone role), Manfredo's wife Fiora (an obvious soprano role), and her lover Avito (an obvious tenor role). No reorganization of incidents was required: all Montemezzi had to do was decide which long speeches should be trimmed down and which bits of conversation could

---

[1] Olin Downes, 'The Quest of a Drama to Sing – Montemezzi and "Three Kings,"' *New York Times*, 9 March 1924, section 8, p. 6.

be eliminated altogether. His compositional process was then shaped by the conviction that:

> Not for a moment could the music advance divorced from poetry. From beginning to end music and poetry must progress side by side. Only in this fashion could I attain that unity which justified the title 'music drama.' The music had to be the exaltation of the drama, augmenting its efficacy; setting poetry in an ideal lyricism and a passion bursting forth with the fury created by the dramatic incidents but all this without having recourse to devices that had nothing to do with effects of a sort that might falsify the title of 'music drama.' This principle I followed through the entire length of the opera.[1]

L'Amore dei Tre Re has impressed many critics, in its own time and since, as an almost perfect synthesis of words and music, Benelli's richly poetic language naturally unfolding into Montemezzi's luscious score. Many *Literaturopern* give the impression that melody has been suppressed in the interests of a minute interpretation of the language of the play. *L'Amore dei Tre Re*, by contrast, gives the impression of being shaped from compressed melody, melody which may be seldom unleashed in a way comparable to its use in the popular operas of Puccini and Mascagni, but nevertheless always potently present and worked into a system of musical motifs that is easy to recognize and brings a strong sense of structure to the whole. Thus Montemezzi fulfilled his ideal of what a 'music drama' should be, while at the

---

[1] Letter of Montemezzi to Herbert F. Peyser, summer 1948, quoted in Peyser, 'For Deeper Enjoyment of *L'Amore dei tre Re*,' *Opera News*, 10 January 1949, 4–6, 30–31, p. 5.

same time offering enough purely musical interest to satisfy the tastes of audiences raised on more obviously popular fare. The score is strongly influenced by Wagner, and it soon became a critical commonplace to call it a very individual synthesis of Wagner and Debussy. That describes what most listeners hear, but in terms of the *Literaturoper* tradition it might be better described as a fully achieved attempt to find a midway point between *Pelléas et Mélisande* and *Salome*, a project in which Wagner quite naturally became a key point of reference. The overall balance achieved between a fairly conventional and very easy-to-follow plot, Benelli's lofty poetry, Montemezzi's Wagnerian score, the dramatic demands of a play and the musical demands of an opera, or 'musical drama,' is quite extraordinary, and in my view establishes *L'Amore dei Tre Re* as the definitive Italian *Literaturoper*. It was enthusiastically received at its La Scala premiere on 10 April 1913, and soon became hugely and deservedly successful, especially in America, as has already been discussed.

La Nave

The two essays that comprise part one of this book describe how Montemezzi went on to compose his second *Literaturoper*, *La Nave*. Placed together they suggest that he first conceived of the new opera in April 1914, though the second essay was clearly designed, confusingly, to give the impression that the initial idea came many months prior to the First World War. April 1914 was a year after the premiere of *L'Amore dei Tre Re*, and it is important to note the suggestion in the first essay, by Vincenzo Bucci (1878–1958), a prominent journalist and one of the editors of the *Corriere della Sera*, that Montemezzi did seriously consider reverting to the specially written libretto, but was unable to find one of sufficient quality to satisfy him.[1] Like most of the earlier

---

1 See below, p. 34.

composers of *Literaturopern*, he felt no special commitment to the form, despite its giving him his greatest success. Though they agree on a moment of conception in 1914, the two essays differ significantly on what happened next. Bucci reports Montemezzi stating, in 1918, that after being impressed by the imaginative vision of D'Annunzio's *La Nave*, he was overwhelmed by the difficulty of setting it as an opera, and did not look at the play again for a long time, until he was made aware of its relevance to the war nearly a year later. The second essay, written by Montemezzi himself nearly twenty years later, emphasizes by contrast many weeks of study and planning, 'wavering between renunciations and firm purposes':[1] all this, seemingly, before the wartime significance of the work dawned on him. The two accounts are not as incompatible as they appear at first if it is recognized that Montemezzi was making the same point in different ways: that is, that *La Nave* was supremely challenging, and that the war was the mighty catalyst which led him to set the play. Read another way, the essays do seem tacitly to acknowledge what many of the opera's subsequent critics have stated in no uncertain terms: that *La Nave* was not really suited for setting as a *Literaturoper*. Earlier accounts of thought processes are usually more reliable than later ones, and in my view the later account was a defensive response to the criticism the opera had received. By 1938 Montemezzi wanted to emphasize that *La Nave* was not just naïvely chosen for its wartime topicality, but that a long process of artistic deliberation had preceded the decision to compose the opera.

Whatever went through Montemezzi's mind in 1914, by spring 1915 we are on firm, verifiable ground. Around March that year the composer made a definite decision to set *La Nave*, Tito Ricordi, who may have independently seen operatic possibilities in the play,[2] was enthusiastic about the project, D'Annunzio's

---

[1] See below, p. 46.

[2] See below, p. 314.

permission was readily obtained, and Tito himself quickly – one suspects too quickly – prepared a shortened version of the tragedy that Montemezzi began to compose on 25 April, St. Mark's day, St. Mark being the patron saint of Venice. The following month Italy entered the First World War, so most of the composition was done in the war years, and clearly considered as a form of patriotic war work: Montemezzi states in his essay that 'my wish to make a work of art was fed by the wish to make also a work of propaganda.'[1]

The propaganda was clear enough. D'Annunzio's play drew on, and set out to encourage, the popular *irredentism* (from *irredento*, 'unredeemed') of the time: the belief that the Italian peoples should be united in a Greater Italy including the parts of northern Italy still, after three wars of independence, in Austrian hands, as well as the former Venetian possessions across the Adriatic. The majority of Italians, even those who did not wish Italy to fight, welcomed the advent of the First World War as a chance to fulfil this dream of the country recovering its great destiny. The war party, in which D'Annunzio became very prominent, believed that conflict with Austro-Hungary would allow Italy to recover the *irredenta*, the lost territories. On the other hand, the anti-war party led by Giovanni Giolitti (1842–1928), the former Prime Minister who commanded the largest faction in parliament, believed that Austro-Hungary could be persuaded to abandon some of its Italian possessions in return for a promise of Italian neutrality. Montemezzi belonged to the war party, but he seems to have decided, even before it became clear that Italy would join in the conflict, that *La Nave* was of immense contemporary relevance, and Tito Ricordi apparently agreed. But a great deal of political relevance is seldom beneficial to the long-term attractiveness of a work of art, and Montemezzi was giving hostages to fortune, as I argue in the

---

1 See below, pp. 46–47.

later introductions to the different productions. *L'Amore dei Tre Re* had incorporated a layer of political symbolism in which Fiora is the soul of Italy forcibly wedded to the foreign invader, but it was a timeless symbolism that could be relished or ignored according to the predisposition of the spectator. By contrast, the nationalistic message in *La Nave* was unmistakable and not for all times and all places.

Connected to the explicit nationalist politics of *La Nave* was the cultural politics of setting a play by D'Annunzio, Italy's most famous, and most notorious, writer. Before the war he already had an international reputation as a writer, legendary womanizer, and Italian nationalist. In the period of Italy's neutrality, D'Annunzio was a leading spokesman for war, and when Italy actually entered the conflict in May 1915 he soon established himself as a bona fide war hero (see illustration on p. 49). During the period in which Montemezzi was composing his new opera, D'Annunzio was constantly in the newspapers as a result of his military exploits, into which he threw himself with real bravery as well as the desire for self-aggrandizement that informed most of his actions. Thus Montemezzi was setting the play which, at an artistic level, best supported the campaign in which D'Annunzio was now very publicly risking his life.

Furthermore, setting the poet-warrior's plays as *Literaturopern* had become something of a trend in the 1910s, and *La Nave* was the last, and arguably the most ambitious, of a wave of D'Annunzian operas. Ildebrando Pizzetti, Mascagni and Zandonai had all written notable examples that Montemezzi would have known about by 1915. In 1911 or '12 Pizzetti had completed *Fedra*, commenced in 1909 at D'Annunzio's prompting. If Dargomïzhsky's ideal of keeping the music subservient to the drama and the words is accepted, *Fedra* might claim to be the greatest Italian *Literaturoper*, and it certainly pleased D'Annunzio. But *Fedra* is a connoisseur's opera with very little of the popular appeal that Montemezzi had been able to develop in *L'Amore dei*

Tre Re. Significantly, Pizzetti was unable to get it produced until March 1915, after *L'Amore dei Tre Re* and Zandonai's *Francesca da Rimini* had decisively proved the theatrical viability of Italian *Literaturopern*. It seems clear, though, that Pizzetti would have abandoned the *Literaturoper* form even without this delay. In 1914 he started work on a second D'Annunzio opera, but this time writing his own more thorough-going adaptation of *La Fiaccola Sotto il Moggio* (1905). Even this level of compromise was not enough, however, and after working for a year or so he 'condemned and destroyed without hesitation or regret [the new opera] ... realiz[ing] that if he followed the path indicated by D'Annunzio's aesthetic he would never succeed in translating his own dramatic theory into reality.'[1] Thereafter Pizzetti preferred to write his own librettos.

Mascagni's *Parisina*, written in 1912–13 to a text by D'Annunzio, is in many ways the most problematic Italian example of the *Literaturoper*. That problem is most clearly evident in the fact that when D'Annunzio planned to stage *Parisina* as a spoken play in 1921, Mascagni experienced a sense of betrayal, and begged the poet to desist – unsuccessfully. Mascagni never forgave D'Annunzio this supposed treachery. If he regarded *Parisina* as a *Literaturoper*, then, Mascagni also regarded it as somehow quite distinct from earlier examples: a libretto written as a play especially for him. In his standard biography of D'Annunzio, John Woodhouse refers to *Parisina* as 'a pot-boiler ... which exploited material not used for *Francesca da Rimini*.'[2] This verdict is so much at odds with Mascagni's belief – shared by some of his critics – that he was setting a masterpiece, that there have naturally been very different views expressed about the merits of the resulting opera. What is undeniable is that *Parisina*, an

---

1 Guido M. Gatti, *Ildebrando Pizzetti*, trans. David Moore (London: Dennis Dobson, 1951), 28.
2 *Gabriele D'Annunzio: Defiant Archangel* (Oxford: OUP, 2001), 264.

attempt to be minutely faithful to D'Annunzio's text, though in a more melodic idiom than Pizzetti, has never been successful on the stage. When premiered at La Scala on 15 December 1913, the opera was over four hours long – well over twice the length of *L'Amore dei Tre Re*. Drastic cuts were quickly made, but *Parisina* was never to enter the regular repertoire. Nevertheless, the fact that one of Italy's two most famous composers had chosen to write such an epic *Literaturoper* – even if we need to qualify that term slightly – did much to raise the profile of this new species of opera.

The really successful D'Annunzian *Literaturoper*, as noted already, was Zandonai's *Francesca da Rimini*, premiered at the Teatro Regio, Turin, on 19 February 1914. Zandonai had conceived the idea of a *Literaturoper* based on D'Annunzio's tragedy (1902) – D'Annunzio's earliest play in verse – in 1912, and once arrangements were concluded with the poet, it was Tito Ricordi who abridged and rearranged the play, to the approval of D'Annunzio: 'Bravo, Tito; you're really a man of the theatre; your arrangement is perfect ...'[1] This praise doubtless did much to convince Tito that he could adapt *La Nave* with similar success. Zandonai composed his opera through the second half of 1912 and 1913. He was, like Montemezzi in *L'Amore dei Tre Re*, able to infuse a great deal of melody into his opera, and, unlike Montemezzi, he had the benefit of a plot based on an already well-known story. *Francesca da Rimini* pleased both public and critics, and much could be written on its merits and demerits relative to those of *L'Amore dei Tre Re*. In my view, Montemezzi's opera is superior in that the action is much more concentrated, and the world outside the castle in which the story unfolds, and what goes on there (principally the comings and goings of Manfredo and Avito), is strongly suggested in the music without

---

[1] Konrad Claude Dryden, *Riccardo Zandonai: A Biography* (Frankfurt am Main: Peter Lang, 1999), 117.

being enacted on stage. By contrast, Zandonai's more episodic opera requires that a large-scale battle – not strongly linked to the main action – be fought on stage, and it is very hard to make stage battles convincing. The advantage that Montemezzi had in this respect, however, would be squandered in his next *Literaturoper*.

Leaving aside the wartime relevance of *La Nave*, then, it is likely that Montemezzi would, in any case, have considered it a natural and logical career move to set a D'Annunzio play around 1915. He had composed the most successful Italian *Literaturoper*, but of the five major Italian composers of *Literaturopern* he was the only one who had not set a D'Annunzio text; he would also have known that Benelli, still mainly known as the author of *La Cena*, was widely regarded as a follower of D'Annunzio. Yet the belatedness of Montemezzi's turning to D'Annunzio was itself a problem, for the poet had written a comparatively small number of plays in verse – his earlier plays were in prose, and Italian composers had not yet accepted the principle of the prose libretto – and the most suitable of those plays for operatic adaptation had already been claimed by other composers. There can be little doubt, I think, that *Francesca da Rimini*, despite its battle, and *Fedra*, partly written in the knowledge that Pizzetti would compose it, were the pick of the bunch, though *La Figlia di Iorio* had real potential, too. Montemezzi may, in any case, have chosen *La Nave* for political reasons, but the choice of a less suitable play than his rivals had been able to set was inevitable. Most of the critics who have written on Montemezzi's opera have considered this play at best a very questionable choice and at worst a very bad one. Certainly most of the dramatic advantages that *L'Amore dei Tre Re* had are absent. *La Nave* was a very long tragedy which involved far more cutting (over two-thirds of the lines) than Benelli's play. It was full of secondary characters who, though their roles are not very important, are nevertheless needed to make the story clear. And Benelli's tightly organized structure, with at least three of the four principals very sympathetic characters, is replaced by a sprawling, episodic, 'epic' plot in which none of the main characters comes across as likeable or even normal. Montemezzi considered that *La Nave* was an advance on *L'Amore dei Tre Re* and technically it is, with its beautifully incorporated choral element, but to the best of my knowledge every critic who has compared them has come down in favour of the earlier opera.

Montemezzi clearly strongly believed, and with good reason, in the merits of *La Nave*. The critical consensus can be summed up along the lines that he did well with a badly-chosen text. The complete contextualization of any work of art requires some knowledge of what the artist did subsequently, however, and in this case it is noteworthy that after *La Nave* Montemezzi rejected both the *Literaturoper* and obviously nationalistic subjects. His next operatic project, worked on for several years in the early 1920s but then abandoned, was an opera entitled *Paolo e Virginia* based on Jacques-Henri Bernardin de Saint-Pierre's classic sentimental novel, *Paul et Virginie* (1787), which had already inspired several operas.[1] Saint-Pierre's Rousseauist vision of innocent love in the tropical paradise of Mauritius is as far remote from the world of *La Nave* as one could possibly get, and Montemezzi had a libretto written by Giuseppe Adami and Renato Simoni, the team which had come together in 1920 to write *Turandot* for Puccini. In choosing such a subject, Montemezzi may have been responding to hints from the reviewers of *La Nave*, despite the fact that his 'official' position was that the opera was unfairly undervalued. Guido Podrecca, for example, had judged Montemezzi as most inspired 'in the sentimental, idyllic images,'

---

[1] The earliest certain reference to Montemezzi composing this opera I have come across is in the programme for the 1923 Verona production of *La Nave*. However, earlier references to him working on a new opera probably refer to this work.

Carlo Gatti that he excelled at the 'tender and delicate,' and Ugo Navarra had asserted that he sensed in the composer 'the absolute prevalence of a *lyrical* [as opposed to *epic*] *temperament*.'[1] Such suggestions, in combination with the reviewers' general objection to the *Literaturoper* form, and the difficulty of getting the work staged, probably helped ensure that *La Nave* was not only the last in the line of a particular kind of 1910s Italian opera, but the end of a creative cycle for Montemezzi. As the 1920s dawned, he turned to pastures new.

---

1 See below, pp. 88, 105, 118.

Summary of the Montemezzi–D'Annunzio *Nave*

Scene: An Island in the Venetian Estuary
Time: Circa 552 A.D.

Prologue

VENICE IS being built by the 'Freed Exiles.' A busy scene is interrupted by news that the rivers are flooding and bringing ruin. The people ask 'Where shall we make our home?,' and a mysterious voice answers 'Upon the ship!' (*Su la Nave!*). This is greeted as a miracle. News then comes that the Bishop is dying, and some of the people express the wish that Sergio Gratico should be the next Bishop, just as his brother, Marco, should be the Tribune. We learn that the previous Tribune, Orso Faledro, and four of his sons have been blinded after he was accused of extorting property from his fellow Venetians and secret dealings with the Greeks. A warship is seen approaching, and Orso Faledro and his blinded sons appear; they are expecting the arrival of Basiliola, Orso's daughter. As she approaches in a boat, her beauty is remarked. Basiliola lands, and is appalled to discover the fate of her father and brothers. The Gratico brothers land soon afterwards, bringing news of their success in war and the recovery of holy relics. The people advise Basiliola to withdraw, but she refuses to do so; instead she persuades her four blinded brothers to crouch around the throne set up for the Tribune. The people choose Marco as their Tribune and Sergio as their Bishop. Marco promises them a bright future, and says that God has told them to 'Arm the prow and sail toward the World' (*Arma la prora e salpa verso il Mondo*) – words repeatedly referred to during the remainder of the opera. Basiliola interrupts the ensuing celebrations and, addressing Marco as the 'Ruler of the Sea,' says that his triumph would be incomplete were she not to dance the 'dance of victory' for him. She commences the dance in front of a shaken Marco, but collapses, sobbing. The people believe her crazed, and break out again in praise of their new Tribune.

First Episode

Close to the new city, alongside Marco Gratico's house, is a pit in which those who have fallen out of favour with the new Gratico regime are kept prisoner. The prisoners beg for bread and water, or for Basiliola to come and kill them. Basiliola approaches and they accuse her, knowing she is now the lover of Marco Gratico. Basiliola is eventually so enraged that she takes a bow from one of the guards and starts shooting the prisoners, who beg her not to stop. Eventually they are all killed. Immediately after this slaughter, Traba, the monk, appears, denouncing Basiliola as a 'Jezebel' and predicting her downfall. Traba's words awake Marco Gratico, and Traba upbraids him too, stating that he is 'in the hands of a woman' and betraying his great destiny. Traba tells Marco to throw Basiliola into the pit, but she responds by starting to remove her clothes – 'She resembles a serpent, shedding skin after skin' – and daring Marco to obey. Marco is spellbound, but stung into action when Traba asks him 'Do a man and his own brother / Go to the same adultress?' Basiliola demands vengeance on Traba, but Marco simply tells the monk to go away. Marco describes his confused feelings of desire and hatred for Basiliola, who responds seductively. She avoids his question as to whether she is really Sergio's lover, too: 'Ah, thou shalt soon know what I am.' Basiliola feeds his dreams of foreign conquest, and though Marco cannot help being suspicious of her motives, they end up in a long kiss. Afterwards Basiliola derisively demonstrates her power over Marco by telling him to pick up her scattered clothes.

Second Episode

Bishop Sergio, 'in the first stupor of intoxication,' is hosting a distinctly unchristian feast in his church, into which a pagan altar, adorned with an image of Victory, has been moved. Basiliola is at his side. At the request of the guests, Basiliola dances, 'savagely and with every possible seduction of motion.' A group of the people crowd in at the door, demanding that the church should be purged of 'fornicators and idolaters,' and that Sergio should lose his office. Marco Gratico arrives to interrupt a tense standoff between Sergio's supporters and their opponents. Marco denounces Sergio as a 'Bishop of orgies' and tells his men to arrest him. Sergio responds with threats, and the two brothers, incited by Basiliola and the people, agree to a single combat that will decide the Bishop's guilt or innocence. The brothers draw their swords and fight in the church, Basiliola following every move, and encouraging Sergio, who succeeds in wounding Marco in the face. The fight then starts to turn against Sergio, and Basiliola attempts, unsuccessfully, to throw her cloak over Marco's head, so as to blind him. Marco responds to this treachery by killing his brother. The people acclaim Marco, who promises vengeance on Basiliola. Alarms sound, and news arrives that Giovanni Faledro, Basiliola's oldest brother, is leading an attack on the city. The people now recognize that Basiliola has been acting in cooperation with her brother, and demand her death. Marco orders that she be bound to the pagan altar, then leaves to organize the defence of the city.

Third Episode

Venice has been successfully defended. The big ship *Totus Mundus* is ready for launching. Marco Gratico explains to the assembled people that he will not 'expiate [his] sin' by fasting, but by banishing himself. The people respond enthusiastically, calling on him to 'Redeem the Adriatic!' Various men step forwards, offering to sail with Marco as 'pioneers.' Preparations are made to launch the ship. Basiliola, still bound to the altar, which has now been moved out of the church, interrupts to request a 'glorious death.' She wants to be taken on the ship, then thrown into the sea. Marco releases her, and is clearly once again confused by his feelings. She sees this, and offers, 'without further treachery,' to assist him in his conquest of the Adriatic, 'The Eagle of Aquileia [i.e. Basiliola] on the prow!' Marco welcomes the words as an unintended sign of God's 'manifest,' and orders that Basiliola be fixed onto the ship as a figurehead. This is done, and as the people sing a chorus of praise, the ship slides into the water.

Note on the Texts

THE GENERAL aim throughout this book has been to present the various essays on *La Nave* in a form as close to the original as possible. Thus, although obvious mistakes have been corrected, no attempt to standardize spellings, punctuation or references has been made. *L'Amore dei Tre Re*, for example, has been written with every variety of capitalization, and Montemezzi himself was not consistent on the matter. To impose a standard in such a case would be of very questionable value. To take another example, some reviewers insisted on referring to the different parts of *La Nave* as 'acts' rather than the 'episodes' that D'Annunzio and Montemezzi preferred. In some cases this may have been the result of forgetfulness, but in others it may represent a deliberate insistence on conventional terminology. Either way, it is part of the critical response, and to make the critics always refer to 'episodes' would be clearly misleading.

In the case of quotations from the libretto, I have usually consulted R. H. Elkin's fine translation (1919) prepared for the Chicago production of *La Nave*. In many cases Elkin's translation is given verbatim; in others it has been adapted in the interests of greater fidelity.

Part One

Composing and Staging *La Nave*

La Scala Workshop with 'The Ship' under Construction

(Original illustration to Bucci's article)

1. Vincenzo Bucci, *Emporium*, October 1918.

'La Nave' in the Shipyard
A Launch at La Scala in Milan

BUT ... let's return to La Scala,[1] where the new caulkers are reconstructing Marco Gratico's ship for her new launch, at a time when the Austrians have quite different ships to fear, and, if anything, are working not to increase the size of their fleet, but to fill the gaps made in it by – praise be to the 'great and tremendous' (*'grande e tremendo'*) God of Gabriele D'Annunzio – the audacious Italian torpedo boats.[2]

So, how did Italo Montemezzi conceive the idea of setting the D'Annunzian poem to music?

---

1 The first part of Bucci's article is omitted here. It discusses D'Annunzio as a war hero, notes that his personality is strongly reflected in his imaginative writings, especially in *La Nave*, remarks the forthcoming production of the operatic version at La Scala, discusses the first production of the spoken play in 1908, and presents some evidence that its political message, and D'Annunzio's related comments on the Adriatic, had actually led the Austrians to recognize that they needed to be more vigilant in defence of their naval interests.

2 The Italian Navy had developed *Motoscafi armati siluranti (MAS)*, or torpedo-armed motorboats, and these were widely used in the First World War. They achieved some well-publicized successes, most notably the sinking of the *Szent István*, an Austro-Hungarian battleship, on 10 June 1918. D'Annunzio was strongly associated with the *MAS*. As early as 1888 he had enthused about the use of torpedo boats in naval warfare in his pamphlet *L'Armata d'Italia*; he had written poems about torpedo boats; he had fought on torpedo boats in the war; and he had coined a Latin phrase from the acronym *MAS*: *Memento audere semper* (Remember always to dare).

The young composer, with the sweet intonation in his voice revealing him a native of that beautiful region of Italy which the soldiers of Charles I won't be able to molest for much longer,[1] was telling me, up in the Scala workshops, in front of the sketches painted for the scenery of his opera by the painter Marussig – a trueborn Trieste man – about the genesis of the musical reincarnation of Marco Gratico,

Not long before he had relished the success of *L'Amore dei tre Re*, but with the shortage of good librettos and great stinginess of melodramatic imagination that we suffer from on the Italian operatic Parnassus, Montemezzi had in vain been looking for a new libretto. One day, while dining in a restaurant in Milan, the inspiration came to him: 'What if I set *La Nave* to music?'

The idea was daring; but it seemed excellent to him, anyway. And without losing any time, he called a waiter and sent him, immediately, to the nearest bookseller, to buy a copy of the tragedy. Having received the volume, he began to glance through it excitedly, became engrossed in his reading – forgetting the tender fillet, a beef steak, reddish in his plate – and there he was, all of a sudden, taken back from 1914 to the year 552 of the fruitful incarnation of the Son of God. There it is, the new city built on the shoals, on the ruins and on the mud flats;[2] with the stilt houses (*palafitte*) of larch and alder hiding the huge estuary, with the high sterns of the moored vessels and the unfinished Basilica. Here, amid the harsh fervour with which the new Italic people tames the adverse elements, with eyes already fixed on their great destinies, here

---

1 Charles I of Austria and Charles IV of Hungary (1887–1922), the last ruler of the Austro-Hungarian Empire. Much of the fighting between Italy and Austro Hungary had taken place in the Veneto, including the decisive Battle of the Piave River fought in June 1918.

2 Bucci virtually quotes D'Annunzio's scene direction here, which refers to the city built '*su le velme, su le tumbe e su le barene.*' These are all obscure and archaic terms; translating them involves an element of guess work.

is human drama and epic deeds, the battle of the hero against the obscure forces that attempt to thwart the heroic life, Marco Gratico and Basiliola; here it is, finally, the purple dawn of Venice behind the quarterdeck crowned with trumpets blaring the announcement of glory promised in future centuries to the maritime city.

The Maestro closed the book, dazzled by the grandiose vision. What a subject for a composer, what a sketch to fill out into a masterpiece![1] However, the extent of the picture and the large size of the tragedy, which could hardly be reduced to the small proportions of a libretto, left him perplexed. He went home, threw the book on the table, and for some time did not reopen it.

Some time later, when the conflict had already broken out in Europe, and in Italy there was fermenting the sacred enthusiasm which would push her to be a participant, Montemezzi, in Trentino,[2] meditated again over the project. The place, the proximity of the event, the significance that his opera would assume in the coming hour, revived in him his purpose of setting *La Nave* to music.[3] Returning to Milan, he went straight to Ricordi and stated his intention to him. The publisher found it excellent. It was necessary to reach an agreement with D'Annunzio: the poet's consent was obtained without any difficulty. But what about the shortening of the tragedy? How to cut

---

[1] The literal reference is to the *canovaccio*, or written sketch on which an actor would freely improvise in a theatrical performance.

[2] Bucci literally writes 'a small strip of Trento land' (*un lembo di terra trentina*) here. Trentino was in Austrian hands until the end of the First World War, but the suggestion may be that Montemezzi had been to the border region, perhaps around Lake Garda, that could still claim to be Italian.

[3] It was not yet clear that Italy would enter the war, but for Montemezzi's assurance of the relevance of the prospective opera, see general introduction, pp. 19–20.

through the fir and the oak of those four gigantic episodes in order to make them as lean (*smilzi*) as was necessary?[1] This time Tito Ricordi himself grasped the double-edged axe and with his leonine courage put himself to the job.[2] Under his strokes, the rich, luxuriant eloquence of the D'Annunzian heroes was reduced to sparing and concise talking; some characters collapsed, dead;[3] the crowd that with its presence and its tumult fills the tragedy, had to swallow, similarly, many words; in the end, the three thousand plus lines of the poem became the seven hundred lines of a libretto in which, it's true, much was sacrificed to the needs of the music, yet the strong dramatic structure was left intact and, in its surviving fragments, the original form was preserved inviolate. The double-edged axe had cut with rough, yet neat, strokes. And the adapter became so passionate about his work, and identified himself with it to such an extent, that having completed it he telegraphed the composer: 'I've finished *La Nave*'…

Italo Montemezzi was therefore able to devote himself to his opera.[4] As a homage to the glorious patron saint of the Lagoons, he started work on the 25 April – Saint Mark's day – 1915. Three years of work, interrupted by short periods of rest, it cost him to produce the new composition, the merits of which will be judged in a few days by the audience at La Scala. Before that judgement is given, let's leave the maestro to the anxieties of waiting for the curtain up and see how Guido Marussig, the

---

1 Bucci associates the effort necessary to prune the tragedy with the efforts of the early Venetians, described in *La Nave*, to build their city and their ships.

2 In fact Tito Ricordi had already shortened *Francesca da Rimini* for the very successful opera by Zandonai: see general introduction, p. 22.

3 In other words, some characters were cut completely, their dramatic importance being considered insufficient to merit their retention.

4 There is the popular Italian pun on work / opera here.

Tito Ricordi, c.1918

creator of the designs for the scenery and costumes of *La Nave*, has contributed to the imminent spectacle.

We won't introduce Guido Marussig to the readers of the *Emporium*. All those who have some familiarity with modern art, all those who visited the Venice Biennales from 1905 to 1914,[1] know this imaginative painter for whom reality is nothing but the firm ground from which his imagination takes a leap to rise into the sky of poetry. Although very young – as 'a young artist' is usually fifty years old, and he is only thirty-three – Marussig has already exhibited works in Paris, Munich, Brussels, Leipzig, Dresden, Amsterdam, Barcelona, and San Francisco in California. His works, whether paintings, sculptures, decorative arts or scenography, can be recognized among a hundred others. He belongs to the group, that is now numerous in Italy, of the so-called decorative landscape painters, although he brought to this group a trend that is wholly his own, a clean and clear-cut style that's like his Pisanellian profile.[2] Venice and Trieste are the sources from which Marussig draws most. [Bucci goes on to emphasize Marussig's deep historical acquaintance with these cities, especially Trieste, where his art has won him the patronage of the municipal authorities.]

Who, therefore, could have been more appropriately entrusted than Marussig, endowed as he is with a rare scenographic and decorative sense, assisted by special archaeological and historical knowledge, with the designs for the sets and costumes of *La Nave*? And Gabriele D'Annunzio thought of him when consulted on the staging of the opera, and wrote about him to

---

1 The Venice Biennales, major international exhibitions of contemporary art, had been founded in 1895. There were Biennales in 1905 (the sixth), 1907, 1909, 1910, 1912 and 1914; because of the war there were then no more until 1920.

2 That is, in the style of the great Medieval artist Pisanello (*c*.1395–1455), whose painted portraits and portrait medals mostly show the sitters in profile.

Ricordi, who in fact then entrusted the painter from Trieste with the task of preparing the designs.

Marussig devoted himself to the job with enthusiasm. He searched, examined thoroughly, consulted the chronicles, the historical accounts, the monuments of the ancient Adriatic civilization for the elements necessary to translate into pictorial visions the wonderful descriptions contained in D'Annunzio's stage directions; and on this material he worked as a poet, he interpreted as a poet. It would be necessary to reproduce here, beside the designs, the originals that Marussig drew from in order to give an adequate idea of his researches: Santa Fosca in Torcello, the Euphrasian Basilica in Parenzo, the Mausoleum of Galla Placidia and the churches of Saint John the Evangelist, Saint Apollinaris in Classe and Saint Vitale in Ravenna, the Pomposa Abbey, the cathedral of Saint Justus in Trieste and the small Lombard Temple of Cividale all provided him with valuable elements.[1] His conscientiousness, his passion as a researcher, is found in the smallest details. As an example, it is possible to compare the tablecloths and hydriae portrayed in the apse of Saint Vitale with the tablecloths and hydriae drawn for the feast of the second episode; or let's compare the costumes of those Magi who, in a mosaic in Saint Apollinaris, present their gift to the Virgin, or the tapestries and dresses of the 'Offering of Theodora to religion' in the same church, with the costumes and tapestries created by Marussig for *La Nave*, and it will be pos-

---

[1] This list of buildings includes three that are close to the date of the action of the play (552): the Basilica of Sant'Apollinare in Classe and the Basilica of San Vitale in Ravenna were both completed in the 540s, and the Euphrasian Basilica, in what is now Poreč in Croatia, was built in the 550s. Two are significantly earlier: the Mausoleum of Galla Placidia and the church of Saint John the Evangelist (also built by Galla Placida) in Ravenna date back to the mid-fifth century, though the church was significantly altered in medieval times. The other buildings all date from several centuries later.

Mosaic of the Three Magi,
Sant'Apollinare Nuovo, Ravenna

Mosaic of Empress Theodora,
San Vitale, Ravenna

Marussig's Costume Designs for the Prologue
(Original illustration to Bucci's article)

sible to notice how and upon what foundations the imagination of the artist has built.¹

However, Marussig, as we were saying, is first of all a poet, and in composing the scenes where the tragedy takes place he wanted, needless to say, to create a work of poetry; he wanted the spectator to find himself, when the curtain was raised, not in front of a pedantically realistic (*verista*) reconstruction – which, in any case, was impossible to attain – but in front of a 'vision.' His scenery, in perfect stylistic harmony with his costumes, circumscribed, bordered and joined together like large polychrome windows, like mosaics or ancient panels, bears a strong decorative stamp that creates, around the action performed on stage, the same ideal atmosphere in which the characters live and breathe as is found within the pages of the poem. The scenic descriptions of D'Annunzio always start with the word '*appare*' ('appears') because in his dramas each episode is indeed an 'apparition,' a projection of life into a dream.² Marussig precisely endeavoured to give to the totality of the scenery, the props and the costumes, not the character of a real scene, but that of a pictorial apparition.

As I'm writing, machinists and scenographers are working in the workshops and workrooms of La Scala to create this spell. On huge canvases, covering the entire floors of enormous rooms, often with rails crossing them to make the conveyance of materials easier, the '*ramazzette*' – as they call, in their jargon, the broad knives used to paint scenery – move back and forth unceasingly

---

1 Bucci appears to be a little confused here. The famous mosaic of the three magi is in the sixth century Basilica of Sant'Apollinare Nuovo, while the mosaic of the Empress Theodora – not conventionally referred to as Bucci titles it – is in the Basilica of San Vitale. Both are reproduced here: see p. 40.

2 In *La Nave* the scene directions at the start of the Prologue and the three episodes do indeed all start with the word '*appare*,' though this is not true for all the other directions.

and, little by little, here are the wheels of a mill, the hump of a bridge, the stilt houses along the estuary, the top of a ship, the Basilica decorated (*istoriata*) with mosaics, the cypresses on the edge of the Fuia Pit; here is the whole city emerging once again from remote antiquity and appearing in the air, as Ruggero's castle does at the sorceries of the wizard Merlin.[1] While the scenographers make the new city, in a nearby workshop the machinists build the great ship, already erected with her planking, her quarterdeck and her oars on the building-slips, from which the audience will see her glide, like an authentic ship in real waters, amid blares of *buccine*[2] and sung Hallelujahs.

And to say the truth, this *Totus Mundus*, to which Giovanni Ansaldo, the stage engineer at La Scala, has been devoting his efforts for a long time, is a vessel nearly in perfect order.[3] From her keel to her quarterdeck she measures a good five metres, she bears the weight of many people and would need only a prow – invisible from the auditorium and therefore eliminated – to be more than a pretence. However, in the huge workshop Ansaldo – a trueborn Genoese – is this time happy to work for the maritime power of the Adriatic rival, so the pretence is perfect.[4] It is like being in the *Arzanà* (naval dockyard) of the Venetians. Nothing is missing: not the strong pitch boiling in a

---

1 Bucci's reference is obscure and probably misrecollected. I suspect he was thinking of the enchanted castle in which the magician Atlante imprisons Ruggero (more often written Ruggiero) in Ariosto's *Orlando Furioso* (1516).

2 The *buccina* was an ancient brass instrument, formed from a very long, curved brass tube; it was used by the Roman army. Montemezzi does indeed score for *buccine*.

3 Giovanni Ansaldo (1857–1929), a renowned stage technician who started working at La Scala in 1899 and remained there until the end of his life.

4 Genoa and Venice were traditional rivals, and Bucci's point is that in the past a Genoese shipbuilder would not have worked for Venice, a fact that undoes the illusion.

huge smoking cauldron at one end of the large room, nor someone hammering at the bow and someone else hammering at the stern, nor someone who makes oars and winds the shrouds, nor someone who patches up topsails and reefs.

So, if someone finds that the ship being built at La Scala is too small to redeem the Adriatic, it doesn't matter. In these times, other vessels travel those waters and, however bitter (*amarissimo*) they were made for us by the late lamented Tegetthoff, our sailors will be able to sweeten them.[1]

---

[1] Bucci refers to Wilhelm von Tegetthoff (1827–71), a famous Austrian naval commander. The reference is primarily to the Battle of Lissa, fought on 20 July 1866 in the course of the Third Italian War of Independence. Count Carlo di Persano, the commander of the Italian fleet, had been ordered to seize Austrian possessions along the Dalmatian coast, but his fleet was attacked and defeated by Tegetthoff's, ensuring that Austria would remain the dominant power in the Adriatic until the end of the First World War. It was D'Annunzio who influentially described the Adriatic as *amarissimo*, in protest at its domination by Austro-Hungary.

2. Italo Montemezzi, *Scenario*, April 1938.¹

How I Wrote the Music for 'La Nave'

On 3 November 1918, at La Scala, Milan, *The Ship* (*La Nave*) entered the sea among the exaltation of people shouting: 'O Lord our God, redeem the Adriatic! Restore the Adriatic to Thy people! Give the whole Adriatic to the Venetians!'² On the same day, the Italian troops entered Trieste. A miraculous coincidence.³

As a result, the bombardment of Pola, organized by Gabriele D'Annunzio, that he intended to have coincide with the first performance of *La Nave*, didn't take place.⁴

I started thinking about setting *La Nave* to music in April 1914, immediately after *L'Amore dei tre Re* had had its baptism at the same La Scala.⁵ The first sensation I felt on reading that enormous tragedy was one of bewilderment. I thought, in order to tackle the tragedy and translate it into sounds, it was necessary to have plentiful courage. It was so large, with nerves of steel, with extremely dramatic roles, the People the

---

1 This was a special issue of *Scenario* devoted to D'Annunzio, who had died on 1 March.

2 These are lines from the final chorus of *La Nave*.

3 For more on this 'miraculous coincidence' see below, pp. 56–57.

4 Pola was a naval base, and D'Annunzio was indeed planning to bomb the shipping there before hostilities came to an end, but I have found no corroborative evidence that he intended this to coincide with the premiere of *La Nave*. It is, however, easy to imagine him boasting of such a synchronization of war and art to Montemezzi. D'Annunzio had already been involved in three bombing raids over Pola: see Robert Wohl, *The Spectacle of Flight: Aviation and the Western Imagination, 1920–1950* (New Haven, CT: Yale UP, 2005), 54.

5 The date is confirmed in the preceding article by Bucci, but it can hardly be said to be 'immediately after' the premiere of *L'Amore dei Tre Re* on 10 April 1913.

protagonist ... Yet so beautiful! And I spent weeks and weeks prying into its proportions, studying its characters in depth.

Impossible! I thought I would be throwing myself into a quagmire and abandoned the idea. I devoted myself to reading other things, easier and more sentimental; but those epic figures, stirring in a gigantic picture, were beating at my imagination, not allowing me peace.

More weeks of research, in pursuit of a new musical structure capable of containing dramatic elements of such importance. And the vision seemed to clarify itself; yet the task was too arduous! This way, months went by, wavering between renunciations and firm purposes, without positive results. Who knows how long I'd have remained oscillating like that had a new development not occurred: The Great War![1]

During the eleven months of our neutrality,[2] nobody could think that we, even despite Hon. Giolitti's famous 'quite a lot' (*parecchio*), could continue to stay out of it.[3] The Adriatic idea dominated me, and my wish to make a work of art was fed by

---

1 For the rather confusing chronology here, see general introduction, pp. 17–18.

2 In fact Italy was neutral for ten months.

3 In early 1915 Giovanni Giolitti, the leader of the anti-war party in Italy, made a serious error by allowing the publication of a letter he had written to Camillo Peano, one of his supporters, in *La Tribuna*. The letter, written on 24 January, included the statement: 'I believe in the present conditions of Europe, much can be gained without war, but information for a complete judgment is lacking for one who is not in the government.' Unfortunately some editorial changes were made to the letter as published on 1 February, and most significantly the word *molto* (much) had become *parecchio* (quite a lot). See Alexander De Grand, *The Hunchback's Tailor: Giovanni Giolitti and Liberal Italy from the Challenge of Mass Politics to the Rise of Fascism, 1882–1922* (Westport, CT, and London: Praeger, 2001), 202. De Grand notes that this change 'gave the impression of a shoddy deal' and 'galvanized both neutralists and interventionists'; the letter became a huge talking point up and down Italy, dividing the country.

the wish to make also a work of propaganda. My courage no longer knew obstacles and I set about realizing my dream.

The project was enthusiastically welcomed by my publisher, Ricordi. Tito Ricordi himself wished to try and trim the tragedy that was then, after being discussed and touched up, presented to Gabriele D'Annunzio. He approved of it, and in the quietness of my old home (in Vigasio by Verona) I started my work.

It was the 25 April 1915, St. Mark's day. I had not chosen it at random. He was the Saint who had to help me too in such an arduous trial. At least, this was my hope. After two and a half years the composition was complete, and I was setting about the instrumentation.

At this point, two pieces of news reached me at the same time: one was that Maestro Serafin wanted *La Nave* for a great opera season at La Scala, Milan, which also had a charitable purpose for singing artists, that would take place the following year, and … the other was the call-up of my contingent! Farewell to my beautiful dream! … it was the autumn of 1917.[1]

It was at that moment that the courage of the madmen came to my rescue with an idea that was my salvation. I came to know that D'Annunzio was in Venice at the Casa Rossa[2] and went to visit him. He was very kind, and wanted to take my situation to his heart.

He sent me two letters at the Hotel Danieli,[3] one for my Chief of Staff in Verona and one for me. The letter for the Chief was simple and logical. It asked him to grant me reduced office

---

1 In fact Serafin can hardly have made a firm offer to produce *La Nave* this early. Though the Lyrical Artists Association (*Artisti Lirici Associati*) had approached the city authorities of Milan with a plan to manage La Scala in September 1917, no agreements were made until the following April. For more on this, see below, pp. 55–56.

2 This was D'Annunzio's house in Venice, rented since October 1915.

3 A luxury hotel in Venice, formerly a palace.

hours (I was in the noncombatant army), because my duty could be dealt with by any other soldier, and the instrumentation of *La Nave*, it said, could be done only by its composer. The letter he wrote me was the following:

> *My dear Montemezzi,*
> *here is the letter, which I hope is effective.*
> *I'm waiting for news.*
> *I'm eager to know your opera and I send you my very best wishes, and I'd like to send you, as well, the most vehement inspiration. Goodbye.*
> *Yours*
> *Gabriele D'Annunzio*[1]

The Chief of Staff consented, and I took advantage of this gesture that, given the time, was exceptional indeed, to devote myself to my score by working nine hours a day for nine consecutive months.[2] The opera was completed in time, and I was able to please Maestro Serafin for the season at La Scala.

So it happened that we arrived at the night of 3 November 1918. Those who were present will never forget it.[3]

---

[1] This letter was published in facsimile. Here and in his other quoted letter to Montemezzi, D'Annunzio uses the formal *Le* for the second-person pronoun.

[2] Montemezzi's account of how he applied to D'Annunzio for help in avoiding military service is incomplete to the point of being disingenuous. He first applied to D'Annunzio on this matter on 6 October 1916, he applied again in April 1917, and on 9 October 1917 he successfully requested not just a period of exemption but a complete release from military duties. For Montemezzi's letters to D'Annunzio on this subject, see Adriano Bassi (ed.), *Caro Maestro (D'Annunzio e i Musicisti)* (Genova: De Ferrari, 1918), 97–105. And see Raffaele Mellace's commentary on this below, pp. 312–13.

[3] Though this account suggests otherwise, Montemezzi himself was actually not present at the premiere of *La Nave*: he was ill, as most of the newspaper reviews noted.

Gabriele D'Annunzio, c.1919
A Contemporary Postcard of Italy's Poet-Warrior

How my poor opera managed to keep itself on its feet that night, tossed about between the hails of an indescribable enthusiasm for the Victory, I don't know. Just think that the performance could only start after three quarters of an hour of national anthems and songs, as well as the 'hurrahs!' and shouts of an incredible crowd wild with enthusiasm.

And then, hear this: while Maestro Serafin, already on the rostrum, was about to start the second act, Tito Ricordi appeared on the proscenium with a telegram in his hands, shouting: 'Rejoice, Italians! This morning our troops entered Trieste; today at 4 pm they entered Trento!'

The second piece of news was not yet known, and I let you imagine what happened! After which … we could start the second act. And so on! … Luckily the opera had a run of ten nights.

And the Comandante wasn't there![1] He was at the real scene! From which he later sent to Milan, while we were getting ready to receive Wilson (the Messiah!) with an imposing performance at La Scala, that famous message saying: 'Distrust that smile that will show you all the thirty-two teeth! …'[2]

I later visited the Comandante, in Venice, where he wanted to

---

[1] 'Comandante' was a title D'Annunzio bestowed upon himself, at the time of his Fiumean adventure; thereafter it was widely used.

[2] Woodrow Wilson and his wife attended a performance of *Aida* at La Scala on 6 January 1919 as part of his triumphal five-day visit to Italy, where he was greeted everywhere by cheering crowds who recognized that without American aid Italy would have been defeated in the war. Again, Montemezzi's chronology is unreliable, for he confuses this celebratory visit with the anti-Wilson spirit that began to develop a month or so later, after the Peace Conference had started. By April, D'Annunzio was whipping up popular opposition to the American president, and on 4 May 1919, haranguing a crowd at the Augusteo in Rome, he made the reference to Wilson's 'smile of thirty-two false teeth' (*sorriso dei trentadue falsi denti*) that got widely reported in the press (see Mario Giannantoni, *La Vita di Gabriele D'Annunzio* [Milan: Mondadori, 1933], 482). This was not a special message for Milan.

present me with his little book 'Letter to the Dalmatians'[1] with the following dedication:

> To Italo Montemezzi, who struck up the cry:
> 'Give the whole Adriatic to the Venetians!'
> Gabriele D'Annunzio

Later he wanted to present me with another one, that I'm sorry I couldn't recover among my papers; but I take pleasure in transcribing here the dedication that I remember perfectly, and that proved the passion which stirred him at that time. Here it is:

> To Italo Montemezzi, who cannot have led off
> in vain into the cry: 'Give the whole Adriatic to
> the Venetians!'
> Gabriele D'Annunzio

And here is the letter that led to the audition of *La Nave* at Levi's home in Venice:[2]

> My dear Maestro,
> forgive me for not being able to see you yesterday. I was very busy all day, until late.
> Would you like to come today to Casa Rossa, at 4.45 pm?
> Bring the prints.
> We'll go to Ugo Levi's home, who is a very good musicologist, and who will also be able to help us with regard to the planned performance.
> Yours sincerely
> Gabriele D'Annunzio

---

1 *Lettera ai Dalmati*, published in January 1919.

2 Ugo Levi (1878–1971) came from a wealthy banking family and was a collector of musical manuscripts. In 1916 D'Annunzio had commenced a love affair with Levi's wife, Olga; hence no doubt his desire to have the first hearing of *La Nave* in Levi's house.

The audition took two nights, first because the poor composer, at the piano, didn't have lungs adequate, or rather, fit, to support the strain; then because the Poet, interested in the musical development, in the adherence of the words to the music, in the treatment of the crowds, etcetera, lingered over details, commenting extensively and with his marvellous speech that kept us spellbound!

Then I saw him again in Fiume, in His Fiume, within an atmosphere of heroes.[1] Then at the Vittoriale, where we discussed a project by the architect Torres of staging *La Nave* in St Mark's Square.[2] The faithful painter Marussig was also present at the conversation. The sketches for the four acts were commented on and discussed by the Poet, the way he only could do, giving wise advice and with the intention of succeeding in the realization of the grandiose enterprise upon his arrival in Venice.

But the Poet didn't move from the Vittoriale. And I didn't see him anymore.

---

1 Montemezzi travelled to Fiume in November 1920, in the company of Toscanini and the La Scala orchestra, who had been invited to perform there by D'Annunzio, and the composer Adriano Lualdi. See Lualdi, 'D'Annunzio e la Musica,' *Piazza delle Belle Arti* 5 (1957–58), 144–68. Montemezzi's idealized memory of an 'atmosphere of heroes' is strong evidence of his commitment to the nationalist cause at that time.

2 Giuseppe Torres (1872–1935) was a Venetian architect. His plan for a performance of *La Nave* in St. Mark's Square was developed in autumn 1922, and it must have been around this time that the final meeting between D'Annunzio and Montemezzi took place. See Raffaele Mellace, 'Prolegomeni a una lettura della Nave. Una collaborazione tra D'Annunzio, Montemezzi e Tito Ricordi' in *D'Annunzio musico imaginifico*, ed. Adriana Guarnieri, Fiamma Nicolodi and Cesare Orselli, *Chigiana* 48 (2008), 417–53, p. 423, n. 35.

Part Two

First Production

Milan, La Scala, 3 November 1918

Cast:
Basiliola . . . . Elena Rakowska
                            (Rakowska-Serafin)
Marco Gratico . . . . Edoardo de Giovanni
                            (Edward Johnson)
Sergio Gratico. . . . . Francesco Cigada
Orso Faledro . . . . Oreste Carozzi
Traba, the monk . . . . . . Giulio Cirino

Director: Tullio Serafin
Stage and Costume Design: Guido Marussig
Conductor: Tullio Serafin

10 performances

La Scala, Early 1900s

Introduction

LA SCALA had a difficult time during the First World War. After the 1916–17 season, Uberto Visconti, who had been managing the theatre, terminated his contract, informing the Milanese authorities that it was impossible to stage good productions in wartime conditions.[1] In September 1917 the Lyrical Artists Association (*Artisti Lirici Associati*) presented a plan to run La Scala if they could get some financial support from the city. The disastrous reversals which Italy suffered in the war that autumn meant that further discussion was put off until the following year; nevertheless, the Lyrical Artists Association made provisional plans for a spring season that would include *La Nave*. Tullio Serafin (1878–1968), the great conductor, was chosen to direct the season, and his relationship with Montemezzi and enthusiasm for the new opera probably had something to do with the selection. Serafin had been a close friend of Montemezzi's since their days together at the Milan Conservatory in the 1890s. After the composer's death, he would describe Montemezzi not only as the '[g]reatest of contemporary Italian composers' but 'an intimate friend, an associate in music for over half a century, and a real brother.'[2] He was thoroughly persuaded of the merits of *La Nave*, which he considered 'the greatest of Montemezzi's operas.'[3]

When talks between the Lyrical Artists Association and the Milanese authorities commenced in April 1918, it was proposed that the planned spring season should be presented in the autumn. The theatre opened again in September, with the

---

1 For this and other information in this paragraph, see Carlo Gatti, *Il Teatro alla Scala nella storia e nell'arte (1778–1963)*, 2 vols (Milan: Ricordi, 1964), 1:264–66.

2 'Italo Montemezzi – An Appreciation,' *Opera News*, 19 January 1953, 10–11, 31, p. 10.

3 Ibid. 31.

organization running it now called the Italian Society of Lyrical Artists (*Società Italiana fra Artisti Lirici*, or *SIFAL*). This delay meant that the premiere of *La Nave* on 3 November coincided exactly with the end of the war: it was the very day that Italy signed an armistice with Austria and Italian troops entered Trento and Trieste. The coincidence of related political events was quite remarkable, and perhaps unprecedented in the history of opera. Montemezzi's thoughts on the matter can be read elsewhere in this book;[1] here, Serafin's can be given:

> One always calls them 'historical nights,' but that one was 'historical' indeed. The house was chock-full. After the first act, which received a lot of applause, I had gone down into the orchestra pit to start the second, in fact I was already on the rostrum, when the lights came on again, the curtain opened slightly and Tito Ricordi appeared, saying loudly: 'The Italian troops have entered Trento!' Don't ask me to describe what happened in the house. I struck up the Marcia Reale [national anthem], but who heard it, amid that loud noise of clapping, amid those shouts of joy? I managed to perform the second act and when, after the interval, I went back on the rostrum, the same scene was repeated. Again the lights, again the curtain slightly opened, and again Tito Ricordi came forward to say: 'The Italians have landed at Trieste!' It was a fantastic frenzy, with people hugging each other, waving handkerchiefs, laughing and crying.[2]

---

1 See above, pp. 45, 48–50.

2 Quoted from Teodoro Celli and Giuseppe Pugliese (eds.), *Tullio Serafin: Il Patriarca del Melodramma* (Venice: Corbo e Fiore, 1985), 96–97.

This remarkable coincidence of politics and art has often been represented, even by Montemezzi himself, as amazing good fortune. Yet it is very questionable whether it actually benefited *La Nave* in the longer term, and even in the short term its impact was arguably partially negative. On one hand it gave Montemezzi's opera the air of a spectacular *pièce d'occasion*, but on the other hand the serious artistry of his grand *Literaturoper* failed to provide an adequate vent for popular enthusiasm: the absence of singable tunes was widely remarked.

If the public response, despite the heady atmosphere, was, according to the most sympathetic review, 'only occasionally truly enthusiastic' because of the absence of a clearly popular element in the opera,[1] so most of the critics found the opera defective in various ways. *La Nave* prompted a great deal of serious, analytical, insightful and on the whole impartial criticism; there can be no question that the critics recognized Montemezzi as an important composer, and the opera as a major work meriting a deep and thoughtful response. None of them, however, were prepared to give *La Nave* unconditional approval. Though there were, inevitably, a good many differences between the critics, there was also a striking consensus concerning what was good and what was problematic about the new opera. On the positive side, Montemezzi's treatment of the orchestra and chorus won high praise. On the negative side, D'Annunzio's play was judged unsuitable for operatic setting, this leading to the related problem of long sections of dramatic recitative with little lyricism; furthermore, Montemezzi's very obvious debt to German music in an overtly nationalistic Italian tragedy bothered many reviewers. The production itself, with well-received set and costume designs by Guido Marussig (1885–1972), a very talented artist, then much in vogue, who had been recommended by D'Annunzio himself, won high

---

1 See below, p. 72.

praise, and the parts of the reviews concerned with the presentation of *La Nave* can have left Montemezzi no reason to feel displeased at the way his most ambitious opera had been given to the world. The criticisms focused on his selection and treatment of the D'Annunzio play.

The seven critics of the first production of *La Nave* featured in this book can be now introduced:

The most widely read review was probably that in the leading newspaper, the *Corriere della Sera*, and this was also the most positive (it is noteworthy that when, in 1933, Casa Ricordi published a promotional pamphlet devoted to Montemezzi, this was the only review of *La Nave* that it quoted). The review is unsigned, and therefore probably editorial. As Vincenzo Bucci was one of the editors, and as he had already written on *La Nave* at length, in the essay included in this volume, he would seem to be an obvious candidate. Yet the review appears to be by another hand: it is, for example, hard to imagine Bucci, who had made so much of Marussig's sets in his earlier essay, simply stating that they gave 'a good effect of unity' in the review itself. I am therefore inclined to attribute the review to another of the *Corriere*'s editors, an exact contemporary of Montemezzi who also had strong theatrical and operatic interests: Renato Simoni (1875–1952). Simoni grew up in Verona, where he commenced a career in journalism in the 1890s. In the early 1900s he began writing plays with considerable success. It is more than likely that he knew Montemezzi personally, and he was also close to Casa Ricordi, for he supplied the libretto for Giulio Ricordi's own opera, *La Secchia Rapita* (1910). In 1920 he began working with Giuseppe Adami on the libretto for Puccini's *Turandot*, and soon afterwards the same team, as noted in the general introduction, worked on an abandoned *Paolo e Virginia* opera for

Montemezzi. Altogether there are good reasons to suppose that Simoni, if he was the reviewer of *La Nave*, would have wanted to be generous, and this might explain why the *Corriere* review was substantially more positive than the others. The subtlety of Montemezzi's dramatic insights, his fidelity to D'Annunzio's poetry, his dramatic recitative, orchestration and melodic inspiration were all warmly praised. On the negative side, the absence of tuneful arias and the excessive influence of Wagner and Strauss were remarked – yet these alleged faults were lightly touched on in comparison with other reviews.

The *Corriere della Sera*'s main rival, *Il Secolo*, carried a much less enthusiastic review by Gaetano Cesari (1870–1934). Cesari, the chief librarian at the Milan Conservatory, was a very distinguished critic, editor, and music historian whom Toscanini would describe as 'the very best among Italy's finest musicologists'[1] – though admittedly this was at a juncture when he was trying to get Cesari his job back, the latter having fallen out of favour with the Fascist regime. After graduating from the Milan Conservatory, Cesari moved to Germany where he studied for many years, finally obtaining a doctorate from the University of Munich for a thesis entitled *Die Entstehung des Madrigals im 16. Jahrhundert* (The Development of Madrigals in the Sixteenth Century) in 1908. The same year he returned to Italy, where he quickly established himself as an informed critic of the contemporary musical scene, and, more significantly, as a key figure in the movement to revive earlier Italian music, especially that of Monteverdi. Cesari considered *La Nave* a bad choice for adaptation as an opera, though unlike other reviewers he was mainly concerned with the principal characters, whom he found unsuited to musical development. He objected, rather more strongly than Simoni,

---

[1] *The Letters of Arturo Toscanini*, ed. Harvey Sachs (London: Faber and Faber, 2002), 110.

Designs for the Prologue and First Episode
Guido Marussig

Designs for the Second and Third Episodes
Guido Marussig

to the Wagnerian character of the music – interestingly, Cesari judged that Montemezzi's musical debt was wholly to Wagner, not to Strauss – and the misplaced associations introduced by Wagnerian reminiscences. Cesari felt that Montemezzi was at his best in the choral scenes.

A very different review was published in *Il Popolo d'Italia*, the heavily political and nationalistic paper founded by Mussolini in 1914, which frequently included flaming editorials over the signature of the future dictator. The reviewer was Guido Podrecca (1865–1923), who had become famous in 1892 as one of the founding editors of the ferociously satirical magazine *L'Asino* (The Donkey). So fierce were *L'Asino*'s attacks on political and clerical corruption that Podrecca was arrested several times and in 1898 forced into exile in Switzerland. He returned to Italy in 1902, where he soon became a prominent figure in the Socialist Party, and entered parliament as a socialist deputy in 1909. He was expelled from the party in 1912, on Mussolini's initiative, on the grounds that he was a 'reformist' rather than a true revolutionary, but continued in parliament as a member of the Italian Reform Socialist Party. The outbreak of the First World War smoothed over any differences between Podrecca and Mussolini: both were committed to Italian involvement. Podrecca, a skilful public speaker, gave a number of speeches in early 1915 urging the necessity of war. He argued that the Germans were driven by a belief in their ethnic and cultural superiority and wanted nothing less than German domination of the world. In a combative vein, Podrecca argued against the Germans that it was actually the Latin 'genius' which had achieved far more in almost every field of human endeavour. His account of Wagner, included in one of these lectures, is worth quoting here, for though it can only come across as a shockingly biased argument, even when some allowance is made for the context, it points unerringly to the cultural fault line that made many Italian critics uneasy about *La Nave*:

... Richard Wagner [is sublime], but he – as Lombroso says – is not an ethnic genius but a universal one, and in his art whatever is German is ephemeral, whatever is Latin is immortal.

Nor did Wagner find his audience in Germany.

From the Emperor, who, because of his professional aesthetics can only understand military arts – he said of Wagner's music: 'It may be good, but one cannot march to it!' – down to the Berlin people, Wagner is admired there more for national pride than because of conviction.

And it is in Italy that – as a refugee – he looks in Venice, La Spezia, Rome, Sorrento, Palermo for the inspiration and the picturesque setting for his dramas; it is in Bologna, Rome and Naples that he finds the initial firm supports for his superb ascent.

Gluck and Wagner made polyphony the tool to express their feelings; yet, would they have been able to do so without Pier Luigi da Palestrina, who created it ... ?

...

And when Wagner himself, seized with Teutonic exaltation, ends *Die Meistersinger*:

'Even if the Holy Roman Empire collapses
Art will live in the genius of the German'

he forgets that he himself had acknowledged that art as having come to him from Palestrina, the greatest polyphonist, and in the same way Vincenzo Bellini – who, with his melody, had risen to the purest peaks of inspiration – gave to Wagner, in the finale of *Norma*, the feeling for his melodic masterpiece: the death of *Isolde*.[1]

During the war, Podrecca became a prolific frontline war correspondent for *Il Popolo d'Italia*, while also writing the paper's opera reviews. He clearly knew a lot about opera, even if he lacked the technical knowledge of music possessed by most newspaper opera critics. As Wagner was strongly associated with German claims to cultural superiority, one might expect Podrecca to have taken a dim view of an epic and overtly nationalistic Italian opera that was clearly Wagnerian in its musical content. In fact, the matter was touched on only indirectly, and it is clear that Podrecca, perhaps the second most positive of the 1918 reviewers, was more inclined to welcome Montemezzi as a 'Latin' genius capable of meaningfully synthesizing the real musical advances made by Wagner into the Italian operatic tradition. Whether Montemezzi had actually managed to do this in *La Nave* is one of the major questions that agitated Podrecca's review. More theoretical than other reviewers, he discussed at length the Romantic notion of the organic work of art: the complete harmony of form and content. He felt that Montemezzi had not fully achieved this, but not so much because of an extraneous 'German' element as because D'Annunzio's play itself was insufficiently organic.

G. B. (Giovanni Battista) Nappi (1857–1932), a minor composer, was the dean of the Milanese opera reviewers and 'one of the most influential and authoritative Italian critics of the time.'[2] He had become the music critic for *La Perseveranza* in 1885, and also wrote for other newspapers and periodicals;

---

[1] *Genio e Kultur (Latini e Tedeschi)* (Rome: Tipografia Editrice Nazionale, 1915), 80–81, 83.

[2] Michael E. Henstock, *Fernando De Lucia: Son of Naples: 1865–1925* (London, 1990), 199.

his views were highly respected, and it is noteworthy that Montemezzi had apparently consulted Nappi about his choice of *La Nave* at an early stage of working on the opera.[1] Nappi wrote one of the two longest reviews of Montemezzi's new opera (the other being Ugo Navarra's). The first part, published on 4 November, is omitted here; it dealt with the production itself, and is summed up in the statement: 'Concerning the execution [of the work] there is but one word: magnificent.' The only comment on *La Nave* itself concerned the opera's immense difficulty and the vocal straining demanded of the principals. The second part of the review, published the following day, included Nappi's analysis and judgement of the drama and the music. His verdict was not encouraging. Though clearly well-disposed towards Montemezzi, whom he regarded as a very talented composer, Nappi declared strongly against the whole *Literaturoper* phenomenon as well as finding plenty of faults in D'Annunzio's *La Nave* both as a play and as a basis for a *Literaturoper*. Commenting on the wave of D'Annunzio operas in the 1910s, he asserted categorically that 'Gabriele D'Annunzio is a new Circe, who lures our musical maestros to perdition.' Nevertheless, having strongly declared against the text, he allowed that Montemezzi had done an extremely good job with intractable material, even though he too, like other critics, expressed some concern at the strong influence of German music and absence of singable melody. A useful perspective on Nappi's review is supplied by the recognition that both he and Montemezzi were great admirers of Alfredo Catalani (1854–93), one of the first Italian composers to create a meaningful and individual response to the German music drama. Commemorating the 25th anniversary of Catalani's death earlier in 1918, Nappi had stated:

---

1 See below, p. 93.

> We [the critics at *La Perseveranza*] all believe that Catalani would have been able to create a wholly Italian music drama that would better respond to the exigencies of the music of today, and that would have dragged this musical genre away from the hybridity from which it has struggled to free itself for far too long.[1]

This is clearly what Nappi was looking for from the younger Italian composers, and what he failed to find in *La Nave*.

Carlo Gatti (1876–1965) reviewed *La Nave* for the celebrated and influential weekly magazine *L'Illustrazione Italiana*. Gatti, another minor composer, was a professor at the Milan Conservatory where he had previously been a student under Catalani. Though he was active as a critic in a wide range of publications, he was more of a scholar and is remembered for his important biographies of Verdi (1931) and Catalani (1953) and his major study of La Scala (1964). He also did much editorial work. Gatti's review of *La Nave* is the trickiest one to assess. Though he asserted that the opera deserves 'the highest praise,' and made much of it having caught the public mood, the list of 'faults' he went on to itemize must have struck Montemezzi as depressingly long: the opera is too Wagnerian, too slow moving, the harmonisation and orchestration are too old-fashioned, there is too much 'tonal restlessness,' too much monotony, insufficient characterization. On the positive side, Montemezzi's treatment of the chorus was praised, along with his ability to move the audience in the more affecting passages. Overall, one gets the impression that Gatti disliked *La Nave* but wanted, for whatever reason, to appear encouraging.

Of all the Italian reviewers featured here, the most obscure is Ugo Navarra, and all I am able to say for certain about his

---

[1] See Domenico Luigi Pardini, *Alfredo Catalani: Composer of Lucca*, trans. Valentina Relton, ed. David Chandler, 2nd edition (Norwich: Durrant, 2011), 106.

career is that he was active as a critic in various publications from about 1900 to the time of the Second World War. His first independent publication appears to have been *Note Illustrative ai 'Maestri cantori di Norimberga' di R. Wagner* (1902), followed some time later by *Note Illustrative al Parsifal di Riccardo Wagner* (1914). Clearly Wagner was Navarra's biggest enthusiasm, and he apparently had a special interest in *Parsifal*, to which opera he published an introductory guide in 1924. He also had strong musical connections in France and wrote on the Italian operatic scene for French publications. He was the music critic for the fortnightly *Corriere di Milano*, and apparently intended to have a review of *La Nave* ready for the issue of that paper which appeared on 5 November. In that issue, however, there was just a brief note praising the performance and stating that the main review had not been available for inclusion in time. Navarra thus had much longer to work on his review, and it is tempting to suppose that it was this which led him to expand its scope, for he eventually produced a lengthy essay that examined *La Nave* in greater depth, and with a wider sweep, than other reviewers. He thought well enough of this to publish it separately as a pamphlet, *Critical Notes on Gabriele D'Annunzio's Lyrical Tragedy* La Nave *Abridged by Tito Ricordi for the Music of Italo Montemezzi* (*Noterelle Critiche sulla Tragedia Lirica di Gabriele D'Annunzio* La Nave *Ridotta da Tito Ricordi per la Musica di Italo Montemezzi*). This was the first – and for long the only – independent publication devoted to the composer's music, so it has achieved a prominence in the Montemezzi bibliography beyond its deserts.

Navarra's essay started with the bold thesis that the Italian people have never had a real predilection for tragedy in the theatre, and therefore Italian writers have seldom, if ever, produced tragedies that really work theatrically. D'Annunzio is described as no exception to the general rule, though *Francesca da Rimini* is regarded as partially successful (and therefore Zandonai's opera based on it is judged the best of the D'Annunzio *Literaturopern*). D'Annunzio's *La Nave* is analysed and found to be a bad play, however fine it may be as poetry – Navarra's main objection was that the principal themes, and the motivations of the characters, are too obscure. The libretto prepared by Tito Ricordi is then found to be even more unsatisfactory, for it is shortened but not simplified, and Navarra highlighted an issue that the *Literaturoper* has always struggled with: 'the *reverential fear* of not changing a single detail in the original text.' This led in turn, Navarra argued, to far too much '*musical declamato*' and the suppression of a more lyrical impulse. And Montemezzi's essentially '*lyrical temperament*,' Navarra concluded his analysis, made *La Nave* the wrong choice for him, on top of its general unsuitability for musical setting.

Giacomo Orefice (1865–1922) was the only important composer to review the first production of *La Nave*, which he did in the monthly *Rivista d'Italia*. Having trained at the Liceo Musicale in Bologna, he had initially pursued a career as a pianist, but in the 1890s began to devote himself to opera. His first major success was *Chopin* (1901), an episodic opera about Chopin, utilising the Polish composer's music. *Mosè* (1905), a more ambitious work, received very good reviews, and it briefly looked as though Orefice could establish himself as an important opera composer. But his operatic career quickly declined just as Montemezzi's was starting to take off, and it is sad to note that three of his last four operas have never been performed. In 1909 he became a teacher of composition at the Milan Conservatory, and remained busy as a performer and critic for the rest of his life. In his most active years as a composer, around the turn of the century, Orefice had been strongly influenced by the international musical scene. In the 1910s, however, like many of his contemporaries, he became increasingly attached to the idea of reviving and extending a specifically Italian tradition of composition. He was, though, strongly opposed to superficially nationalistic music, as revealed in a strong statement of 1917:

> These Wagnerians, these Straussians, these Debussians of yesterday, who today are moved by considering the destiny of Italian music, smell of *opportunism*, to use a political metaphor. Today we are all nationalists in music. But we are not all nationalists in the same way ...[1]

With views like this, it is not surprising that Orefice was disinclined to welcome an opera which seemed to be strongly nationalistic in intention while remaining Wagnerian in its musical essentials. Most of his review of *La Nave* was taken up with the argument that the opera is far too Wagnerian, and that Montemezzi had not even learned from the best of Wagner, but rather relied for long stretches on 'that *musical manner (maniera musicale)* as opposed to music which Wagner used to create much of his operas.' This led naturally to the opinion, expressed by other critics, that there was too little 'genuine lyricism' in *La Nave*. And, almost as though to present Montemezzi's achievement in the most ironic light, Orefice argued at the end of his review that the composer had failed to be inspired by the nationalistic vision of Venetian greatness that D'Annunzio had offered to his readers as a genuinely lyrical idea.

Overall, the critical response to *La Nave* was disappointing. Simoni – if he was the reviewer in the *Corriere* – was appreciative, but perhaps too obviously partial, and Podrecca was cautiously positive, but most of the reviewers found more to fault than to praise.[2] Montemezzi would always claim subsequently that *La Nave* was undervalued, and that the 1918 audiences had been

---

1 Quoted in Adriano Bassi, *Giacomo Orefice: Tradizione e avanguardia nel melodrama del primo '900* (Padua: Franco Muzzio, 1987), 57.

2 Giannotto Bastianelli (1883–1927) was another reviewer who judged *La Nave* seriously defective. See below, pp. 309–10.

enthusiastic, but it is difficult not to conclude that his confidence as an opera composer was deeply shaken. Between 1904 and 1918 he had produced four full-length operas; between 1919 and his death in 1952 he would complete just two one-act operas, the first of which was not heard until 1931. *La Nave* was the end of Montemezzi's brief career as an unquestionably major opera composer.

1. Unsigned review attributed to Renato Simoni,
Corriere della Sera, 4 November 1918.

'La Nave' at La Scala

THE THEATRE was very crowded for the first performance of *La Nave*, the tragedy by Gabriele D'Annunzio abridged by Tito Ricordi and with music by Italo Montemezzi. The expectation was intense. It was a great success: there were four curtain calls for the artists and maestro Serafin after the prologue, three after the first and second acts, and two at the end of the opera. The composer, who was indisposed, did not attend the performance.

There was also applause for the scenery of the third act.

The music is beautiful. All the qualities already present in germ in the score of *Giovanni Gallurese*, and which had arrived at a high degree of development in that of *L'amore dei tre Re*, appear even more intensified in today's score, which thus represents a clear step forward in Montemezzi's artistic career. In *La Nave*, again, the quality that most stands out to claim the attention of the critic and the admiration of the audience is the clarity and constancy of dramatic insight. The music adapts itself to the play's events with surprising ease, not only in what concerns their manner and form, but also their degree and rhythm. This way and that way, whether fast or slow, simple or complex, glowing with colour or softly and modestly hued, it truly forms a new clothing of sound through which the poetic matter of the libretto can be seen clearly in the fullness of its lines, in the variety of its attitudes, without anything being altered of the original balance between the lights and shades of fantastic evocations, the surges and cessations of human passions, the thickening and rarefying of the veil of symbols. Therefore, since everything in the poetry is reflected precisely in the music, one of the most serious questions that melodramatic music must confront, the matter of how to establish proportion and relation between the parts and the whole, both with regard to the quantity of matter and the dynamism of feelings, is resolved with the simplest and most appropriate unity.

As to more strictly technical qualities, the music that is most praiseworthy in *La Nave* is the dramatic recitative, which is always of perfect expression, very often being an expansion, as eloquent as effective, of the melodic movement already inherent in the spoken phrase.

The composer made extensive use of this recitative, thus avoiding the danger of accumulating many *ariosos*, which the melodramas of the modern Italian school have certainly overused. The treatment of the chorus, which in the libretto of *La Nave* has the importance, and indeed the office, of a character, is also very well done by Montemezzi, with an interesting liveliness of colours and rhythms.

The instrumentation and harmonization are excellent, with a modernity of intentions and methods that yet never becomes eccentrically neurotic (*bizzarria neurotica*). The melody, though seldom completely original, is nonetheless rich and spontaneous; extremely free and sinuous in its lines, it too has the merit of adapting itself, like the dramatic recitative, to the passionate movements of the several characters, thus coming to perfectly reproduce their psychology.

Such a large set of merits amply justifies the brilliant success that Montemezzi's new opera met with last night. On the other hand, some of its imperfections explain how that success, even though it had all the warmth and grandeur of a sincere success, was only occasionally truly enthusiastic. Namely, in the music of *La Nave* some formulas that have been borrowed from the melodramatic music on the other side of the Alps appear too insistently: in Basiliola's wild passion, the echo of Salome's can be heard too often; in the structure of the ensemble pieces, in the development of the melody, in some details of the harmonization, the reflection of Wagner's art is too evident. Furthermore, the melodies in closed form (*forma chiusa*) are used with such parsimony that the opera cannot but sound difficult to an Italian audience. So, for example, the pursuit of realism in the people's songs at the end of the opera prevented every rhythmic and melodic softness, while it is exactly at this point that one would have expected a hymn with broad, regular lines, in which could be expressed the enthusiasm of the unanimous people. If, however, these imperfections were able to diminish the immediacy and intensity of the impressions of the larger public, they are not such as to compromise, with the critics, the high overall value of the new score.

The performance was excellent. Rakowska Serafin (*Basiliola*) and De Giovanni (*Marco Gratico*) were tackling parts of exceptional difficulty, especially because of the high *tessitura* and roughness of certain intonations, but passed the test in a really admirable way, without displaying any sign of tiredness in their vocal efforts, and without showing any variation in the unremitting perfection of their technique. The baritone Cigada (*Sergio*) and the bass Cirino (*Traba*) were also very good. The chorus behaved extremely well. The orchestra was excellent, conducted with great refinement by Serafin. The costumes were beautiful. The sets, which were designed by Marussig, give a good effect of unity. The machinery was also very successful, including that used to launch the ship, *Tutto il Mondo*,[1] in the final scene.

---

[1] In fact, as other reviewers correctly noted, the ship is called *Totus Mundus*.

Gaetano Cesari (1870–1934)
Described by Toscanini as Italy's finest musicologist

2. Gaetano Cesari, *Il Secolo: Gazzetta di Milano*, 4 November 1918.

'La Nave' by Maestro Montemezzi at La Scala

Having overcome the obstacles which trapped her in sight of the Venetian lagoon, *Totus Mundus* finally unfurled her sails in the wind to the sound of *buccine*[1] and applause. *The Ship* descended, creeping on her smoking keel, to cradle herself on the waves of the very bitter (*amarissimo*) Adriatic,[2] as if driven by a yearning toward the far East and a wish for the attainment of less symbolic successes. *La Nave* had everything in its favour: from the significance of its prophetic relationship to current events, to the excellent performance given by Maestro Serafin with the contribution of a number of first-rate artistic factors, such as make the event worthy of our Scala.

Under the fascination of such diverse forces, yet all acting to one end, and certainly seized with the interest that Italo Montemezzi had aroused in them with *L'Amore dei Tre Re*, the audience, as magnificent as one only sees in extraordinary circumstances, joined its efforts to those of the industrious workers on stage, so that securely and happily could proceed the opera of the launch.[3]

As well as the manifestations of approval that burst out here and there during the performance, there were a total of a good 12 curtain calls, of which 4 were after the Prologue, 3 after the First Episode, 3 after the Second Episode and 2 at the end.

---

1 See above, p. 43 and n. 2.

2 It was D'Annunzio who influentially described the Adriatic as *amarissimo*, in protest at its domination by Austro-Hungary. See above, p. 44 and n. 1.

3 Cesari puns: '*l'opera del varo*' means both 'the opera of the launch' and 'the work of the launch,' both referring to the spectacular artistic and technical climax at the end of *La Nave*.

Given the outcome recorded here, there are grounds for hoping that *La Nave*, in spite of the perfidies of the sea and the difficult demands made on the chorus, will not ingloriously hold the waters, and that in the season at La Scala it will remain to represent a conspicuous result achieved by the *Society Among Opera Artists*.[1]

The idea that flashed through Montemezzi's mind of setting *La Nave* to music was already contained in part in the D'Annunzian tragedy itself.

Even without taking into account those moments in the play for which D'Annunzio thought he might one day avail himself of the collaboration of Ildebrando Pizzetti,[2] some outward aspects of the tragedy designated it as easily suited to music. Apart from the state of Dionysiac exaltation which D'Annunzio intended, and that, had it really been present in *La Nave*, would have been the best tinder to inflame the composer's imagination, the wealth of picturesque elements, the lofty poetry of the sea, the evocations of the far East,[3] and the fantastic blend of Christian with pagan rites could not but exercise a powerful attraction upon the theatrical composer.

All in all, though, to the eyes of those who try to fix in sounds the various attitudes (*atteggiamenti*) of external reality, *La Nave* perhaps erred toward the excessive, and certainly did not fall short; it might have appeared plethoric, but not poor.

The passions agitating the hearts of the tragic characters in *La Nave* – magnificent in their verbal expression in this literary tragedy where, by exaggerating the truth to the point of absurdity, they reveal the strong side of the poet – descending as they

---

1 See introduction, pp. 55–56.

2 Pizzetti composed the incidental music for *La Nave*, though D'Annunzio had written much of the play before the collaboration with Pizzetti – a then unknown composer – was established.

3 I.e. the Eastern Roman Empire.

do into certain abysses of the human psyche, racking some of its intricate and even contradictory aspects, and making the voice of the most ferocious cruelty prevail over and within every other voice: would they enable the composer to find the note that stirs up a corresponding emotion and provokes an equivalent tremble?

Let's remember that those who successfully attempted something similar in the field of opera had to limit themselves to quite simple types of perversion that were clearly expressed, as in *Salome*.

Basiliola, on the contrary, though she contains within herself one or more mysteries which can be deciphered with the reader's good will, when transported to the domain of music can only disclose her barrenness (*sterilità*) to the musical scenic action. The scoffing ferocity of *Basiliola* – an exaggeration or an idealization, as you prefer, of the most ruthless feminine volubility – though capable of inspiring some good verses, cannot, we believe, find enough sounds to render it within the range of music, nor orchestras yelling sufficiently to emphasize it properly.

Marco Gratico, the hero of the tragedy, does not seem in turn any more musical a character than *Basiliola*.

His love, savouring of lechery, dims, rather than illuminating, his spirit of adventure and glorious ambition to achieve freedom and conquest. As the *Prince of the Sea*, and as the elected head of a people of workers living together, according to Cassiodorus, 'in equality, poor and rich, without the stain of vices and envy,'[1] Marco Gratico, instead of being conceived of as larger than

---

[1] Cesari quotes, not very precisely, from Book XII, Letter 24 of the *Variae* by Cassiodorus (*c*.485-*c*.585), a selection of the official correspondence Cassiodorus wrote between the 500s and 530s as a servant of the kings of the Ostrogoths. This letter contains the earliest, much quoted, account of the inhabitants of the Venetian Lagoon. See *The Variae of Magnus Aurelius Cassiodorus Senator*, trans. and ed. S. J. B. Barnish (Liverpool: Liverpool UP, 1992), 178.

nature, seems imagined out of it, or against it; so much so that we are not convinced of the fusion in one human being of the great idea he represents with the atrocity and needlessness of his crimes!

The point of gravity of Marco Gratico's heroic personality is on the sea. It is the sea that absorbs, it is from the sea that his moral beauty emanates. But because of this, the composer who would wrap *La Nave* in music will be deflected into devoting his shaping talents to the depiction of a natural element: the sea and the symbolic *Ship* offering him material more malleable than that making up the maritime tribune of the lagoons.

It was inevitable that these constitutional weak points of the tragedy would remain in the libretto, intelligently drawn from it by Tito Ricordi, and affect the inner structure of Italo Montemezzi's music.

The best part of his opera seems to be in the decorative fragments (*frammenti decorativi*) and the ensemble scenes where the chorus has an important part. In these fragments it appears to us that he has achieved the integration between the plastic, poetic and musical elements accepted as the aesthetic basis of the modern lyrical drama. For this reason, the tumultuous, industrious life of the rising Venice, divided by factions and by faith, seemed to us, in the *Prologue*, very lively and well described; and the processional chorus accompanying the urns of the Holy Bodies (*Corpi Santi*) appeared full of gravity. Moreover, the popular elevation of Marco Gratico to the tribunate was effective, expressed through the monologue '*O genti della patria nuova*' (O peoples of our new country)[1] and culminating, in developments of larger proportions, at the end of the opera. In the *Second Episode*, the orgy kept within

---

[1] This is the opening address of the speech Marco Gratico makes when elected tribune. The speech ends with a promise of future glory for Venice.

a reasonable measure of sonority, and the animated *Judgement of God* (*Giudizio di Dio*),[1] gave us the impression that the scenic elements had found an adequate musical expression, sufficient to sculpt as well as agile and flexible enough to run parallel to them.

In the *First Episode*, on the contrary, and in all the other fragments in which the characters lay their problematic souls bare, Montemezzi's music seems to cease being clearly planned; it appeared to us like a supra-construction (*sopracostruzione*) standing only artificially joined to its base.

Certainly, what contributed to make this impression stronger, in no little measure, was the Wagnerian character of the music, especially prevalent in the *Second Episode*. The musical images through which Montemezzi tried to fix the obscure moods of Marco Gratico and Basiliola recalled to our minds, with too much evidence, other operatic figures and other feelings rendered, at other times, with material very similar to his own yet perfectly done. Isn't it true that Basiliola's bestial titillation (*voluttà*) as she eliminates her lovers in the Fuia Pit assumes an almost parodic tone in Montemezzi's orchestral draughts, where there resounds impetuously a reminiscence of the love pangs of the dying *Tristan*?

Such incompatibilities, it is necessary to acknowledge, seemed less sharp where the stage action and musical commentary could tolerate, without necessarily excusing, the reminiscence. Thus the procession of the Holy Bodies, imbued with a *Parsifalesque* atmosphere, did not lack effectiveness, nor did the memories of Isolde's ship, recalled by that on which the tribune nails the Faledra, result in incompatibility.

On the other hand, the music of *La Nave*, compared to that of *L'Amore dei Tre Re*, reveals exactly a progress in this: the assimilation of various styles is now limited to the assimilation

---

1 Basiliola's insistence that Marco and Sergio fight. See below, pp. 112–13.

of only one, the Wagnerian, and from this point of view it has become technically more perfect. We no longer find Debussy beside Wagner. Montemezzi now takes beautiful walks with only the latter at his side as a guide, no longer paying attention to the former. Nevertheless, he shows that he has learned quite a lot in these excursions *à deux*. The hand of the orchestrator has become more confident, and through the equality (*uguaglianza*) of his style he has also reached a relative equality of technique.

From this, and from Montemezzi's ability to mould neatly, with effective contours, musical material which is still impersonal, *La Nave* derives a feeling of clarity and homogeneity sufficient to confer unity on the work and make us forget several episodes in an old-fashioned style interspersed here and there between the more noble fragments.

To say that Maestro Serafin took care of the staging of the opera with the feelings of an artist and the heart of a brother would be an understatement. And to add that, thanks to him, to the painter Marussig, and to the stage engineer (*macchinista*) Ansaldo,[1] the performance on the stage, both in its musical and decorative aspects, conferred on *La Nave* a special attractiveness, is only to say what is right and proper.

By availing herself of a very keen intuition, able to render the innermost traits of the part of the Faledra, and with a voice suited to expressing the role properly, Rakowska overcame a difficult trial. The tenor De Giovanni, a studious reproducer of the figure of Marco Gratico, was not her inferior, while Cigada gave to bishop Sergio a stamp of violent harshness very typical of the D'Annunzian character. Cirino, who with the hair shirt of the Traba monk looked like a reincarnation of the Wildean John the Baptist, did well in his part, and the same can be said of Turro and Carozzi.

---

1 Giovanni Ansaldo. See above, p. 43 and n. 3.

A special tribute of praise, finally, must be paid to the chorus and Clivio,[1] the chorus master, to whose ability, accompanied by his good will, we attribute the successful performance of the perilous choral dialogues.

Before the spectacle, a grandiose patriotic demonstration took place. All our anthems, and those of our allies, were performed amidst shouts and delirious cheers.[2]

---

1 Achille Clivio (dates unknown).

2 It is possible that Cesari did not write this final paragraph, which appeared below his signature.

Tullio Serafin, 1919
Director and Conductor of the Milan Production

(Photograph inscribed to the Argentine
composer, Julián Aguirre)

3. Guido Podrecca, *Il Popolo d'Italia*, 4 November 1918.

Theatrical Novelties

'La Nave'

D'Annunzio–Montemezzi

TWELVE HOURS to devote to art. A quick intermezzo between a collapsing tyranny[1] and ten peoples who have freed themselves. I'm coming from the winning battle, that involving arms, and tomorrow I'll return to see Italy seated in Trieste.[2]

But isn't this battle, too, fought at La Scala tonight, a battle for our Italy, for its musical becoming (*divenire*), for its artistic primacy?

Didn't the German aeroplanes, when furiously attacking Venice and Vicenza, where Titian painted and Palladio built, attempt to annihilate our ideal patrimony just as in France they destroyed part of its industrial patrimony?[3]

Italy will return to a primacy in the world: that of art, the most pure and bloodless primacy, and in this none will be able to

---

1 The Austro-Hungarian Empire, which had ceased to exist on 31 October.

2 It appears that Podrecca was actually dispatched to Trento instead, from where he was soon telegraphing enthusiastic reports to *Il Popolo d'Italia*.

3 Italy, already at war with Austro-Hungary, had declared war on Germany on 28 August 1916. The Fourth German Bomber Squadron was transferred to the Italian front in December 1917, and industriously supported the existing Austrian bombing campaign. The Germans bombed Vicenza on 31 December 1917, and Venice on the night of 27–28 February 1918, when a total of 281 bombs were dropped. For these facts, see Alan Kramer, *Dynamic of Destruction: Culture and Mass Killing in the First World War* (Oxford: OUP, 2007), 56. Kramer supports contemporary Italian assumptions that the Germans were deliberately targeting sites of cultural value.

contend with her. For this our youth should work, following the traces of the great masters, with their eyes fixed on the future.

We don't want to be passive, nor futurists. We are people with a good sense of timing (*tempisti*). We feel that in the rhythm of the centuries our time has arrived, and we want it illuminated with beauty, beauty that is the eternal light of Italy.

Is *La Nave* a new source of light in Italian art? I wouldn't dare make such a statement before getting to know it better. An opera like this one of Montemezzi's cannot be judged after a dress rehearsal and a single hearing. This is a bad habit of our publishers: preventing critics from attending even the tutti rehearsals and leaving the dress rehearsal to them, alongside the relatives, friends, divas and experienced musicians (*professori d'orchestra*); even worse, they publish the scores not before, but after the performance. It's always the same conventions. Now a musical work – whatever it is, even a very short piece – never can be judged properly after one, nor even after two hearings, if we are to avoid behaving like large audiences, with their respective experts (*relativi competenti*): the audiences who hiss *Il Barbiere* in Rome, *La Traviata* in Venice, *Norma* and *Lohengrin* in Milan![1] It is so difficult to judge the musical value of a genre – an improper

---

1 The premiere of Rossini's *Il Barbiere di Siviglia* at the Teatro Argentina, Rome, on 20 February 1816, was a famous fiasco, mainly because of disruption by members of the audience who objected to Rossini's setting a subject already treated by Giovanni Paisiello. The premiere of Verdi's *La Traviata* at the Teatro La Fenice, Venice, on 6 March 1853, was another celebrated failure, mainly because of problems with the casting. The premiere of Bellini's *Norma* at La Scala on 26 December 1831 was described by the composer as 'a failure, failure, complete failure' (quoted from Stelios Galatopoulos, *Bellini: Life, Times, Music, 1801–1835* [London: Sanctuary, 2002], 222). The first performance of *Lohengrin* at the same theatre on 30 March 1873 was a much cited disaster, thanks to the intense nationalistic opposition Wagner's opera encountered. Podrecca's point, of course, is that all these operas were subsequently recognized as masterpieces by Italian audiences.

word – that is out of the ordinary, that even our very great Verdi could find no melody in the *sinfonia* of *Tannhäuser* that young boys now whistle in the streets.¹ Therefore, I won't express judgments – especially on the thematic essence, that is the beauty of melodic ideas which cannot be understood if they are not in our ears and in our minds – but simple impressions.

Is *La Nave* a musically synthetic creation?²

It is certainly a great spectacle, an imposing conception, but it is not a synthesis. Nor could it have been so, D'Annunzio being in his precious and sumptuous art tenaciously analytic, like Richard Wagner in his magnificent art, and similarly employing grandiose architectures.

---

1 Verdi wrote to Opprandino Arrivabene from Paris on 31 December 1865: 'I have also heard the *sinfonia* [i.e. overture] to *Tannhäuser* by Wagner. He is mad!!!' (see *Verdi Intimo. Carteggio di Giuseppe Verdi con il Conte Opprandino Arrivabene*, ed. Annibale Alberti [Milan: Mondadori, 1931], 61). This was the first occasion on which Verdi heard Wagner's music. I am indebted to Giuseppe Martini of the Istituto Nazionale di Studi Verdiani and Linda Fairtile and Francesco Izzo of the American Institute for Verdi Studies for confirming that this letter must be the ultimate source of Podrecca's statement, though he may have encountered the reference in garbled form.

2 Podrecca's distinction between synthesis and analysis is essentially that between inner imaginative unity and a composite art of details. The distinction can be traced back to Romantic aesthetics, and is central to Giuseppe Mazzini's famous essay 'Byron and Goethe' (1839). Mazzini there contrasts the 'terrible unity' of Byron's work, created by his synthesising ego, with the studied artistry of the analytical Goethe: 'In him [Goethe] there was no subjective life; no unity springing either from heart or head. Goethe is an intelligence that receives, elaborates, and reproduces the poetry affluent to him from all external objects: from all points of the circumference; to him as centre. ... Goethe is the poet of details, not of unity; of analysis, not of synthesis. None so able to investigate details; to set off and embellish minute and apparently trifling points; none throw so beautiful a light on separate parts; but the connecting link escapes him. ... He has felt *everything*, but he has never felt the *whole*.' See *Life & Writings of Joseph Mazzini*, 6 vols (London, 1864–70), 6:75, 76–77.

Nor can the adaptation, I'd rather say the mutilations, by Tito Ricordi, although carried out with respectful acumen, remove this analytical character, precious like a veil by Botticelli or a diadem by Cellini, yet still an analysis. Certainly the stupendous D'Annunzian work, intended for the theatre, possesses some broad, sure lines of synthesis; however, whatever was accessory – as well as the literary, the historical, the real elements – has not disappeared in the adaptation, therefore the composer found himself setting descriptive details to music in order to arrive at the feeling of the work.

Yet is Montemezzi's music a music of feeling, of synthesis, that is, of intuition?

I certainly won't ask the obsolete question of what *genre* it belongs to: whether romantic, classical, naturalistic or idealistic. The work of art, if it is art, is never this or that thing, not romantic passion, not classical composure, not the real and the ideal; rather, it is all these things together which, when they become an artistic image, are simple and synthetic, as the works of our great masters are.

Even less am I concerned with the matter of essence and form which critics habitually bring up when dissecting a theatrical work, and as composers, too, habitually accept, splitting themselves in two in their methods of composition, into melodists and orchestrators. And then we get really absurd aesthetic judgments about beautiful ideas and poor instrumentation, or contrapuntal richness and melodic stinginess.

Well, it's exactly the disproportionate weight that our young composers give to the instrumental aspect, pursuing this element of composition and its complications to the point where it oppresses them, that determines the unnatural distinction between substance and form, whence the suspicion that the exuberance of the latter hides the poverty of the former. Yet if the distinction appears anywhere, there is no longer art, for the intuition is unified and it is manifest as the thought diffused within the image: the thought cannot be drawn out without causing the image to dissolve, just as a jellyfish taken out of the water dissolves in the sun on the beach. Since I'm evoking water and beach here, the inseparability of essence and form can be represented by the blue sea as well, from which it is impossible to extract the colour that forms its pictorial essence or beauty unless by taking its water in the hollow of one's hand.

Maestro Montemezzi cares precisely about making us experience in his opera a form which surpasses and renders pale in the comparison (*sbianca*) all previous Italian orchestrations, and thus the quest for complications and exuberances which are supposed to confer a grand character even when this is not in the image, that is, in the fiction. So our thoughts return to those composers whom we improperly call our classics: to a musical picture Rossini made of a few synthetic lines, to a tragic image by Bellini in which the musical colouring has the sea-depth of the romantic, of the classical, of the ideal and real all together, a non-analysable yet integral expression really comprised of everything.

But my assertion of this unity of form and substance will appear to contradict my search for melodic beauty to judge the level of musical inspiration. The contradiction is only apparent, though, because in music the melodic idea is the very essence of beauty, regardless of the dramatic atmosphere and the harmonic colouring in which it is developed. However the five notes of the bells in *Parsifal* (by an Italian organist, incidentally)[1] or the

---

[1] This is a confusing reference to a now discredited argument, apparently first advanced by Richard Heuberger in the 1880s, that the Grail theme in *Parsifal*, derived from the so-called 'Dresden Amen,' had originally been composed by Giuseppe Antonio Silvani (1672-c.1727). The argument seems to have gained considerable currency in Italy, and it is mentioned in Ugo Navarra's introductory guide to *Parsifal*: 'Richard Heuberger, the noted Viennese critic, formulated the hypothesis that it was composed by the organist of Saint Stephen's basilica in Bologna, Giuseppe Antonio Silvani; some music of his is still sung in Dresden.' See Navarra, *Parsifal: Guida attraverso il poema e la musica* (Milan: Bottega di Poesia, 1924), 97.

theme of *Siegfried* are harmonized, their essence is supremely beautiful in itself, just as Bellini's or Beethoven's themes are even when divorced (*avulsi*) from their orchestration.

This essence, which after all is still called inspiration, can be seen especially in Montemezzi's sentimental, idyllic images, broadly understood; more so here than in the visions of greatness and force where the expression seems to be entrusted to the new techniques rather than to intimate emotion. When we still have impressions of *Mosè*[1] ringing in our ears, an opera in which the grandiosity of the situation is rendered through an incredible simplicity of means, and when we recall the tremble that goes through those who listen to the finale of *Norma*, entrusted to some instrumental unisons, then the scream (*urlo*) of a hundred dissonant instruments may convey to us a grandiosity of dimensions and sonority, but certainly not of thought. Shall we say that maestro Montemezzi is a strong contrapuntist? Good heavens! It is his duty to be so, otherwise one couldn't be the sort of opera composer who thinks of art as a battle and an apostolate, though one might get the sort of easy audiences and box office successes that such young artists certainly cannot expect.[2] A strong instrumental composer, then, Montemezzi is unquestionably; yet this acknowledgment, that the audience made with respect, could be the conviction of a work of art that should appear homogeneous, limpid, transparent.

Do we get this musical feeling? Or is the music supported by other, extraneous elements meant for effect? I said I'd like to reach a decision on this with better knowledge, but meanwhile I really must notice the gripping effectiveness of the tragedy as

---

[1] Rossini's opera *Mosè in Egitto* (1818) had been revived at La Scala on 12 September 1918 and proved very popular, playing for thirteen performances.

[2] In other words, Podrecca regards Montemezzi as a composer committed to artistic innovation, and not just interested in commercial success.

a whole. Many components contribute to this effectiveness: an exceptional staging, an exceptional cast of artists, and the mood of the audience resonating in unison with the prophetic, magnificent D'Annunzian vision.

Of this vision, the most striking interpreter is certainly Marussig, whose aesthetic intuition is truly inspiration and creation. He revived the symbol by dematerializing the means of expression painting had placed at his disposal, making them a harmonic vibration (*vibrazione armonica*). I'm tempted to say, after this initial impression, that to me Montemezzi seemed more of a painter and Marussig more of a composer. The difficulty the composer faced in setting to music D'Annunzio's words, so precise, clear, and detailed, that say everything and leave nothing unthought-of, did not present itself to the painter, who felt the work in his own way, without making himself a slave to the exuberant stage directions. The D'Annunzian verse is, in its full sonority and highly imaginative intensity, some of the least suitable for musical setting.

Ansaldo[1] was Marussig's collaborator, and he set the *Ship* against the warm yellow tones of the Eastern sky, stylizing it with lines signifying dominion and greatness, as strong as the majesty of its secure launch.[2]

Tullio Serafin pervades the master souls (*anime signore*) and the mob, who will together be a *civitas*, in a wild consonance that puts life into the picture. Serafin's stature as an orchestral director is demonstrated by his miraculous conducting of this opera, in which he gave light to every elegiac recess, to every sentimental height, to every abyss of horror, to tormenting Dantesque coils, to creatures made of ferocity and lust, of degradation and greatness, over which the triumph of the race flows, sweeping away everything.

---

1 Giovanni Ansaldo. See above, p. 43 and n. 3.

2 See the scene design reproduced on the rear cover of this book.

Together with Serafin, maestro Clivio[1] made the masses eloquent, arranging them in groups and actions in perfect correspondence with the tragic resonance of their passions.

And Montemezzi's choruses have stupendous clarity of line and structuring.

Only artists like Rakowska, Di Giovanni, Cigada, Cirino – together with some good names – Carozzi, Treves, Bonfanti, Novelli, Marucci, Malfatti, Pezzettoni – could effectively frame their own dramatic and vocal figures in the grandeur of such a setting. As for Rakowska Serafin (*Basiliola*), it would be pedantic to examine her voice or her attitude, her registers or her action, when everything about her is harmony and wholeness, when in her representation *Basiliola* is an animated bronze in which all the fictions (*finzioni*) of the artist – who possesses perfect means – merge in the most shining reality!

With Di Giovanni (a first-rate dramatic power and an inexhaustible voice after the awful strains that the score demands) she makes a couple admirable for their passionate expression and plasticity.

Cirino and Cigada are excellent in the short and rough (*rudi*) parts.

For the record, there were several curtain calls after every act for the artists, for Serafin and Marussig, as well as acclamations and good wishes for the Maestro, who was absent because of an indisposition.

So, it was a complete success. We had the impression of being in front of a powerful work by a confident and mature talent.

Montemezzi's musical psyche, although imbued with Wagnerism, has the Italian clarity in the flow of its themes and the decisiveness of its procedures.

There are some pages of the score – the whole of the prologue, the seduction duet and the third episode – that are gripping. If

---

[1] Achille Clivio (dates unknown), the chorus master.

the season allows, I'll analyse them in detail, with the hope of being able to eliminate all the reservations of an aesthetic nature mentioned earlier, and in any case paying due homage to a man who brings into art a personal and lively force.[1]

---

[1] It appears Podrecca never wrote the more detailed analysis that he hints at here. He published a lengthy historical note on an anachronism in Marussig's stage designs in *Il Popolo d'Italia* for 5 November: 'With Regard to "La Nave": A Christ out of His Time' (A Proposito della 'Nave': Un Cristo fuori di tempo). He reviewed *La Nave* again in the recently founded periodical *Rivista di Milano* for 20 November 1918. This shorter review went over much of the same ground as that in *Il Popolo d'Italia*, from which it quotes (and it also incorporates material from the note on representations of Christ), but the overall tone is more affirmative, and clearly Podrecca had overcome most of his doubts. His initial impression, he says, later 'became clearer and more intensive,' and his conclusion states that in the course of the victorious war, 'in the temple sacred to Art a young composer was winning a different battle, a prelude to those victories that will reconsecrate our artistic primacy in a world without weapons and without tyrants.'

Elena Rakowska, Early 1920s
The First Basiliola and Tullio Serafin's wife

4. G. B. Nappi, *La Perseveranza*, 5 November 1918.[1]

About 'La Nave' by maestro Italo Montemezzi

IT WAS reasonable to imagine that Italo Montemezzi, encouraged by the brilliant success of his previous opera, *L'amore dei tre re*, and convinced that his artistic nature was fervidly in love with tragic subjects, would set himself the challenge of a grander and more arduous task in the same area that he had ventured into with such good fortune.

Therefore a tragedy on a private subject could not suffice him: he needed one framed by a vast historical stage.

However, I believe that nobody could have expected the maestro to give his attention to *La Nave* by D'Annunzio, and to fall in love with it to the extent of making it his own, adorning it with notes in its original form, as he had previously done with the poem of Sem Benelli.

Although in that earlier work he had been able to overcome the many difficulties he met with in setting to music a text not conceived for the art of sounds, who would have encouraged him to do a *bis in idem*?[2]

I was in fact among those who failed to comfort Montemezzi with approval when he revealed his new purpose. I remembered D'Annunzio's tragedy having read it – I had not seen it in the theatre – and, however much I admired the poet's eruditon and the sumptuousness of the literary work, I got the impression

---

1 As noted in the introduction, this is the second part of Nappi's review. The first part, published the previous day, was an enthusiastic review of the production and performance.

2 Nappi quotes the Latin legal phrase *ne bis in idem*, or *non bis in idem*: 'not twice in the same [thing].' This refers to the legal principle by which a person cannot be prosecuted for the same crime twice, and by alluding to the idea Nappi is able to insinuate that the composing of a *Literaturoper* is something of a crime against true operatic art.

– strengthened after a fresh examination of the play – that it lacked the requirements necessary for the stage or, to put it better, that it demanded more than the stage could give it.

D'Annunzio's aim was very noble: a lofty aim, too broad though to accommodate itself to the stage, which settles for something *less* that nevertheless maybe surpasses ... the *more*. In other words, the stage is satisfied with taking in those events that have a real substance of humanity, those events that speak of the real life that everyone lives – and probably will live – even though this life is lived by going through the perversity and the wickedness fomented in man by the instinct toward evil, unfortunately more deeply-rooted in him than the principle of good.

Now, in *La Nave* – whatever can be maintained to the contrary – what's missing is exactly this substantial element that gives life to a theatrical work, because the tragic event that should be the fulcrum of the production is instead merely the complementary part.

I am not so presumptuous as to claim any originality in stating that it is not *Basiliola* nor *Marco Gratico* who are the columns, or pillars, on which the poem is based. It is the people who are the *Deus* of the tragedy; that primitive, rough, fanatic people who are meant to be – according to D'Annunzio – the symbol of the strength and power that will triumph later and write, with indelible letters, one of the greatest pages in our history.

The *meat* of the D'Annunzian tragedy (please forgive this prosaic word which, however, renders the concept perfectly) is exactly this people who, unconsciously, by the impulse of their instinct, want the prow of their 'ship' to set out on the course to civilization, progress, the intellectual uplifting of the large human family.

But the heart of the tragedy, what constitutes the *pathos* in its proper sense, is small; in fact, it appears even smaller – it looks like an anachronism – when seen through the magnifying glass of the melodrama.[1] And it is exactly *pathos* – the vital essence of every production intended for the stage – that *La Nave* is lacking in, because Basiliola's hatred – a legitimate hatred calling for revenge – is sullied by the turpitudes of the young woman, who is made the more despicable by the morbid, unrestrainable force of her lustful instincts.

Perhaps *Salome*'s psychological morbidity is more excusable, as well as the pretended love of a courtesan like *Delilah* who acts as she does because it may be advantageous for her country.[2] *Basiliola* should be, or rather is, the only dominant figure in the tragedy, but how nasty she is!

Marco Gratico, then, is a weak man, a weak-kneed hero, but there is no need for us to elaborate a reproach for him because he has a glimpse of conscience left to judge and condemn himself.

I've entered into judgements like this, for though they may seem very distant from my objective, they are actually, on the contrary, very close to it. They are intended to prove what *La Nave* lacks in order for it to be, more than a work for the theatre, a work suitable for music, regardless of its melodramatic exteriority, which is essentially decorative. It is perhaps this exteriority which attracted Montemezzi and made him fail to recognize the poverty of the passionate content (*contenuto passionale*) of the story.

Yet, he should have realized that the dazzling verbosity of the poem, the *erudition of the stage directions*, the *very heavy historical truth* (I'm availing myself of the concisely summarizing words of criticism used yesterday morning by my very good colleague *g. f.*)[3]

---

[1] In other words, the opera makes clearer than the spoken play the insufficiency of the 'heart of the tragedy.'

[2] A reference to Camille Saint-Saëns' opera, *Samson et Dalila* (1877), which was well established in the international repertoire.

[3] *G. f.*, whom I have been unable to identify, was another writer for *La Perseveranza*; he had written a special review devoted to the scenery and staging of *La Nave*.

would have been an encumbrance in the course of that very thin dramatic rivulet which seeps with difficulty through the D'Annunzian production.

Isn't the stripping of the flesh off the poem, carried out by Tito Ricordi with his well known surgical skill, the major criticism that can be brought against the work? He tried to lighten, to prune, even to eliminate characters of a certain importance, such as the *Deaconess Ema*, so as to give the poem a cut (*taglio*) suitable for music; but did this important process of condensation help to bring into relief the tragic part and the protagonists and their characters? Did it assist our understanding of the various intentions of the literary work, including its ethnic and ethical relations? I don't think so.

The relations existing between many scenic episodes and some of the characters of D'Annunzio's *La Nave* – as some wanted to find – even making wrong comparisons –[1] become of minor importance, in my opinion. As to the references, to the dramatic affinities, let's remember the old saw: *Nihi sub sole novi.*[2]

Therefore, it's not these correlations that can damage the opera, but again it's the tragedy in its poetic format that has forcedly been put to music.

As I've said on another occasion – (I don't mean to offend the Poet but, on the contrary, to pay homage to his ... seductive virtues) – Gabriele D'Annunzio is a new Circe, who lures our musical maestros to perdition.

So far, they haven't realized that D'Annunzio's poetry is music in itself, a spoken symphonic poem that says everything, even the things that exceed the limits of our understanding. They haven't realized that music, with the special virtues of its broad, indeterminate language – music that can live on its

---

[1] In other words, the 'relations' between the action and the characters of the spoken play noticed by some literary critics.

[2] I.e. *nothing new under the sun.*

own but that on contact with words demands such an intimate union as to make one think it has sprung up from the same spring of inspiration – music doesn't adapt itself, doesn't bend willingly to celebrate a morganatic marriage with the D'Annunzian word, which is a much worse *despot* than Marco Gratico. Besides, this word needs no alliances to proceed in its conquests of the ideal.

Further, in order for music to address a large audience, it must in the first place be composed around concepts, around words, that they can understand immediately, without having to carry a copy of the libretto to the theatre ... and a dictionary, too.

But if this large audience fails to understand the arcane meaning of the words, they are unlikely to form an exact concept of the dramatic event, of its aims, and, consequently, they will not appreciate the aims of the music.

What is more, music badly needs – particularly after the dramatic evolution it has gone through recently, and is still going through – the greatest variety of metres, perhaps even an irregularity of rhythms and accents, in order to be able to develop new, fresh, original ideas. Music wants to proceed through diverse routes, not to be channelled into the one imposed on her by the austere-sounding hendecasyllable, nor to be restricted to developing her sphere of action within an environment hermetically closed to her will of expansion (*volontà di espansione*), almost forcing herself to keep watch with the *sonetto a rime obbligate*.[1]

If our maestros think that the D'Annunzian theatre can excite their imaginations, they should make use of it. However, just as nobody has set to music (the ingenious mistake made by

---

1 'A "Sonetto a rime obbligate" is one [sonnet] in which fourteen words are supplied to the poet as compulsory rhymes, and his task is to fill up each line and to weave them all into a poem. Even without these obligatory restraints the sonnet is not always successful, and with them the poet may be said to be dancing in chains.' See William E. A. Axon, 'An Early Essay by Panizzi,' *The Library* NS 3 (1902), 141–47, p. 143.

Mascagni with Heine's *Ratcliff* is an exception)[1] in their original format the tragedies by Monti, Alfieri, Shakespeare, Schiller and Racine, nor the dramas of Victor Hugo, they should rewrite the works by our Poet, to give them a really lyrical format. Didn't Verdi himself do this, even at the end of his glorious career, availing himself of the collaboration of another illustrious poet?[2]

In this way, our musicians will facilitate their job, while at the same time having more guarantees concerning the result and the life of their operas.

With the above-stated judgements I think I have pointed out the considerable passivity of Montemezzi's new score. But his effort, his study beyond comparison (*che non ha confronti*) to overcome the huge difficulties of his undertaking are certainly admirable. He showed a steel temper, an unbreakable confidence in his own powers. He worked with faith, enthusiasm and – we ought to render him this honour – he placed at the disposal of this enterprise a complex of intellectual qualities and artistic virtues that not many musicians possess, despite their smattering of critical-aesthetic ideas.

Those who, in the last few days, saw and approached the composer of *La Nave*, must have been impressed by his calmness, his serenity. He was convinced he had given the best of himself to his work, and that he had not taken upon himself a task superior to his powers. He felt that his opera – though discussed as well – would be appreciated; and he wasn't wrong.

It's true he didn't overcome all the obstacles, but those he was able to overcome enabled him to lay down good foundations for his opera, making it organic and robust.

---

[1] For Mascagni's *Guglielmo Ratcliff*, the first Italian *Literaturoper*, see general introduction, pp. 8–9.

[2] Verdi's last two operas, *Otello* (1887) and *Falstaff* (1893), had librettos adapted from Shakespeare by Arrigo Boito.

Someone said – rightly – that the maestro's imagination didn't soar to the upper spheres of genius. I greatly suspect that from now on these spheres will have such visits frequently ...[1] But no one could deny that perhaps it was the restraints imposed on him by the libretto that prevented these very lofty flights.

On the other hand, Montemezzi has not yet revealed his true creative personality to us. As I said yesterday morning, though he is an ingenious absorber of the expressions (*espressioni*) of modern art, he is not yet able to attain that process of assimilation that hides the origins, their provenance. However, the sources Montemezzi draws on offer us the best guarantees. His musical creations are not polluted, fortunately for us, by heterogeneous, inorganic substances.

Too much Wagner, too much Strauss in the music of *La Nave* was said two nights ago. I agree. Yet, indisputably – at least this is my opinion – Montemezzi has Italianised and softened their Teutonic procedures.

Were there blatant, unbearable anachronisms between the culminating situations of the tragedy and the music? Was the maestro unable to see the grandeur of the picture of *La Nave*, so as to carve the characteristic traits of its decorative lines and those of its scenic figures? Did he not take care that every act should proceed with the utmost unity? Were there differences of style, banal episodes and abstruse passages? Personally, I feel that such criticisms are misplaced. On the other hand, I would agree with those criticisms aimed at pointing out that the maestro has too often forgotten the traditions of *our singing* which, willy-nilly, is the vital substance of Latin art. I'm not referring to the singing of the orchestra, which, on the contrary, can be said to always sing eloquently in this opera, often with broad, warm

---

1 Nappi appears to mean simply that working with such unsuitable material has cramped Montemezzi's inspiration, which will now be free to take wing again. It is just possible, though, that he knew Montemezzi had decided to abandon the *Literaturoper* altogether: see general introduction, pp. 24–25.

waves of Italian melody, notwithstanding its thick polyphonic fabric; no, I'm referring to the *singing* of the human voice.

I know what our excellent friend Montemezzi can say to me: 'But the fragmentary character and particular structure of D'Annunzio's verses and libretto didn't allow me to make use of singing.' With this answer he will have fully confirmed my deep-rooted opinion: namely, that D'Annunzio's poems cannot be set to music as they were conceived and written.

I'm not disregarding the fact that Montemezzi frequently and effectively makes use of dramatic recitative; on the other hand, though, he makes excessive use of the would-be sung declamation, which in most cases is shouted declamation. It conspires against verisimilitude, for though it's true that people don't habitually sing in real life, it's also true that they don't shout their feelings – whether of sorrow, hatred, love, etc. etc. – except in moments of excessive cerebral excitement. Declamation, the way modern composers use it, and as it has been loaned to Montemezzi, is often very monotonous and irritating to the ears, and at the same time it compromises the singers' throats with disorderly, sudden changes of vocal register and very high *tessitura*.

All this is exotic stuff. Today, more than ever, we must free ourselves from the forms and systems that do not belong to us. It's *us* now, in music too. The time of artistic imports is over, when they can compromise the roots, the trunk of our ancient music traditions. These reflections do not deprive *La Nave* of its preeminent merit: that of being a re-affirmation of a very noble mind, of a skilful maestro, of a composer who, in his art, pursues the highest and most disinterested ideals.

Let's allow that Wagnerian and Straussian rays pass through *La Nave*. They cannot be burning beams, destructive of the sound disciplines of art and the laws of beauty.[1]

---

[1] Nappi seems to be alluding to the story of Archimedes setting fire to Roman ships by concentrating the sun's rays on them with mirrors.

As I wrote yesterday morning, Montemezzi's symphonic and choral work unconditionally deserves the admiration even of those not well versed in music. However, his whole opera deserves consideration, for its breadth, its fullness and the discerning application of the themes, which is not elevated into a now antiquated system; finally, the opera deserves consideration for its harmonic element, that doesn't infringe the modern, balanced dictates appropriate to this branch of the art of sound. Montemezzi should be praised for not having gone to scrape in the field of the *ars nova* those harmonic formulae, the latest figurines of musical fashion, without which, in the opinion of many, it's become impossible to make art properly.

Montemezzi is a sincere person, unlike some of his too cerebral colleagues, who pose as prophets of the art of tomorrow.

Tomorrow's art will be whatever it will be. Meanwhile, we ourselves should wish that today's art be correspondive to the soul, the heart of those who create.

In my opinion, it was in this way that Montemezzi composed the music of *La Nave*.

[Nappi concludes with a rather untranslatable reflection, riddled with puns, on the amazing fact that the premiere of *La Nave* coincided with the Italian victory in the war, and the wish that this will bring the opera luck: '*La Nave* is closely tied to the history of the completed Italian Risorgimento.']

Edward Johnson as Marco Gratico

5. Carlo Gatti, *L'Illustrazione Italiana*, 10 November 1918.

'LA NAVE'

O<small>N THE</small> night of the 3rd instant was performed at La Scala, for the first time, in the adaptation by Tito Ricordi with music by Italo Montemezzi, this naval tragedy by Gabriele D'Annunzio. It came at the right time to exalt the glory of our Homeland, wholly reconstituted and turning in freedom toward its radiant new destinies.

Maestro Montemezzi had the peculiar fortune of recognizing in every listener's heart the same throbs that must have moved his own when he set about composing this opera:[1] throbs caused by a too complete joy given the reality that must have been just a dream for the maestro when he began his work, but that now, on the contrary, on that unforgettable night, appeared to us more beautiful than a dream; clear, firm, and precise before our eyes. The intoxicating reality was the announcement, made in the opera house, of the martyr cities (*città martiri*) finally returned to us thanks to the valour and the sacrifice of our combatants, our Homeland made larger, more powerful, more august.

And Maestro Montemezzi will have rejoiced at this fortune happening to him, even though, perhaps, the news was able to claim part of the attention that should have been given to his music. But this is the pride of true art and the precise mark of its excellence: when it becomes the natural expression of simultaneous passions and mixes with them. Therefore we deem it right to bestow the highest praise upon the new opera, acknowledging its right to aspire to this pride.

We know: it has its own faults, and they are not small.

---

[1] Gatti's implication seems to be that Montemezzi was present at the premiere of *La Nave*, but, as other reviewers noted, this was not the case: the composer was unwell.

It's easy to recognize that *La Nave* derives directly from the Wagnerian opera its tones and forms; that the conversation of the characters is too slow, and the meaning of the words often sacrificed to the musical line, created separately; that the harmonization isn't excessively appealing to our modern sensibility, accustomed as we are to the chords that Montemezzi repeats; and that the instrumentation pleases us most of all for the sobriety with which it reproduces colours we already know well. One can feel, also, some discomfort from the excessive tonal restlessness of the musical periods, which are too short; from the questionable good taste with which they start their development, moving, for the most part, from the overused and weak second inversion of the perfect chord, then concluding and suddenly resting on a key that's nearly always different from the one in which they developed; and one might ask why the opera, despite containing an abundance of expressive means, is, in the end, slightly monotonous. The same monotony weighs on whole acts, which do not differ much from one another in character. And a more serious fault is that the figures of the different characters do not always have the necessary prominence: let's take as an example Basiliola, who is not, in the music, the sensual, bewitching and perverse female that the poet fully realized in the wonderful verses of his tragedy.

Yet Montemezzi has traits that reveal his value as a dramatic composer. He was able to infuse ample, vehement life into the character of Marco Gratico and into the chorus. In the chorus, the double tragedy that tires the spirits of the prince of the sea is extended and continued: it becomes the tragedy of the origin and the decadence of the early Venetians. It is a great merit of the composer that he has given back to the chorus its expressive force: something that, in recent times, had been fading in operas and musical composition in general.

But the note of pity melts the heart of Basiliola when she returns to see her blinded brothers, and when she whispers enrapturing love promises to the young tribune;[1] and we rejoice that the maestro was able to make the hidden fibres of our hearts vibrate so intensely, and move us at her prompt, loving, delicate sentiment. Therefore we say: Montemezzi may abandon the clothes he chose to wear because he thought the audience would like them. They are clothes of a foreign style, and they don't suit him.

There remains his own clothing, simple and distinguished, with which he can adorn himself and please the audience. His passion may remain tender and delicate: it will prove dear to our souls tired by many sentimental complications. His technique will be more than sufficient for his needs of expression, even if he abandons some of the wealth accumulated by studying and working on the models of the great composers arisen in recent times beyond our borders.

We love to accompany with all our affection composers such as Montemezzi, for they assure a bright future for our art. This affection is shared by the most illustrious great minds and noblest souls that honour our art. Here is one: maestro Tullio Serafin, who always gives all his fervid talent, inexhaustible activity and most affectionate cares to the young – this autumn season at La Scala proves the point. For *La Nave* he prepared an admirable

---

[1] Gatti's statement here is odd, as it is far from clear whether Basiliola's 'enrapturing love promises' (*promesse estasianti d'amore*) to Marco Gratico are ever motivated by, or combined with, pity. The only occasion on which she is described as whispering to him occurs in the Third Episode, after Marco has offered to release her: 'The fettered woman turns and whispers to him, stealing at him from beneath her narrowed lids those long slow glances before which all his opposing courage melted away.' It is possible for the viewer to interpret her offer to abandon 'treachery' at this juncture as genuine, and inspired by pity, but it was certainly not how D'Annunzio understood the matter. In a direction for this scene not included in the opera, he wrote 'Once more, once more, the temerarious female casts the dice on the ground and plays with her demon' (*La Nave* [Milan: Treves, 1908], 241).

performance, helped by excellent artists and by choral as well as orchestral forces worthy of their fame.

And here is another precious and affectionate collaborator of Montemezzi's: the painter Marussig, who had daring solutions for scenic stylization and synthesis that are ingenious and evocative. Once more, La Scala opera house accomplished its task in a lofty way: it introduced to the world, in the noblest manner, an opera and a composer deserving praise and fame.

6. Ugo Navarra, *Corriere di Milano*, 19 November and 3 December 1918.

La Nave

Lyrical Tragedy in a Prologue and Three Episodes by D'Annunzio and Montemezzi[1]

In a book I've written, publication of which has been delayed by the circumstances of the war, I devote a good deal of space to pointing out and analysing those various elements of historical and psychological character which led me to dare conclude that, 'if in Italy a national theatre exists, it is essentially a comic theatre and only with very rare exceptions a tragic theatre.'[2] A newspaper article dedicated to reviewing an opera obviously does not allow me to examine such a concept in detail here. However, it seems to me that anyone with any notions of our literary history, if they examine both our past heritage and contemporary culture, will come, with little difficulty, to similar or identical conclusions: especially if they have a clear vision of the huge difference existing between dramatic literature and 'performable' ('*rappresentabile*') theatre – an ugly yet effective adjective describing something that can possess scenic vitality.

This phenomenon is perhaps constitutional to our race. We are the authentic and most direct descendants of the Romans, and it seems that not even the deep transmutation which took place with the passage from the pagan to the Christian world has significantly affected the aesthetic attitudes of our people in this regard.

---

[1] As noted in the introduction, this review was also published separately as a pamphlet, *Critical Notes on Gabriele D'Annunzio's Lyrical Tragedy* La Nave *Abridged by Tito Ricordi for the Music of Italo Montemezzi* (Milan, 1918).

[2] The book Navarra refers to here appears not to have been published.

It is common knowledge, thanks to the unanimous testimonies of contemporary writers, that the people of Rome had little predilection for tragedy, and that the mediocre authors of pale imitations of the Greek tragedies, especially those of Euripides, never came close to the importance of Plautus and Terence.[1]

In this respect, Italian theatre is not very dissimilar. Our comic playwrights of the sixteenth century, though they did not create a national theatre, were possessed of such virtue that the influence of their productions was felt well beyond the borders of our country, and they were even considered the real fathers of the French theatre.[2] Some of their works could still be staged nowadays, and indeed sometimes are revived to the enjoyment of audiences, in the same way that Goldoni's masterpieces remain gloriously alive, and are performed almost every day.[3]

In the domain of tragedy, by contrast, whereas in London and all over the world the immortal genius of Shakespeare excites

---

[1] This is a very tendentious argument relying less on 'unanimous testimonies of contemporary writers' (such testimonies were, in any case, concerned more with literary quality than popularity) than on the survival of the comedies of Plautus and Terence into a later age and the corresponding loss of early Roman tragedies, which consequently received much less attention in later discussions of Roman theatre. Yet tragedy was, for centuries, a very important part of that theatre: see A. J. Boyle, *An Introduction to Roman Tragedy* (London and New York: Routledge, 2006). It was Seneca's tragedies that survived into a later age, and there has been a long-standing debate on whether they were written for theatrical performance or for private reading and recitation (Boyle 192). This may have prompted Navarra's belief that tragedy in Italy had always been more a literary than a theatrical form.

[2] A reference to the famous *Commedia dell'arte*, or improvised 'comedy of craft,' which has long been recognized as having had an enormous influence on French theatre, most notably the plays of Molière.

[3] Carlo Goldoni (1707–93) actually started his career writing tragedies, but the greater part of his theatrical work is in the field of comedy, and his most popular comedies, written between the 1740s and 1760s, became a permanent part of the Italian repertoire.

and moves every new generation, and whereas in France a real crowd will rush each week to pay a renewed tribute of admiration to Corneille and Racine, our poverty is so complete that even that little bit of Alfieri which still seems capable of taking the heat of the stage no longer finds interpreters, nor would it ever be enough to constitute a repertoire.[1] But on the other hand, who would consider staging Manzoni's *Adelchi* or Monti's *Aristodemo* or Niccolini's *Arnaldo*?[2] Nobody, right? It's because our tragedy, since the dawn of the Renaissance, was always essentially *literary* and never *theatrical*. There is a whole tradition representing the strange incapacity of the Italians to rescue their tragic theatre from the unnatural environment of the 'book' in which it is doomed to vegetate, and this incapacity is still everywhere evident after the numerous tragedies, so significant for their loftiness of thought, offered us by Gabriele D'Annunzio and Sem Benelli. It's a typical case that the latter, after revealing himself a true *man of the theatre* in dramas and comedies, failed in his most prominent qualities when approaching the tragedy.[3]

D'Annunzio's Tragedy

The figure of D'Annunzio as a dramatic poet is a very complex one. Putting aside the excellent poetical form, always exquisite,

---

[1] Vittorio Alfieri (1749–1803), generally considered the founder of Italian tragedy because he did so much to raise the cultural standing of the genre. Of his plays, *Saul* (1782) was much the most securely established in the repertoire. In 1932 Joseph Spencer Kennard estimated that 'No other tragedy has been so often performed in Italy.' See *The Italian Theatre: From the Close of the Seventeenth Century*, 2 vols (New York: William Edwin Rudge, 1932), 1:153.

[2] *Adelchi* (1822) by Alessandro Manzoni (1785–1873), *Aristodemo* (1786) by Vincenzo Monti (1754–1828) and *Arnaldo da Brescia* (1843) by Giovanni Battista Niccolini (1782–1861).

[3] This is a significant comment given that Benelli's first tragedy was *L'Amore dei Tre Re* (1910). See general introduction, p. 15.

with which his dramatic creations are adorned, if we set ourselves to observe them simply from the point of view of their theatricality, we notice, not without some amazement, that in each of them the *mother idea* (l'*idea madre*) could have generated a succession of scenes susceptible of arousing passion and interesting the audience, but that, with one exception, this mother idea remains stifled, or appears obscured and nearly lost amid too many extraneous elements. At the same time, the absence of a logical progression of events highlights the fact that those eternal maxims of Aristotle cannot be violated with impunity, of which perhaps the most unbreakable is that of 'unity of action.'

I mentioned one exception: *Francesca*.[1] It's not difficult to recognize the reason. This play turned out to be more organic than her sisters, because here the poet's sometimes too fervid imagination was restrained by his use of an existing plot, and one that didn't allow, under penalty of deforming its lines, excessive ornamentation and arabesques in the pitiful story of the two lovers.

Therefore, of D'Annunzio's tragedies set to music, *Figlia di Iorio, Parisina, Fedra, La Nave* and *Francesca*, only this one, with a score by Zandonai, appears as a happy marriage of the two elements uniting to form a work of art.[2]

The original text of *La Nave* is not only too long for a theatrical performance (many cuts had to be made even before its first performance at the Teatro Argentina in Rome), it is also excessively rich in dramatic 'motifs.'

Three of these appear with particular prominence, and they can be found in the excellent adaptation prepared by Tito Ricordi, which cuts several thousand lines and some secondary characters. The grim loves and burning hatreds of *Basiliola* pass prominently into the foreground of the picture. However, it can be intuited that in the mind and the intentions of the poet

---

1 *Francesca da Rimini* (1902), D'Annunzio's earliest play in verse.

2 For these *Literaturopern*, see general introduction, pp. 11–12, 20–23.

they had to remain an episode, like the rather different affair of Margaret in *Faust*,[1] meaning that the leading idea of the tragedy should have remained the *ship*, since from this the play takes its title, which would otherwise have been *Basiliola*. However, if the process of stripping the flesh off the plethoric poem led to such a transmutation of the essential values of the tragedy, it wouldn't be fair to hold the adapter too responsible, because it is the scenic substance of what was supposed to constitute the basis of the dramatic idea that ran out, it having received insufficient *effective* (*fattivo*) as opposed to *verbal* development.

And it is possible to see that perhaps there flashed for an instant at least in the author's mind the idea that the protagonist of the tragedy was actually those rough, brave people, the primordial inhabitants of the Venetian lagoons, admirable and superb in the harsh travails they endured to build a homeland for themselves, and, when freed from the last vestiges of the Greco-Byzantine civilization, rising to the dignity of a free nation, teacher and master of its most sublime destinies.

From the poem to the libretto

Of these three different conceptions, the superimposition of which does not appear so evident in D'Annunzio's original and integral text, the one personified in the form of *Basiliola* dominates the libretto from end to end. The residual elements of the other two, reduced to simple ruins, isolated and lonely, without any apparent cause and effect relationship to the story of the Gratici and Faledri, are forced to assume the character of pleonastic accessories; a confused perception of them muddles the audience's clear vision and hampers their comprehension of the drama not less than the fifty and more archaic terms impossible to find in the best dictionaries.

---

[1] Goethe's *Faust* (1808). Navarra presumably intended an ironic analogy, Margaret being the complete antithesis of Basiliola.

Thus forcedly limited to having to consider only the '*romance*' of *Basiliola* – the one character of the tragedy possessed of an intrinsic life – how very disjointed and incomplete we find the total *penetration* of her psychology! The logical progression of the various factors that should lead the spectator step by step toward the catastrophe, and which is the very dynamic of the dramatic action, can be perceived only in very broad lines. For example, it is anything but clear whether the Gratici really were responsible for the blinding of all the males of the Faledra race; but even accepting such a premise as true, none of the many episodes far less necessary to the economy of the action shows us how *Basiliola*, in her great hatred, managed to seduce the two brothers and be at the same time the paramour of both. And why, after the revelation of such incest by the *Traba* monk, doesn't Marco Gratico – whom the news leaves completely cold – burst into invectives at the woman? And how is it that instead, without showing himself struck in his religious feelings (he who often appears to us as a mystic), or hurt in his male dignity, he descends in his jealousy as a lover to kneeling before the haughty and untamed woman? Even less can we understand why this mannequin of a weak-kneed hero later rises up unexpectedly against his brother and provokes him to mortal combat. And then that bishop, who does not hesitate a moment before preparing for the nefarious crime that he might commit in killing his brother: he too stands outside ordinary humanity, and his action strikes us as even less realistic, since until this juncture his personality is unknown to the spectator.

But the point in the play which appears most supremely obscure, because of the lack of any preparation for its overwhelming burst of passions, is precisely this brotherly duel that the author has *Basiliola* name the 'judgement of God' ('*giudizio di Dio*'). A judgement for what? For the bishop's heresy, it is said. However, it does not seem that this is the best 'jurisdiction' ('*foro competente*') to solve the controversy. Is it not rather about who will finally enjoy the beautiful *Faledra*? This would appear more likely. But then we cannot clearly see why the honourable Deity would have an interest in attending such a dirty contest.

Among the many observations that a fleeting analysis of the tragedy suggests, those detailed here demonstrate that we should pardon the excellent Montemezzi a great deal if various parts of his composition appear defective.

From the libretto to the music

Given these faults in the ground on which the musical construction was to be erected, however, why is it that the Veronese Maestro, who had already revealed himself an intelligent opera composer, did not think of repairing them? Once Montemezzi had proceeded past the consideration of whether D'Annunzio's *Nave* was a good or bad choice, and even granting that he had seen or sensed in the play enough positive elements suitable for an opera, when accepting it he should have considered immediately the very special requirements of the opera theatre and asked, perhaps the poet himself, for those indispensable alterations that by strengthening the course of the action would make the play more agile, more organic, and not dependent for many essential details on stage directions and verbal hints that are easily missed.

What is the benefit and use, to the general economy of the tragedy, of the whole episode, bordering on the grotesque, of the prisoners possessed with crude sadism in the Fuia pit? The idea was presumably to characterize the type of the fascinating and perverse woman, but in the lyric theatre it simply constitutes a sheer encumbrance for the composer. Oh! and how much more opportunely that precious time could have been given over to the insertion of a new scene in which *Sergio Gratico* could reveal more of his character and his relationship to the whole of the tragic action.

In the first act[1] the composer has one of his best moments, as the

---

1 I.e. the Prologue.

crowd expresses its joy at the arrival of the *Gratici*; it's a situation Montemezzi felt strongly and represented very happily. So, when the chorus reaches the climax of its vehement peroration, the music, and perhaps the action, too, spontaneously generates the feeling that there is a necessity or opportunity for the phonic edifice to be crowned, before the passing of the procession, by the awaited and acclaimed hero saying a word to the people that responds to their feelings, to the flame of admiration and affection with which they will exalt him shortly afterwards. Instead, seized by the *reverential fear* of not changing a single detail in the original text, Montemezzi is forced to freeze the forward impetus of his music and to proceed to the chilly motion of the processional march.

Our illustrious friend Nappi observed that the transformation of the tragedy into a libretto should have demanded an elimination of the monotony of the verse, with its always uniform metre.[1] I don't know whether to agree. Mascagni was able to compose his best work on Maffei's hendecasyllables, while Massenet was not paralysed in his inspiration when composing *Thaïs* over the rhythmical prose of Louis Gallet.[2] And the opinion is quite widespread that the matter of the melic poetry is prejudicial, and that the composer can be granted greater freedom, sparing him every tie to the verbal rhythm.

On the contrary, what I deem ruinous to anyone still seduced into adding his music to D'Annunzio's verses is the acceptance of the order and cut of the scenes as they appear in the original text. Certainly the art of libretto writing is a hybrid art, but it is not as base as is commonly maintained, and the crisis of our musical theatre is perhaps due in great part to the librettos. It is

---

1 See above, p. 97.

2 This is high praise for Mascagni's *Guglielmo Ratcliff* (1895), the first Italian *Literaturoper*, for which see general introduction, pp. 8–9. Massenet's *Thaïs* (1894) is regarded as one of his greatest works. Navarra's point is that these operas prove that metrical variety is not necessary for musical inspiration.

necessary to give the composer opportunities for *action*, because the audience will only understand the words a little, or even badly, and with all their attention dedicated to the music they do not want to be distracted into having to decipher psychological complications or confused enigmas.

Therefore, if a true librettist had reconstructed the threads of D'Annunzio's creation, it is possible he would have known better how to highlight the importance of the *Ship*, the real protagonist. We can observe an analogous case in *Mosè*, where, in order to make the action more interesting, the little matter of the loves between *Amenofi* and *Anaide* was inserted; however, the authors carefully avoided spoiling the grand architecture of the sacred drama by giving too much prominence to this, which always remains a minor episode.[1]

Had something similar been done with *La Nave*, the first to benefit would have been Montemezzi himself, for the enormous superiority of the first and fourth acts over the other two in a musical point of view reveals that he *felt* the dramatic motifs of the 'primordial people' and of the *Ship* much more than the story of *Basiliola*, to which the central acts are exclusively dedicated.

But I'll discuss this further in the next issue, as well as the musical content of the score and its relation to and blending with the tragedy, for want of space here.[2]

The work of art

Jules Combarieu,[3] one of the finest musicologists of recent times (who died prematurely during the war), attracted atten-

---

1 Navarra refers to Rossini's opera *Mosè in Egitto* (1818), which had recently been revived: see above, p. 88 and n. 1.

2 The first part of Navarra's review ended here.

3 Combarieu (1859–1916) wrote several influential studies of the history and evolution of music.

tion when still very young by maintaining the following thesis for his degree in Literature at the Sorbonne: 'From the point of view of rhythm, modern music resembles the musical poetry of the Greeks as much as it differs, in all points of view, from modern poetry.'[1] And in his learned and brilliant work he describes the relations between the two elements in modern opera theatre thus: '*Le poète est le maître du musicien, mais c'est un maître qui achète sa souveraineté par les plus grands sacrifices, et ne prend le sceptre que pour revêtir le plus pauvre costume.*'[2]

Is D'Annunzio a master of that sort? Of course not. He is much more of a despot than his *Marco Gratico*, and his powerful personality tends to dominate imperiously; hence, in the clash between two opposing wills, it is nearly always the composer who comes off worse. In vain have composers of very strong fibre ventured on setting D'Annunzio's lines, for each of them, whilst managing to create a few pages of great value, saw his efforts become sterile when he aimed at making his melody *adhere* to the verse by the poet of the Laudi,[3] so musical yet so difficult to set to music. In many cases the vigour of the verbal expression or description is so full and powerful that Euterpe can add nothing to what Melpomene inscribes so definitively.

It is probable that in setting about his hard task Montemezzi asked himself the dreadful question: how could he better manage to ensure that the work of art resulting from the union of poetry and music would appear as an organic *whole*, with a perfect balance and blending of the various elements?

---

[1] *Les rapports de la musique et de la poésie considérées au point de vue de l'expression* (Paris, 1893), xv.

[2] Ibid. 356. The statement translates: 'The poet is the master of the musician, but a master who acquires his sovereignty through the greatest sacrifices, taking the sceptre only to don the poorest costume.'

[3] Between 1903 and 1918 D'Annunzio published five volumes of poetry, under the general title *Laudi*.

The solution he sought is revealed by his score itself: it is the constant adoption of the *musical declamato*. The formula is certainly in accord with the principles informing modern opera; yet, *est modus in rebus*,[1] and however great the composer's ability in varying and giving agility to this oratory, and Montemezzi's is, no one can avoid the sense of uniformity and weariness that the spectator experiences, especially if, like us, he still has a weakness for preserving ... the superstition of *singing*.

I would not deny that in recent years I have happened to hear in Paris several lyrical dramas and tragedies, praised to the skies by the French critics, in which every trace of singing, understood in its broadest sense, was rigorously banned. Among the most illustrious examples I remember Gabriel Fauré's *Prometheus* and Vincent D'Indy's *Fervaal*, both of which various eminent musical friends in France proclaimed to me, with the utmost seriousness, as the most sublime masterpieces of their contemporary music, setting them even above *Pelléas* and *Arianne*.[2] However the good audiences, on the contrary, found them supremely boring and, abandoning the Opéra, ran in droves to hear again *les italiens* (Puccini, Leoncavallo, etc.) at the *Opéra Comique*.

Now, God forbid! I wouldn't think of putting the *Tosca*s, *Pagliacci*s, and various *Butterfly*s, the delight of the Parisians, before the present most noble and worthy work by Montemezzi.

I linger over this anecdote just to point out that we Italians have an illustrious tradition of singing, by virtue of which our musical theatre was and still is sovereign ruler on all stages around the world. By voluntarily renouncing what was always

---

1 I.e. there is measure in all things.

2 The references are to Faure's *Prométhée* (1900), which had been revived, with a reduced orchestration, in 1917; D'Indy's *Fervaal* (published 1895, premiered 1897), last performed in 1913; Debussy's classic *Literaturoper*, *Pelléas et Mélisande* (1902); and Paul Dukas's *Ariane et Barbe-bleue* (1907), another *Literaturoper* on a play by Maeterlinck.

one of the leading features of its fortune, we really abjure one of the most distinctive characteristics of our national personality.

In his wonderful evolution, Verdi, by freeing himself from the old-fashioned customs of the *recitativo secco*, was able to attain that model of dramatic declamation that is *Otello*'s monologue: *Dio, mi potevi scagliar tutti i mali* (God, you could have thrown every evil at me). But the Great Old Man, in that very passage, showed that it was not at all unbecoming to the effectiveness of his inspiration to give a movement of lyrical excitement to the moment when his hero's soul swells with memories and he weeps over the destruction of his love dream.

I heard the unavoidable apostrophe being thrown about around me: The author lacks inspiration! And the even more common charge: There is no melody! Nothing could be falser! Evidently the *musical declamato* cannot be moulded into a melodic form, at least according to that which is commonly designated by that term; yet the modern composer who, like our Author, knows the resources of the instrumental symphony, has a hundred voices in the pit on which to confer the prestige of a more winged eloquence. In this regard, I only regret the stubborn frequency with which he appears to take pleasure in swiftly breaking up the happiest phrases which, like Minerva from Jupiter's brain, seem to emerge complete from his imagination; one has to conclude that he feels an aversion to letting the musical discourse flow for some bars.

The character of the music

If I've come to the persuasion that the absence of any *oasis* of singing in the voices of the individual interpreters is intentional, a response to the rigid observance of a preset formula, it is because I remember, and very pleasantly, the Montemezzi of *L'Amore dei tre Re* and even more because I always seemed to sense in him the absolute prevalence of a *lyrical temperament*.

His character in this respect is attested by several *moments* in the new work, which really required a quite different strength (*nerbo*), and a quite different dramatic impetus, in the musical translation. Whatever might be D'Annunzio's flaws in his capacity as a writer for the theatre, no one would dream of contesting the power of the *epic* conception always immanent in his tragic poem.

Now epic poetry and lyricism have at all times been the two opposite poles of the artistic vision and manifestation; and from this derives the contrast between the composer's temperament and the requirements of the situation revealed in some scenes, such as that in which the wild figure of the *Traba Monk* is prominent, and that still wilder scene of the *Fuia Pit*.

The Anchorite's dreadful invectives, stirrers of the biggest storms in the characters' souls, appear very much superior in their plastic rawness to the honest but colourless orchestral comment that accompanies them!

And what of the other scene? Admitting at once that nobody would have been able to draw out of it anything useful to the musical progress of the tragedy, is it nevertheless imaginable that it could be effectively represented with music that is, apart from two or three slightly more vigorous yet inexpressive bars, all whipped cream and sugar (*lattemiele*)? A true musical dramatist, a Richard Strauss for example, would surely have found some turbid chords, some vehement movements with disorderly rhythm, some unusual instrumental mixtures, some mysterious phonic effects ... in short, some devilry that could give shape to the horror, the dread, the disgust provoked by the sadistic ravings of those madmen and the dreadful carnage the *Faledra* inflicts on them.

This first half of the second act is, as to musical value, of the same stature as the following act.[1] However, it's useful to make a clear

---

[1] Navarra's terms of reference are confusing: by 'the following act' he means the Second Episode, which he then proceeds to discuss.

distinction here: whilst in the former the fault was in the libretto, in the latter we cannot ignore the composer's responsibility.

The wildness of the orgy; the now famous dance of the seven candleholders; the contrast of the people's factions; the fratricidal duel; the announcement of the enemy raid; the litanies – all these are so many dramatic or scenic motifs of assured theatricality offered to the composer's inspiration. By repeatedly attending the performance of this grand scene, so correct in its proportions, so concise, fervent, agitated I would almost say in its movement, I was unable to avoid the incoercible idea of what could have been done with it by Modest Mussorgsky. And if I felt so much nostalgia for the composer of *Boris*, it is because neither musically nor dramatically does Montemezzi persuade me here. In the dances he was perhaps obsessed by the worry of doing things differently from his predecessor in the same undertaking;[1] what's certain is that they appear anaemic, whereas they demanded the greatest vividness of the orchestral palette.

In the duel, that sobriety for which everybody likes Montemezzi, and finds him worthy of sincere praise, deprived him of the boldness to fully raise himself to the loftiness of the tragic moment. And finally, in the finale of the act, being the expert contrapuntist that he is, how could he not notice what an immense horizon would have opened before him had he adopted the *canto fermo*[2] to give the hieratic chorus a powerful prominence over the harmonic construction of its instrumental polyphony? Alas! From the *Miserere* in *Trovatore* to the *vespers* in *Gioconda*,[3] we all know too well the very stale method of having the soloists replying with

---

[1] I.e. differently from Pizzetti, who had written the incidental music to the spoken play.

[2] The *canto fermo*, or *cantus firmus*, was the 'fixed song' or pre-existing melody that typically formed the basis of a polyphonic composition prior to the sixteenth century.

[3] Verdi's *Il Trovatore* (1853) and Ponchielli's *La Gioconda* (1876).

high notes over the background of the homophonous choir, and we really expected something more modern from a work that bears the august date of the capture of Trento and Trieste.

The happiest pages

Conversely, the best confirmation that Montemezzi is essentially a *lyrist* is offered by the love duet, which resulted in one of the most exquisite pages of the whole score and is without any doubt the only episode of *Basiliola*'s drama capable of exerting a sincere fascination over the listener's soul. Here the followers of the most forbidding aesthetics owe the composer a large tribute of admiration, because no little asperity made each compositional step very difficult, and because he never for an instant betrays the effort.

How complex and contradictory are the feelings of the two characters! Lust, seduction, anger, dissimulating hatred, jealousy, pride, sincere vehemence and feline deceitfulness: all the passions which can violently agitate the depths of the human soul. And all of these, or nearly all, the music manages to illustrate with its countless possibilities of expression, assuming a variety of attitudes and a ductility of language thanks to which the spectator fails to notice the almost excessive duration of the dialogue. Indeed, without fatigue he reaches that final *sustained* (*filata*) note of the soprano under which the orchestra concludes its always interesting commentary as the act ends delightfully.

I have already said that the prologue and most of the final episode are well above the rest of the work, because they were deeply *felt* by the composer: the dramatic motif of the *primordial people* dominating and forming the substratum of the former and that of the *Ship* providing the foundation of the latter.

The crowd, in both, has its own individuality and reveals, with a nice variety of musical attitudes, the moods it passes through. Even though in rare cases (such as the *Alleluia*) the starting point (*spunto*) and form seem a bit old-fashioned, on the whole the lines of the choral polyphony are of a majesty, yet nevertheless an elegant simplicity, such as perhaps not many contemporary composers would be able to produce. The technique of the contrapuntist reveals here its value and modernity, understood in the best sense, and gives the measure of the intense, continuous and noble aspiration of Montemezzi to a loftier ideal, toward which to direct our melodrama.

Besides the chorus, what one often listens to with pleasure, even when it betrays some *défaillance* in relation to the tragedy, is the orchestra.

The symphonic discourse in *La Nave*, like that already found in *L'Amore dei tre re*, is fast, fluent, and rich in ideas; it interests us not with stylistic precocities, nor with rare harmonic expedients, but with a certain personal fascination of its own (as *Falstaff* would say[1]) made of impetuous agitation and languid evanescences, of querulous chirping in the woodwinds, of exquisite fullness (*rotondità*) in the strings (in the preferred Italian way), of abrupt and powerful blasts from the brass, used with praiseworthy good taste.

While on this theme, it's impossible to pass over in silence *the procession of the catechumens* (novices), entirely built as it is on short chords struck from the strings (*strappate*) marking and emphasizing the solemn rhythm with a new and strange effect; thanks to its very characteristic aspect, this magnificently composed passage will certainly remain lastingly impressed in the memory of the listeners.

As to the overall character of the music, from the point of view of the different artistic schools, there would have been a curious ideological conflict had the tragedy borne the genuine

---

[1] Navarra adapts Falstaff's words in Act 2 of the Verdi-Boito *Falstaff*: 'un certo qual mio fascino personal!' ('a certain personal fascination of my own!'). There is no direct equivalent in Shakespeare, where Falstaff, at this point, says 'Setting the attraction of my good parts aside, I have no other charms' (*Merry Wives of Windsor* 2.2).

and austere stamp of the classical tradition. This is certainly not the case, though; hence that flavour of eclectic *neo-romanticism* that can be perceived in the musical development of the new work, in which flicker (*guizza*) some reminiscences, or at least some refractions, more harmonic than melodic, of *Tristan* and *Parsifal*, without disturbing the overall aesthetic impression of the work of art. Free from every banality and every pursuit of facile success, valuable for the sense of measure that informs the whole, the opera certainly suffers from the defects of its source (*vizio d'origine*) discussed above; however, it remains a valuable document of the stern conscience of a young man who brings honour to the current musical generation and toward whom the Italian opera theatre can turn its eyes with full confidence.

The performance and the success

In a more than full house, blazing with lights, if the quivering nerves of the magnificent audience had found in the music a flame of communicative ardour equal to that which was stirring them, if *Marco Gratico*'s formal address concluding in the famous incitement *Arma la prora e salpa verso il mondo* (Arm the prow and sail toward the world), one of the most significant moments of D'Annunzio's poem, had contained in itself those tones that touch the heart and shake all its fibres, the consecration of the new work would have assumed triumphal proportions.

Instead, the success was very good, yet calm. It was expressed on the first night through numerous curtain calls for the wonderful interpreters, and this remained the case at the subsequent performances, which were attended – to prolonged acclaim – by the composer, previously confined to bed because of an indisposition.

The *Sifal*[1] could not have attested its intentions in a nobler way than by staging with such loving care this work of great proportions.

---

[1] See introduction, pp. 55–56.

The real and authentic creation of the inconstant and complex character of Basiliola made by Signora Serafin-Rakowska marks an august stage in her career as an artist. Indefatigable under the weight of an overwhelming vocal part, she was able to find such subtleties in the byplay, and had a mobility of expression in her countenance that would make a great actress envious.

Edoardo de Giovanni brought the radiance of broad central notes and well sustained high notes, and was appreciable also for the clarity of his diction and the intelligence with which he tried to give an appearance of life to *Marco Gratico*.

The baritone Cigada performed very well, with a powerful voice; really typical in the guise of the *Traba Monk* was the bass Cirino; the bass Carozzi was excellent, and praise needs to be extended also to Bonfanti, Treves and the others who performed the minor roles with ability and conscientiousness.

Tullio Serafin, the inflamed animator of the numerous orchestral and choral forces, a confident and faithful interpreter of the composer's intentions, reached the ideal of what it is legitimate to ask of a great conductor. Certainly much is owed to him if this performance proved in everything very worthy of being recorded in La Scala's Roll of Honour.

The staging, all beautiful, demands some special mention in order to pay homage to Guido Marussig, from Trieste, the creator of the scenery. When a work of art is integrated with a decorative element as brilliantly conceived as the backdrops and costumes by Marussig, we can talk of a real and exquisite artistic collaboration with regard to the painter, too; in the present case we are indebted to him if the spectator's aesthetic enjoyment was enhanced and made more complete.

7. Giacomo Orefice, *Rivista d'Italia*, 30 November 1918.

Musical Review

WE CERTAINLY find wealth and a profusion of means in *La Nave* by Italo Montemezzi; and an organism – still on the subject of this primary factor of the vitality of an opera[1] – healthily and strongly formed. Yet this organism does not possess its own individuality. Or, to be more precise, in its musical structure *La Nave* follows the Wagnerian opera faithfully; and that is too personal and characteristic to lend itself to any experiment in assimilation.

Already in *L'Amore dei tre re* Montemezzi had attempted this trial. And there he certainly obtained a more justified success, because the Wagnerian formula, made more fluent and lean (*snella*) in that opera, fitted, in a certain way, the general character of the poem, and that of some of the main characters, Teutonic and barbaric in the very expression of their sentiments of love.

I certainly am not liable to any suspicion of nationalist exclusivity.[2] But in *La Nave*, where even in the men's primitive roughness and the wild habit of their exploits there is revealed, according to the poet's intentions, the *Italian soul*, the constant use of a musical formula that, through an inevitable association of ideas, reminds us of the most famous heroes of the Wagnerian opera, irritates us by its striking contrast.[3] On the other hand –

---

1 Orefice reviewed three La Scala productions together, and has just been discussing Renzo Bianchi's *Ghismonda*.

2 Like most Italian composers of his generation, Orefice had admitted foreign influences, including Wagner, into his music.

3 The same charge can and has been brought against Orefice's own operas. In his standard study of the composer, Adriano Bassi writes, in the course of his analysis of *Mosè*, 'For the umpteenth time, the Wagnerism enters the scene, reproducing sonorities that are now familiar and reminding us of mythological episodes that do not belong to our Latin culture.' See Bassi, *Orefice*, 99.

Giacomo Orefice (1865–1922)
The only important opera composer
to review *La Nave* in 1918

it must be said – what Montemezzi has absorbed and transfused in *La Nave* is certainly not the best part of the Wagnerian art. It is that *musical manner* (*maniera musicale*) as opposed to music which Wagner used to create much of his operas. It is heavy and often inconclusive; Wagner himself didn't attach any importance to it as an expression of his musical thought, though he considered it necessary for the expression of his philosophical and poetical ideas. It is that part of the Wagnerian operas which in Italy it is customary to *amputate* as vigorously as possible, in order to arrive sooner at those moments that subjugate us with the grandiosity of their structural lines and fascinate us with the spell of their expressive beauty.

Many *cuts* would need to be made to *La Nave*, according to this criterion, in order to effectively *join* those pages of the score where – without resorting to absurd and unnecessary comparisons – we can still state with certainty that Montemezzi makes *music*, in the most noble and complete sense of the word.

So, while the opera starts with a very graceful instrumental page, in the sounds of which, although simple and soft, is contained all the poetry of the evening hour over the sea and almost a presentiment of the destinies that shall rule it, it is then necessary to cross broad fields of musical *dryness* (*siccità*) – which the skilful and elegant discourse of modulations, together with the varied and pleasant succession of orchestral movements and sonorities, is insufficient to embellish – to arrive at a new passage of genuine lyricism: the *apostrophe of Basiliola* to her blinded brothers. The same happens later, before we arrive at the *procession of the Holy Bodies*: this too is not excessively convincing in its formal structure, although it has a colour, halfway between the liturgical and the heroic, that is very appropriate. It is the same again before the *scene of the parliament*[1] which, over the fabric of the rhythmic pattern

---

[1] Presumably the scene in which Marco Gratico is elected tribune.

in the *buccine*,[1] concludes with a beautiful unity of form and a powerful balance of sonorities.

Nor fuller of true musical substance appears the *scene of Traba* that separates, in the first episode, the scene of the *Fuia Pit* (which, despite an abundance of discussion and criticism, still seems to me a noteworthy example of construction and synthesis) from the *duet between Gratico and Basiliola*, more than ever impregnated with Wagnerian marrow, that nevertheless has not only tones of great effectiveness and a broad melodic breath, but also a leading line through which beats a secure pulse (*sicuro polso*).

Proceeding further, and still considering the opera from this point of view, which is necessarily the true one, in the second episode we no longer find the *ubi consistam*.[2] We do find it in the third episode, wholly built on fragments from the preceding episodes, in the introductory prelude and in some other passages that merely reproduce music already heard in the course of the opera, although neglecting to *intensify the expression*, as the hastening of the tragedy to its catastrophe should have required.

Certainly, failing to appreciate the merits of that part of Montemezzi's opera – the largest part – that seems to me, I repeat, more deliberate and decorative than substantial and felt, would be to do him an injustice. The author of *La Nave*, in fact, now possesses his innate talent as an opera composer in all its maturity and supports it by the most refined means of expression and technique. He has an intuition for the musical situation, the confident perception of the theatre, the exact sense of the balance between stage and orchestra, that is so difficult and rare. He handles voices and instruments with pointed confidence. He harmonizes with elegance and clarity. Most of

---

1 See above, p. 43, n. 2.

2 Fixed point and/or solid ground.

all, and this is a quality that surpasses even the previous ones, he never lacks taste and measure.

And it is exactly thanks to this *bone structure (ossatura)*, to all these elements that are like the nerves, the muscles and the living blood of the opera, that the musical organism of *La Nave* appears, to those who do not expect to find in it, additionally, an original animating spirit, strongly constituted.

We ought to assign to Montemezzi, as the author of the musical architecture of the opera, a merit even superior to that of the *librettist*. I shall not talk of the *poet*, since precisely everything that comprises the *poetic element* in the *tragedy* of *La Nave* disappears in the *opera* of *La Nave* (disappears, fatally, as I have already said, because of the very union between words and music) to leave uncovered (*scoperto*) only the *theatrical element*. Now *La Nave*, like all D'Annunzian theatre, is valuable for what the characters say, rather than for what they do. The composer who decides to set this theatre to music finds in it a music – *already made*, therefore – of words, and on the contrary a remarkable absence of any substantial dramatic element. That is, when there are not, as often happens in *La Nave*, characters and scenes depicted that have such an obvious counterpart in others dramas and other operas as to impose on the composer a huge challenge to avoid resorting to plagiarism.

There was, it is true, in the tragedy, or rather around it, a great element of lyricism, capable of arousing the impetus of the composer. Yet perhaps this is precisely what the composer *felt* the least. I should be understood as referring to the vision of the primordial Venice; of the wish for its greatness contained in the tenacious spirit of its people and emanating from the sea itself that the symbolic hero prepares to plough with no return, to the prophetic invocations: '*Arm the prow and sail toward the world!*' ... '*Restore the Adriatic to Thy people!*' What did Montemezzi do with this? He was able to find no corresponding cry in his soul, nor a comparable process of thought.

And this is probably what he will be reproached for most by those who expected that *La Nave* must be, both for the intentions contained within the poem and for the great historical moment when – although fortuitously – the opera saw the light of the day, an affirmation of the Italian spirit.

Part Three

Second Production

Chicago, The Auditorium Theatre, 18 November 1919

Cast:
Basiliola . . . . Rosa Raisa
Marco Gratico . . . . Alessandro Dolci
Sergio Gratico. . . . . Giacomo Rimini
Orso Faledro . . . . Vittorio Arimondi
Traba, the monk . . . . . . Virgilio Lazzari

Director: Cleofonte Campanini
Stage and Costume Design: Norman Bel Geddes
Conductor: Italo Montemezzi

2 performances

The Auditorium Theatre, Chicago, 1929
The Home of the Chicago Opera Company, 1910–1929

Introduction

IN HIS short biography of Montemezzi, published in 1952, Giuseppe Silvestri states that after the production of *La Nave* at La Scala, 'other important Italian theatres' made plans to stage the opera.[1] This was almost certainly on Montemezzi's authority, like much else in the biography. It would not be surprising: a major new Italian opera so attuned to contemporary events, and which had managed 10 performances at La Scala, was bound to appear attractive. Yet none of these planned productions materialized. Possibly theatre managements were put off when they realized the difficulty and expense of staging the work, and possibly Casa Ricordi discouraged such productions until a prestigious international premiere could be arranged. What is more certain is that the movement of history, which had seemed to be working so much in favour of the opera, now began to work in a contrary direction. When the Peace Conference opened in Paris on 18 January 1919 it soon became clear that the international community, strongly influenced by the ideals of the American President, Woodrow Wilson, would not allow a 'Greater Italy' to spread too far around the Adriatic. This led to intense opposition to the peace terms in Italy, and ultimately, in September 1919, to D'Annunzio's famous, or notorious, armed takeover of Fiume, the Adriatic port that is now Rijeka in Croatia. At this point, perhaps, the relevance of *La Nave* briefly peaked, though it was a relevance most impresarios would have been shy of exploiting. But in the following months, as it became clear that the rather farcical Fiumean adventure was doomed, *La Nave* began to stand in an increasingly ironic relationship to modern history; the likelihood of an Italian revival accordingly receded.

---

1 *Omaggio a Italo Montemezzi*, ed. Luigi Tretti and Lionello Fiumi (Verona: Comitato Onoranze a Italo Montemezzi, 1952), 32. Hereafter *Omaggio*.

Against this background, *La Nave* received its international premiere at the Auditorium Theatre, Chicago, on 18 November 1919, where it opened the opera season. The American critics were aware that D'Annunzio was by then the 'Duce' of Fiume, and some of them saw the relevance of this to the opera, but for the most part they were not interested in the politics of the work, and in fact much less exercised by the fact that it was a D'Annunzio text than their Italian counterparts. For the Americans, *La Nave* was, first and foremost, a major new work by the composer of *L'Amore dei Tre Re*, and a huge prestige event for the Chicago company. The Chicago Grand Opera Company had only been created in 1910; until then the city had been dependent on visiting companies from New York for its opera. The company had included *L'Amore dei Tre Re* in their 1915–16 season, and were well aware of the cult following that opera had acquired in New York. To have beaten New York to *La Nave* was a source of local pride, and Cleofonte Campanini (1860–1919), the director, spared no expense to make the production a magnificent one. Some $60,000 was widely reported to have been spent, making it the costliest production in the company's history. To render the occasion as historic as possible, Campanini invited Montemezzi himself to Chicago to conduct the work. It was the first time the composer had travelled outside Continental Europe, and the first time he had conducted in public. His role in the proceedings won high praise.

The American critics had a very different style of reviewing from their Italian counterparts. They were less interested in deep musical and dramatic analysis, and for the most part not concerned about *La Nave* being a *Literaturoper*. They were more concerned with judging the opera as a performance, spectacle and entertainment. As well as recognizing the production as very prestigious and challenging, and an honour to Chicago, they devoted a good deal of their attention to two aspects of the production in a way not anticipated by the Italian reviewers: Rosa Raisa's performance as Basiliola and Norman Bel Geddes' stage and costume designs. Elena Rakowska, who had created the role of Basiliola, and obtained brief but appreciative notices from the Italian critics, would have been amazed to see how much attention her Chicago counterpart claimed, and Guido Marussig, whose designs for La Scala had been well received, would have been surprised by just how controversial Bel Geddes had managed to be. Raisa and Bel Geddes thus need some introduction here.

Rosa Raisa (1893–1963) was born Raitza Burchstein in Bialystok, now in Poland but at that time within the Russian Empire.[1] She came from a middle-class Jewish family. After the 1906 pogrom, in which seventy-five Jews were killed in Bialystok, she made a life-changing decision to immigrate to Italy, pretending to be her cousin's maid. In Italy her vocal talents were soon recognized, and private sponsorship, along with a scholarship, allowed her to study at the Conservatory of Naples. She graduated on 31 June 1911, and made her public debut as a singer the following year. Her first operatic audition was for Cleofonte Campanini, who was organizing the 1913 Verdi Centenary Festival in Parma. She sang in *Oberto*, Verdi's first opera, and *Un Ballo in Maschera*, at the festival, and so impressed Campanini that he offered to take her to America, where he had been appointed director and conductor of the Chicago Opera. At this juncture Campanini persuaded her to adopt the stage name Rosa Raisa – something which caused her considerable anguish. She made a huge impact in the Chicago company in the 1913–14 season, and was widely hailed as an exceptionally promising singer. As the 1914–15 Chicago season was cancelled, she pursued her career in Europe, where she greatly impressed Tito Ricordi and thus won the right to sing the title role in the Modena production of Zandonai's

---

[1] Raisa has been the subject of a superb biography by Charles Mintzer that I draw on here: *Rosa Raisa: A Biography of a Diva with Selections from Her Memoirs* (Boston: Northeastern UP, 2001).

Francesca da Rimini which opened on 26 December 1914. It was the first role she became strongly associated with, and she sung Francesca many times before her Chicago career continued, on a permanent basis, in the 1916–17 season. Raisa's reputation was growing all the time, as she worked her way through the standard repertoire, and by 1919 she was being promoted as the 'World's Greatest Dramatic Soprano' (see illustration opposite). Given this sort of star status, the tendency of American critics to concentrate on performance factors, and the recognition that Basiliola was a very difficult role, it is not wholly surprising that some of the reviews treat Raisa as at least as important as Montemezzi. Her singing was highly praised by all the critics.

Norman Bel Geddes (1893–1958) was born plain Norman Geddes in Adrian, Michigan. In the early 1910s, while working as a commercial artist, he began experimenting with staging plays, and in 1916 gained his first employment as a stage designer at Aline Barnsdall's theatre in Los Angeles. In the same year he married Bel Schneider and changed his name to Norman Bel Geddes (though in the early years at least he seems to have sometimes written it Norman-Bel Geddes). He quickly became well known for his highly innovative designs, and in spring 1919 the Chicago Opera Company hired him, for a fee of $15,000, to design a ballet and two operas, including *La Nave*, for their forthcoming autumn season.[1] It is not clear whether this decision was made with Campanini's approval or not, but in any case Campanini was absent in Europe for much of the period when *La Nave* was prepared, and practical matters were left in the hands of Jules Beck, the stage director, and Herbert Johnson, the business manager. Controversy and conflict followed. Casa Ricordi had sent photographs of the La Scala production to Chicago and expected the American production to be a fairly close replica.

---

[1] Norman Bel Geddes, *Miracle in the Evening: An Autobiography* (New York: Doubleday, 1960), 207. Hereafter Bel Geddes, *Miracle*.

Rosa Raisa Advertisement
Musical Courier, 10 April 1919

But when Bel Geddes saw them, he 'couldn't believe [his] eyes … they were so bad.'[1] He thus completely redesigned the opera, rejecting the sort of visionary realism that Marussig had employed in Milan[2] in favour of his own symbolic and expressionist concept of theatre in which the staging was 'conceived in terms of the psychological state of mind of the characters, and with the scene changing in accord with emotional tension – achieved through exaggeration, emphasis, distortion.'[3] (See illustrations overleaf.) When Campanini, Montemezzi and George Maxwell, Casa Ricordi's American representative, turned up shortly before the premiere was scheduled, there were angry scenes, certain details of which got into the press. Maxwell was completely opposed to the new designs and expressed his feelings in no uncertain terms; Montemezzi, more temperate, also disliked them; Campanini seems to have been angry about the situation rather than the designs. But by this time it was too late to change, and the production went ahead with Bel Geddes' staging and costumes. His work divided the critics, though as usual in such cases the negative point of view was put across more energetically. It is worth noting that, apart from the overall style, Bel Geddes' biggest innovation was to have the prow of the ship facing the audience, rather than the stern.

The Chicago critics can be now introduced:

Karleton Hackett (1867–1935) was the most positive of the Chicago reviewers, and his account of *La Nave* can be considered one of the two or three most positive assessments of the opera

---

[1] Ibid. 213.

[2] For Marussig's style see in particular Bucci's comments above, pp. 38–42.

[3] Bel Geddes, *Miracle*, 131.

to be found anywhere. He was a long term resident of Chicago, where he was the music critic for the *Chicago Evening Post* as well as a vocal teacher at the American Conservatory of Music, an institution of which he later became vice-president and (from 1931) president; he was also the author of a slim volume entitled *The Beginning of Grand Opera in Chicago (1850–1859)* (1913). Hackett's reviews of local productions were generally positive, and this would seem to have had something to do with his personal interest in the Chicago Grand Opera Company, which he had been instrumental in setting up.[1] Nevertheless, there can be no doubting his basic sincerity in finding *La Nave* an opera of great power and beauty, with an outstanding choral role. Like several of the Italian critics, Hackett perceptively understood that *La Nave* is really the story of a people, and his negative criticisms were reserved for the First Episode, in which he felt the epic plot had been lost sight of – this was, of course, really a criticism of D'Annunzio, who however goes unmentioned, along with the fact of Montemezzi's having been constrained by the *Literaturoper* form.

Paul T. Gilbert (1878–1953) was a feature writer for the *Chicago Evening Post* who was later to find fame as an author of children's books. He did not normally review operas, but contributed a second review of *La Nave* to the *Post* in recognition that the work's international premiere was a major event for Chicago. He, too, was very positive, though he regarded *La Nave* basically as a great 'show' with Raisa a great 'star.' It is amusing to speculate on what Montemezzi and his serious-minded Italian critics would have made of such a verdict as: '"La Nave" was certainly a peach of an opera, and you went away feeling that you had seen a show.' Gilbert's only negative criticism of the opera itself, lightly touched on, was that it contained no tunes of the kind that could be whistled.

---

1 Michael T. R. B. Turnbull, *Mary Garden* (Aldershot: Scolar Press, 1997), 75.

Designs for the Prologue and First Episode
Norman Bel Geddes

Designs for the Second and Third Episodes
Norman Bel Geddes

Herman Devries (1858–1949) had been a pupil of Bizet and enjoyed a distinguished career as a bass (and sometimes a baritone) in various operatic roles in the 1880s and '90s. He came to Chicago in 1900, when his performing career was over, and established himself as a leading singing teacher and the music critic for the *Chicago American*. He had been tremendously enthusiastic about *L'Amore dei Tre Re*, and clearly expected great things from Montemezzi, but he was disappointed in *La Nave* – so disappointed, one feels, that he was actually reluctant to go into details. Though still recognizing Montemezzi as 'a great musical genius,' and though accepting that *La Nave* was an extraordinary technical achievement, Devries found in the new opera none of the 'opulent beauty, inspiration and romantic appeal' of its predecessor. It is worth noting that Montemezzi must have taken a copy of this review back to Italy, for it is quoted, in a very garbled translation, in Silvestri's 1952 biography, and it is clear Silvestri undertook no independent research into his subject's American reception.[1]

Edward C. Moore (1877–1935) described himself in 1916 as a 'pianist; teacher of piano; composer [of] songs and part songs; musical editor [of the] *Chicago Daily Journal*.'[2] His long review of *La Nave*, full of praise for Raisa, managed to say very little about the opera itself, which he too found much inferior to *L'Amore dei Tre Re*. He judged the new opera too slow moving, with too much of the vocal writing in the upper register, and insufficient melody. Moore was a smug and self-regarding critic who often gives the impression of being superior to the subjects of his reviews, but unfortunately his views on *La Nave* are important because the much more negative account of the opera that he included in his later book, *Forty Years of Opera*

---

[1] *Omaggio*, 32–33.

[2] *The Musical Blue Book of America 1916–17* (New York: Musical Blue Book Corporation, [1917]), 93. Hereafter *Musical Blue Book*.

in Chicago, gave the misleading impression that it had been a deserved failure.¹

The lengthy review of *La Nave* in the *Musical Leader* was not signed, but this was a Chicago weekly publication and it seems safe to attribute the commentary on such a landmark musical event to the editor, Florence French (1868–1941). Very little is known about her, apart from the fact that in 1900 she cofounded the *Leader* with her husband, Charles F. French (1861–1916), and continued to edit the paper after his death. French again said little about the opera itself, but did briefly make the point, made so much of by the Italian reviewers, that D'Annunzio's play was an unsuitable basis for an opera: she produced one of the more memorable phrases to be found in the American criticism by describing *La Nave* as 'one great symphonic illustration to blank verse.' Like Gilbert and Moore she found a lack of melody.

The review in the weekly *Musical Courier* was again unsigned, but it seems reasonable to attribute it to Jeanette Cox, the paper's regular Chicago correspondent, an obscure figure whom I have been unable to discover anything about. If she was the reviewer, it is noteworthy that the Chicago *Nave* was reviewed by three women, for Henriette Weber wrote a brief and approving notice for the *Chicago Herald*, not included here. Cox's review is one of the most thorough, and best balanced, that the Chicago production received. She discussed the plot and its political significance, and concluded that D'Annunzio's play was unsuitable for an opera and likely to ensure that there were few productions. On the other hand, she found *La Nave* a 'masterpiece' considered as a purely musical work, and Montemezzi a 'master musician' and (perhaps surprisingly) 'ultra-modern.' She noted the Germanic style of the opera and the absence of popular elements.

---

1 *Forty Years of Opera in Chicago* (New York: Horace Liveright, 1930), 202–4. Hereafter Moore, *Forty Years*.

William L. Hubbard (1867–1951) was a talented pianist who studied in Dresden in the 1890s before returning to Chicago and resuming his position of music critic for the *Chicago Tribune*, the city's leading newspaper, in 1899 (he later became the paper's drama and literary critic, too). He was the most scholarly of the Chicago critics, and had been the general editor of, and major contributor to, the 12-volume *American History and Encyclopedia of Music* (1908–10). He possessed an outstanding knowledge of opera, and appears to have been principally responsible for the 160 or so short chapters on the standard operas and operettas in the *History and Encyclopedia*. These reveal that he preferred serious to comic opera and Wagner to Verdi; it is noteworthy that he considered the final act of *Götterdämmerung* to be 'the greatest single act in all opera.'[1] Hubbard gave *La Nave* a long review in the *Daily Tribune* for 19 November, but for the present selection I have chosen his slightly more considered, though not substantially different, review for the *Sunday Tribune* four days later. Hubbard had words of high praise for Montemezzi's score, though still, tellingly, he considered it inferior to that of *L'Amore dei Tre Re*. But discussing the drama more deeply than the other Chicago critics, he found it unsuited to operatic purposes, too confusing, and the characters unsympathetic.

Maurice Rosenfeld (1867–1939), who had been born in Vienna and brought to the United States as a boy, described himself in 1916 as a 'concert pianist; teacher of piano; Chicago critic [for] *Musical America*; musical editor [for the] Chicago *Examiner* (1907–1917); composer [of] works for orchestra and piano; contributor to musical and literary magazines.'[2] In 1916 he founded the Maurice Rosenfeld Piano School. Rosenfeld was highly esteemed in the Chicago musical world. He reviewed *La*

---

1 *The American History and Encyclopedia of Music*, 12 vols (New York: Irving Squire, 1908–10), 2:59.

2 *Musical Blue Book*, 99.

Nave in the *Chicago Daily News* for 19 November, but his later, somewhat shorter, review for *Musical America* is included here, as it would have been much more widely read. Like Hubbard, Rosenfeld praised Montemezzi's new score, but at the same time judged it inferior to that of *L'Amore dei Tre Re* and displaying evidence of 'labour' rather than 'inspiration.' He found *La Nave* as a whole too symphonic and heavily orchestrated.

Taken altogether, the Chicago reviews of *La Nave* must have been a further disappointment to Montemezzi, especially if he compared them to the ecstatic reviews *L'Amore dei Tre Re* had obtained in America. The critics were well disposed towards the composer, and praised what they could, but apart from Hackett and Gilbert in the *Evening Post* they all had serious reservations about the new opera, and those who compared it with *L'Amore dei Tre Re* declared in favour of the earlier work.

The most remarkable fact about the Chicago *Nave* was that it played for just two performances. This was not a comment on the success of the production, or the merits of the opera, but a reflection of a practice – hard to believe nowadays – of bringing out as many operas as possible each season. In the 1919–20 Chicago season there were, in addition to *La Nave*, 19 Italian operas, 14 French operas and 1 English opera presented. Only one of these was put on for more than three performances: *Madama Butterfly* (five performances).[1] Originally the Chicago Opera had intended to bring *La Nave* to the Lexington Theatre, New York, in January 1920, an event announced as early as February 1919:

> The Lexington lobbies have displayed an interesting forecast of Italy's latest operatic sensation, promised here next year. A great poster set up

---

[1] For precise details of the operas and the number of performances see Moore, *Forty Years*, 373.

at the entrance reads 'Lexington Theatre, season 1919-20, Chicago Opera Association ... . Opening night, Monday, Jan. 26, 1920, 'La Nave,' (in Italian,) first time in New York, music by Italo Montemezzi, tragedy by Gabriele d'Annunzio.[1]

A late decision was made to cancel the promised 'sensation,' perhaps mainly for economic reasons: it is surely significant that even without taking such a costly production as *La Nave* to New York, the Chicago company managed to make a reported loss of some $200,000 in the course of their five weeks' tenure of the Lexington.[2] There may also have been lingering discord over Bel Geddes's designs.

An order was consequently given to demolish the sets which had been designed and constructed at great cost, and Edward C. Moore, who had heartily disliked them, would later report with malicious glee that 'the stage force raised a special and quite non-operatic chorus of joy on its own behalf when it was ordered to break up the scenery.'[3] This failure to stage *La Nave* in New York, in front of the many New York critics who were devoted to *L'Amore dei Tre Re*, was the most unfortunate blow Montemezzi's new opera could have encountered, and brought its international career to an abrupt end.

---

1 'Lexington Opera,' *New York Times*, 16 February 1919, 6.
2 'Chicago Opera Company's Losses Here Total $200,000,' *New York Clipper*, 3 March 1920, 6.
3 Ibid. 204.

1. Karleton Hackett, *Chicago Evening Post*,
19 November 1919.

Sig. Montemezzi Scores Triumph in His New Opera

It was worth while bringing Montemezzi from away across the water for the opening of our opera season, and Campanini was justified of his works.[1] 'La Nave' is a tremendous score, far too important a work to attempt to grasp at a first hearing, yet one which leaves an indelible impression of power and sincerity. It is a somber drama and somberly told thru the music. The music is a great symphonic poem conceived on broad lines and sustained with force to the magnificent climax of the final act.

Montemezzi is a new voice come out of Italy, tho we already knew something of his force, one with far other aims than the school of the veristi of a generation ago[2] and not even satisfied with the age old ideal of Italian music to charm by melodic grace and stir by dramatic power. He is a poet with a deeper conception of the meaning of music and with a command of his art which permits him to paint with sweeping strokes of power and beauty upon the widest canvas.

The individuals of the drama do not stand forth from the mass as the essential elements of the tale, but rather as the human bubbles floating on the surface of the mighty stream of life. In no modern work for the operatic stage has the chorus played so important a part. Last evening you felt in them the surge of the

---

1 Hackett's allusion is to Matthew 11:19: 'wisdom is justified of her works.'

2 Hackett's perceptive desire to distinguish Montemezzi from the 'veristi' is important given the subsequent tendency to use *verismo* as an umbrella term for just about all Italian opera from *Cavalleria Rusticana* to *Turandot*.

people, the energy of a race which was to grow into power by its own inherent strength, overcoming whatever of human evil and frailty might impede its path. The opera chorus has been one of the unmanageable elements since the happy old days when it stood contentedly in two unconcerned lines as a mere convention, until composers in despair came frequently to do without it altogether. But Montemezzi had the imagination to find a use for the chorus again, and the swelling volume of choral tone rolled out thru the Auditorium with an elemental power which formed the background of his work.

He gave to the chorus tasks of extreme difficulty, but while difficult the music had meaning and could be sung by human voices after they had been drilled at it long enough. The manner in which the chorus sang last evening was a demonstration of their worth and of the training they have received.

The score was filled with beauty, for Montemezzi has the Italian birthright of spontaneous melody, tho expressed with the utmost freedom of modern thought. Not the graceful tune of pleasant prettiness, but rich, full melodies, singing thru the widest range of contrapuntal weaving and enharmonic change; not merely to delight the ear with passing charm, but to voice the deeper emotions.

One must have time to grow into comprehension of this score. With all its complexities there is power and design therein. The structural quality is there, firm and enduring and so able to wait for full understanding. At a first hearing it sounded as if there were portions of the prolog which might, with benefit, be condensed; and in the first episode, where Montemezzi for the moment got far from the people and the unfolding of the main theme, the music lost something of its vigor. But the last two episodes, or acts, as perhaps they would better be called, were magnificent. Things to hear and to absorb that the full power and beauty of the music might be revealed.

Rosa Raisa sang very beautifully in the prolog in which the music was especially grateful for her voice. Montemezzi has no mercy on his singers, having his own purposes in his mind, and demanding the utmost of which the human voice is capable. Yet he has the instinct for the voice, and while his music makes heavy demands they can be met if the singer have both the natural voice and the acquired skill. Mme. Raisa showed that she had them both. The first episode did not come out so well. The music was not so grateful, and the drama did not tell itself convincingly. If you knew the story you could understand what it was about, but for the general audience which had to catch it mostly by the eye it must have been nearly impossible. The sense of evil was not pervasive. Mme. Raisa must do something about the killing of the poor prisoners with those arrows which she shot from that slimpsy bow. When Eleonora Duse years ago shot those arrows in 'Francesca da Rimini' it seemed to me that she attained the apex of futility in female marksmanship,[1] but Mme. Raisa beat her record last evening. Mme. Raisa is too smart a woman not to find some way out of the difficulty no matter how stringent the police regulations may be about the use of dangerous weapons.

Her costumes were in excellent taste and she made a striking picture to the eye.

---

1 Eleonora Duse created the title role in D'Annunzio's *Francesca da Rimini* – a play specially written for her – when it was premiered in Rome on 9 December 1901. She later brought it to America, where her company played it in Boston, New York and Chicago between October and December 1902.

Mr. Dolci sang very well and played his part with dignity. Mr. Rimini was excellent. Mr. Arimondi, Mr. Lazzari and Mr. Rogerson deserve special words.[1]

It was rumored yesterday afternoon that quite a little gale had been blowing over the question of the stage settings, which served to heighten the general interest, as well as to show that the opera was functioning normally. When there is no excitement about an opera-house you may be sure that the organization is pretty nearly dead, consequently it was good news to hear that things were lively back of the stage.

As far as I am concerned, the stage settings were most gratifying to the eye, imaginatively conceived and making beautiful pictures. The setting for the prolog was symbolic of the ship and aided the audience in getting into the poetic mood. The ship of the final scene was quite a triumph of stagecraft, a tremendous affair which filled the entire stage, yet when the time came it moved down to the sea with impressive steadiness. Doubtless the settings were quite different from what Montemezzi expected, and perhaps another manner of doing the thing would have been just as effective and more to his mind. But as far as I am concerned Mr. Norman-Bel Geddes was entirely successful in his undertaking save for the technicality that he hardly left enough free space for the people on the stage. At times they had to be crowded together in a manner which must have taken considerable figuring on by the stage manager, but they were finally grouped into striking stage pictures.

Montemezzi received several ovations, especially after the first act, in which the singers had their full share. The performance was under his direction, and he showed genuine force as a conductor.

---

1 William Rogerson sang the part of Orio Dedo, the Harbour Master.

Of course 'everybody' was present, and there was a general air that the opera had begun this year under the most favorable conditions. There was not a vacant seat in the house and no tickets had been purchasable for days.

'La Nave' will be repeated next Monday evening, and if you wish to hear something of unusual power, something which will give you food for thought, you would better go.

Rosa Raisa as Basiliola

2. Paul T. Gilbert, *Chicago Evening Post*, 19 November 1919.

'Wonderful!' That's What All Say Of 'La Nave'

Opening Number of Opera Season Unanimously Hailed as a 'Peach'

THE GOOD ship Totus Mundus was launched at the Auditorium last night, and incidentally the 1919–20 season of grand opera.

The unanimous verdict on 'La Navy,' as the dowager in the seat behind me called it, can be summed up in one word – wonderful!

The critics down in the sixth row; the debutantes in the boxes; the music lovers in the gallery; the garlic-scented delegation from Orleans street,[1] all agreed on that. 'La Nave' was certainly a peach of an opera, and you went away feeling that you had seen a show.

I am still haunted this morning by Rosa Raisa's green eyes. Her eyes were like those of some great cat animal. They were dangerous eyes – dangerous and green. Sometimes they were like a serpent's eyes – a green, poisonous serpent that charms its prey by looking at it. Green, poisonous eyes they were, and almond-shaped like a celestial's. They were not human eyes.

New Dramatic World Vamp

In Rosa Raisa the dramatic world has a new vamp. Her face at times was like a Chinese idol's. Again it was as delicious as the face of an angel in stained glass. Sweet, but always passionate.

---

1 Gilbert refers to the impoverished and crime-ridden Little Sicily area of Chicago. This appears to be the only reference in the Chicago reviews to *La Nave* being attended by ordinary Italians as well as the social elite.

Her lips were passionate and her eyes were like glass. She had a sinuous figure and her movements were as creepy as a panther's.

This Basiliola was a sixth century Salome. Only her fingers were not stained red. And she was a seductress not by nature, as Salome was, but to reap vengeance. For early Venetians had a rather horrid Byzantine habit of plucking out the eyes of people who offended them. And they had plucked the eyes from Basiliola's brothers. So she set out to corrupt Marco Gratico.

Had a Chicago girl acted the way she did they would have had her mail forwarded to Hudson avenue until Dr. Hickson could look her over – or some big black thing would have snatched her thru the ceiling.[1] Her kisses were almost embarrassing in length, and she amused herself by shooting down the helpless prisoners in the trenches with a bow and arrow, altho her archery might be improved upon.

She toyed at times with a wicked-looking paper knife. Then she conceived the brilliant idea of sicking Marco on his brother and caused a fratricide. It was she who got up that cabaret show in the church – barefooted dancing girls and big goblets of wine – and no wonder the church members didn't like it and tied this she-tiger to the altar.

Modesty in Girdle Scene

Her only modesty was displayed in the girdle scene, where

---

[1] The police station on Hudson Avenue was used specially for female offenders (see 'Quarters De Luxe Succeed Cells for Women Prisoners,' *Chicago Daily Tribune*, 6 August 1918, p. 10). William James Hickson (1874–1935) was a well-known psychopathologist and criminologist, based in Chicago. The 'big black thing' alludes to the 1885 poem 'Little Orphant Annie' by James Whitcomb Riley, which had been made into a film in 1918. The poem includes a reference to 'two great big Black Things a-standin' by her side, / An' they snatched her through the ceilin' 'fore she knowed what she's about!'

Mary Garden or Theda Bara[1] would have gone the limit. Here she is supposed to dance only in veils. 'I am almost nude,' she sings (in Italian, of course); 'my girdle is so small that if the ends be joined together it could serve as a crown for thy head.'[2] But she was nothing of the sort. Her skirt reached to the ankles and her dress was buttoned up around the neck. There were people in the audience who were gowned less discreetly.

Another thing you liked was the Norman-Bel Geddes scenery. It was almost barbaric in its splendor and reflected that dim, mediaeval atmosphere you admire in old tapestries. The cathedral scene was like a great transparency. And the ship in the last act was colossal. The curtain fell amid a sea of sound and the huge craft, with the seductress nailed to its prow as a figurehead, moved slowly out into the bay. The trumpets were splendid.

The American premiere of the opera was rather a triumph for the composer-director, Italo Montemezzi. After every episode he was led before the footlights by Raisa, Rimini and Dolci, while the chapeau-clat[3] chorus shouted 'Bravo!'

Once or twice Raisa wrenched her hand loose from his and left him there alone and helpless. And once they brought out

---

[1] Mary Garden (1874–1967), the celebrated opera singer, well known to Chicago audiences, as she had been singing there since 1910. She was famous, and sometimes notorious, for the revealing costumes she was prepared to wear in operas like *Salome* and *Thaïs*. Theda Bara (1885–1955), the silent film actress, was similarly famous for appearing in revealing costumes in films such as *Cleopatra* (1917). Bara was nicknamed 'The Vamp.'

[2] Gilbert is misleading here. The words he quotes come from the end of the First Episode, where Basiliola twice states 'I am too naked' (*Son troppo nuda*), and finally, persuading Marco Gratico to pick up her girdle, 'It is so slender, / That if thou close it, thou hast got thy crown!' However this scene is quite distinct from the dance in the Second Episode.

[3] I assume Gilbert intended either 'chapeau-clad' or 'chapeau-claque,' the latter referring to a collapsible top hat designed specifically to be stored under seats in a theatre. In either case, he is obviously referring to the audience.

a jolly little bald-headed man, who was no other than Hugo d'Annunzio, the son of the fighter-poet on whose dramatic work the opera was based.[1]

Conductor Not Nervous

It was just 8:15 when the first violin rapped on his music rack and a bashful, delicately featured man with gray hair and slightly hollowed cheeks mounted the director's stand. This was the first time he had conducted his opera in public, but at that he wasn't half as nervous as I was, who sat just behind him and kept dodging his inspired baton. Next time I will try to get a seat in the prompter's box.

Somehow the glittering horseshoe[2] seemed to lack the glitter of other years. Perhaps because of the high price of diamonds only two tiaras were worn, but there was a good display of ermine and cloth of silver, and the lobby during the intermission was a wilderness of silk hats.

---

[1] Ugo Veniero D'Annunzio (1887–1945), D'Annunzio's third son, had arrived in America in 1918, as the official Italian Government representative of Caproni, the aeroplane manufacturer. He was based in New York, where he later settled permanently. In America he apparently preferred to write his name as Hugo. He did attend the performance of La Nave, but he was certainly not bald, as demonstrated by several photographs collected in Gabriele d'Annunzio, *Carteggio Inedito con il Figlio Veniero (1917–1937)*, ed. Maria Grazia Di Paolo (Milan: Mursia, 1994). Perhaps Gilbert confused him with Pietro Nepoti, the chorus master, who was (see below, p. 168).

[2] This is a reference to the boxes; the Auditorium Theatre was an innovative design that dispensed with the conventional horseshoe shaped balconies. Edward C. Moore explains that the 'golden horseshoe' came about in response to fire regulations: 'a line of boxes, afterwards to become two lines, had been built across the rear of the main floor [of the theatre], thus converting the box tier into a veritable horseshoe. ... at the birth of Chicago's first opera company the boxes extended along both back and sides.' Moore, *Forty Years*, 58.

Maestro Campanini and his party occupied the proscenium box and seemed to enjoy the opera immensely. He had good reason to, because it was not only an artistic success, but about a thousand applicants for seats were turned away.

Little Melodies Lacking

Like many of the modern operas, 'La Nave' has no little melodies that you whistle when you go out – no pretty arias or simple choruses that make some of the old-fashioned operas so popular. But the worshippers' chorus in the cathedral scene and the trumpet chorus as the ship is launched are about as effective as you'd care to hear.

Cleofonte Campanini, 1913
Director of the Chicago Production of *La Nave*

3. Herman Devries, *Chicago American*, 19 November 1919.

Montemezzi and Rosa Raisa Win Honors in 'La Nave'; Opera Criticized

WHEN, IN October, 1915, I reviewed in this column 'L'Amore dei Tre Re' upon its initial performance with the Boston Grand Opera Company at the Auditorium Theater, I said among other things:

'"L'Amore dei Tre Re," presented in Chicago for the first time last night, introduces to the local musical world a young Wagner.

'Ironical as it may appear, the crown of the great Teuton genius seems destined to repose on the brow of a Latin, Montemezzi.

'Will the name place Italy again upon the tablets of musical history as the torch bearer of a new and powerful creator?'[1]

After hearing 'La Nave' last night in its American premiere for the opening of the 1919–1920 Chicago season, I must in all honesty place my preference and my profound admiration with 'L'Amore dei Tre Re.'

Montemezzi's pretentious and stupendous 'Ship' does not transfer the musical affections one whit from the other opera's opulent beauty, inspiration and romantic appeal – for 'La Nave' has none of these.

Commands Consideration

And yet 'La Nave' commands consideration in its amazing formation. That a human brain could have conceived and

---

1 *L'Amore dei Tre Re* was given its Chicago premiere on 6 October 1915, and Devries' review presumably appeared in the *Chicago American* the following day. Two or three issues of the paper were printed each day and unfortunately the one chosen for preservation and microfilming does not include the review.

accomplished so immense an orchestration, so complex a construction, so monumental a feat of technique, is unbelievable.

But we should not have heard 'La Nave' with singers and scenery. It would set more fittingly within the strings and the brasses of our orchestra. For 'La Nave' in my humble opinion is not an opera. It is a symphony.

'L'Amore dei Tre Re' rouses the longing for a rehearing. The more one listens to it, the more one wishes to hear it again.

Will 'La Nave' quicken that same desire? I doubt it, as I doubt that it will see as many performances as its lovely and more pliant predecessor.

However, let this be said – tradition presents many a tale wherein an initial hoot turned to applause. Many a first performance of what now stands immortal in music was greeted with unkindest criticism.

Perhaps in the case of 'La Nave' first criticism may not necessarily mean prophecy.

Montemezzi A Genius

Certain it is that Italo Montemezzi is a great musical genius.

He conducted his opera like the distinguished man of music he is.

He brought to his baton distinction, passion, energy and the orchestra responded gloriously.

First honors among the artists must go to that superb young soprano, Rosa Raisa. Not one bit burdened with the fact that Montemezzi has written his music for a soprano machine rather than for a soprano human, Miss Raisa sang the trying role of Basiliola with grace, charm, and glorious tone. Her matchless voice was again a ringing wonder of volume and luscious quality.

Her Basiliola was a magnificent piece of artistry – and her costumes revelations in rich color and design.

Alessandro Dolci, who seemed slightly fatigued in the Prologue, rose excellently to the vocal requirements of the role of Marco in the last acts.

As for Giacomo Rimini, he is always the earnest, reliable, satisfying artist.

Although the role assigned to Virgilio Lazzari lies a trifle high for a basso, his fine, robust voice carried the dire music of 'Il Monaco Traba' splendidly.

Vittorio Arimondi, always a dependable artist, sang the few phrases of the blind Orso Faledro with authority.

Minor Parts Well Taken

The minor parts were all in excellent hands. Special mention is due Desire Defrere for his ringing tones in the Prologue.[1]

The audience packed the house from pit to dome and recalled the artists and the composer many times after each act. After the second act they brought with them Pietro Nepoti, the excellent chorus master, who is to be warmly lauded for the work of his men and women.

They were not a chorus – they were stars.

'La Nave' is richly mounted. The third act, Atrium of the Basilica, was a gorgeous spectacle and the finale, with its monster ship, was a very definite accomplishment in scenic wonder.

In closing, let me not forget to wish to our generalissimo, Cleofonte Campanini, a fruitful season.

---

1 Desire Defrere (1888–1964), a Belgian baritone who would have a long and distinguished career in America, had sung the role of the Boatswain's Voice (La Voce Del Còmito) heard at the very beginning of *La Nave*.

Montemezzi Rehearsing *La Nave*, 1919
(*L* to *R*) Dolci, Raisa and Rimini

4. Edward C. Moore, *Chicago Daily Journal*, 19 November 1919.

Raisa Opens Opera Season

Italo Montemezzi Conducts American Premiere of 'La Nave' at Auditorium

Brilliancy Of Old Restored

GATHER AROUND and let us discuss the most exciting event of the whole musical season, the opening of grand opera.

The time, last night; the place, the Auditorium.

It was a good deal of an evening, this inauguration of the Chicago Opera association's season. The opening performance involved a new opera, Italo Montemezzi's 'La Nave,' conducted by the composer himself, staged in the most lavish possible fashion, sung by a superb cast, and with one artist taking her rightful place among the world's greatest singers.

She was Rosa Raisa.

If 'La Nave' comes to take its place in the standard repertoire of the Chicago Opera association, it will be because of the same Rosa Raisa.

Season Has Brilliant Opening

For the first time in a number of years the opera season started last night with the brilliancy that a normal opera season should have. In past seasons war abroad and economy at home were reasons why there should be something of a pall over the event, why opera should take only a secondary and half-hearted interest in the minds of its patrons.

But last night began a new page in the history of the company. There was a public that could give its whole mind to the performance, that filled the vast Auditorium to the last seat in the last balcony, that would have filled many more seats could space have been found for them.

It was an audience in gala attire and gala mood, not willing to be swept off its feet by the mere name of grand opera, insistent upon being convinced, but ready and willing to show its appreciation once it had been convinced. This is the customary attitude of a Chicago audience.

Audience in Demonstration

So when the sanguinary climax of the third scene had been reached, the most momentous musically, dramatically and scenically of the entire performance, the audience opened a barrage fire of applause that continued in a manner to make glad the hearts of everyone from directors to cast, with a few special salvos for the composer-director. If there were any who were not happy, they were the ones unable to gain admission.

Montemezzi's music has been set to the words of Gabriele d'Annunzio, the man who changes map lines for occupation and writes plays for diversion. From the pointed comments reported from him concerning his military and political associates, more particularly concerning those who have the temerity to oppose him, one might easily infer that he would be something of a fire-eater in his plays.

Story of Lust and Murder

He is. 'La Nave,' purporting to deal with the history of the founding of Venice, is laid on with all the lurid colors of murder, torture, lust and cruelty that one could well imagine. It is quite possible, even probable, that D'Annunzio did not intend to keep close to historical facts, but to indulge in a certain amount of symbolism. For one thing, the time is placed about 522 A.D., while the histories relate that the basilica of St. Mark's was begun in 810.[1]

A trifle of three centuries is of no great importance in the construction of an opera. For that matter, whatever of historical symbolism there may be in the piece is of no great importance in America, whatever it may be in Italy, because it passes completely over the American head. The beginnings of Italian history are not in the American curriculum.

Seductress Central Figure

The story of 'La Nave' must then stand or fall upon its merits as a dramatic story. The principal figure, the central figure, is Basiliola, a highly improper young person who becomes a very great vamp. She is the daughter of the former ruling family, the Faledri. The election returns going against them, the father and four brothers of the family undergo the pleasant medieval custom of having their eyes put out.

Whereupon Basiliola devotes herself to setting the winners against each other. Of the two brothers Gratici, one becomes the tribune, the other the bishop. Marco Gratico, the tribune, in a fit of jealous rage induced by Basiliola, kills his brother in a duel, and then starts out on a career of maritime conquest.

Just before the ship is launched, they take Basiliola and fasten her to the prow to act as a figure-head. It is the end of her and of the opera. Incidentally, the ship is not named 'Fiume,' as might be imagined,[2] but 'Totus Mundus' – the whole world.

---

1 Moore appears to have been the only critic to make something of this contradiction. The unfinished Basilica forms part of the backdrop for the Prologue and Second and Third Episodes. Moore is wrong with his dates though: D'Annunzio sets his action in *c.*552; work began on St. Mark's Basilica in 828.

2 Of course *La Nave* was written long before D'Annunzio became associated with Fiume. See p. 178, n. 1 below.

Raisa Scores Great Success

Medieval manners were not gentle, and the minds of men and women did not stop at small things. It was this seductress, whose wiles caused a bishop to carry out a sacrilegious orgy in his own church, to be slain by his own brother at the foot of his own altar, who was portrayed last night by Miss Raisa.

And magnificently she did it. She took a long artistic step forward, from being a striking, impressive dramatic soprano, to being a striking, impressive dramatic personage. From the time of her second engagement with the Chicago Opera association she has been a singer whose match was not to be found, a voice that hesitated at nothing in the dramatic repertoire, a beautiful woman, an intelligent artist.

Last night she projected a definite compelling personality as well.

Voice Unequalled in Power

She is a glory to the company and a glory to Chicago, is this lithe, slender woman. Never in this generation was a voice so ringing and powerful. Now that it is overlaid with color, now that she uses it to express emotion as well as to interpret music, now that it reflects the play of expression in her face and the pose of her body, a singing actress has become an entirely different sort of a person.

Montemezzi may well have rejoiced at her being present to take the chief role in his opera. This composer is said to have appeared for the first time as conductor last night. It hardly seems credible. If it is true, he is one of the born conductors, with a well defined idea of what he wants in the performance of his music and a complete certainty of how to go to work to get it.

His profile looks a good deal like the pictures of Hector Berlioz. His features are clearly and delicately cut; he wears hair that is neither too long nor too short, slightly touched with grey; he has the manner of an earnest artist without mannerisms. Possibly another conductor could have found points in his score of which he had lost the perspective, but it did not seem likely in this performance.

Opera Recalls Earlier Work

The unfortunate part of it is that he has not written another 'L'Amore dei Tre Re.' He has not. The score of 'L'Amore' came as near as a score could come to being pure gold. That of 'La Nave' is heavily alloyed. Perhaps unconsciously, there are a good many reminiscences of 'L'Amore' in it.

He has rather extraordinary skill in the mechanics of writing for the orchestra and for voices. Under his hand a musical scene starts with so much suavity and certainty that you prepare yourself to be carried along to an overwhelming climax. But in 'La Nave' the climax is more than likely to elude you.

For one thing, it is too slow moving and there is too much repeated insistence on a particular feature. Montemezzi would seem to have had the idea that if a high note is a good thing, twenty high notes would be twenty times as good. This may be true mathematically, but psychologically it is not.

Abounds with Choral Numbers

Except in the case of an occasional solo passage and in several choral numbers, the heart-touching melody does not appear. Instead of being essential parts of the score they are merely incidents. Important incidents some of the choral numbers are. The chorus of the Chicago company has seldom had more to do, or has done it in a more effective manner.

There was one occasion in the first act when the choristers started on the wrong pitch, with rather painful results. But in all the rest, in the turbulent scenes of the citizens, in the sustained religious and triumphant choruses, practically as much credit is due to these hard-working underlings as to Miss Raisa.

For that reason it may be necessary to explain the identity of one of the people appearing before the curtain at the end of the third act. In spite of extreme and incurable baldness, he was not D'Annunzio, but the chorus master of the company, Pietro Nepoti.

Dolci in Dramatic Role

Enthusiasm over such outstanding features of the performance as Miss Raisa presented causes momentary forgetfulness of the fact that there were other remarkable members of the cast. The singer next most important to her in the performance was Alessandro Dolci

There was good reason that the role of Marco Gratico should be sung by him, because he comes more nearly than anyone in the company to having the voice of the correct type for it. He has a dramatic tenor voice and a very fine one. Some of the big solo singing fell to him, and he did it in highly impressive style.

Giacomo Rimini, the baritone Sergio Gratico, was on the stage quite a bit, but without very much singing to do. What there was turned out excellently. A long cast of minor principals was necessary to complete the performance. They were well cast throughout, with Vittorio Arimondi, Vittorio Trevisan, Lodovico Oliviero, William Rogerson, Constantin Nicolay and Emma Noe coming in for special mention.[1]

Scenery Painted in New Manner

A new feature in the presentation lay in the fact that the scenery and costumes were designed and executed by Norman-Bel Geddes.

---

1 These singers sang the parts, respectively, of Orso Faledro, Simon D'Armario, 'The Survivor' (the last of the prisoners to be killed by Basiliola), Orio Dedo the harbour master, Lucio Polo the pilot, and 'The Voice.'

Therein lay both virtues and faults. The virtues were some beautiful stage pictures. Others were more difficult to discover.

The stage directions for the piece give some definite directions for making the piece practically a period play. They were generally speaking not followed. Fanciful pre-Byzantine decorative effects were substituted. The trouble lay in the fact that they impeded instead of assisting the action.

In three of the four scenes there was something in the center rear, a throne or an altar or what not, which effectively stifled all entrance effect from this quarter. In one scene the light was focused on a blank wall while the singers remained in partial darkness.

In the final scene of Basiliola's forcible location on the prow of the ship only a portion of the audience could see her, and that not plainly. And why in the launching of the ship it should be necessary to have some one not a member of the cast up on the scaffolding, much more plainly in sight of the audience than Miss Raisa, is one of the operatic mysteries.

Errors Invite Correction

It is possible that some of the mistakes can be corrected. Some of the costumes certainly ought to be. Quite apart from the fact that an archaeologist might object to the style of armor worn in the opera, Dolci should have a new helmet. His present one makes him look like the Tin Man in 'The Wizard of Oz.'[1]

But the scene in the basilica was at the start a beauty, and this through the aid of seven members of the ballet corps. If this brief passage affords any standard of judgment, the ballet will be notable this year. The costumes were entirely out of the period, but the line, the pose and the design of the dance were exquisite.

---

1 The reference is either to William Wallace Denslow's illustrations to L. Frank Baum's novel, *The Wizard of Oz* (1900), or to the costume worn in the musical theatre version (1902).

Melodramatics with Montemezzi, 1919
(*L* to *R*) Raisa, Dolci, Montemezzi, Rimini

5. Unsigned review attributed to Florence French,
Musical Leader, 20 November 1919.

Chicago Opera Gala Night Has Most Spectacular of Openings

Cleofonte Campanini Inaugurates Tenth Season With Extraordinary Production – Raisa Proclaimed 'World's Greatest' – Composer in Debut as Conductor – Dolci, Rimini, Lazzari, Arimondi Dominant Figures – Full House Turns Many Away – Seats Held at Vast Premium – 'La Nave' Causes Brilliant Audience to Display Enthusiasm and Recall All Principals – Scenic Production Admired

NOT SINCE the first year of the Chicago Grand Opera Company's existence has there been anything approaching the extraordinary interest shown in the opera at the Auditorium this season as presented by Mr. Cleofonte Campanini and his aids. It must have rejoiced the heart of the distinguished maestro as he viewed from his box the magnificent audience to realize at last his dream of seeing Chicago operatically responsive to his offering.

He beheld the sight most pleasing to a manager's eye – a sold-out house. For this most spectacular occasion of the year the last available seat had left the box office long before the night itself, but nevertheless some hundreds of wistful persons presented themselves at the Congress Street entrance to the theater hoping against hope. Most of them were forced to turn away disappointed. Here and there, however, a ticket-holder on the pavement made good his prevision. It was said that one pair of seats, originally purchased for eleven dollars, changed hands for $20, and were later offered at $40.

[Reflection on Campanini's health.] Campanini and his associates achieved the well nigh impossible, for they had undertaken to produce a work which had met the approval of Italy, and which is one of the most difficult of presentations. Not at all suited to the taste of the American public, which likes action and plenty of it, a story it can understand and much more brightness and life than are contained in 'La Nave' (The Ship), the new opera by Montemezzi. However, a first night audience greeted this spectacular, sombre and tragic work, musically adapted to d'Annunzio's play, with every evidence of approval. Interest had been further aroused by the daily press, which reported that there was considerable difference of opinion regarding the series of pictures designed for the prologue and three episodes of this music drama, and that the composer, who was here to superintend and conduct his work, and the designer of the scenes, Norman Bel Geddes, a young Scotchman,[1] were totally at variance in regard to the staging, scenic arrangements and grouping. Mr. Bel Geddes is a follower and admirer of the work of Ellen Terry's son, Gordon Craig,[2] who to a large degree was the originator of the futuristic style in theatrical pictures. All's well that ends successfully, and while Mr. Bel Geddes' ideas may have been absolutely remote from those of the Italian composer and the writer, Gabriele d'Annunzio, the effect seemed to justify the Scotch designer's venturesome spirit.

It requires some courage to tell the author and the composer that they are all wrong and that he is all right, and one must admire courage wherever it is found, whether scene painter who tells the composer and librettist to go to thunder, or a man who shoots his toe off to get insurance. After all, the end and aim of the theatrical man is to arouse discussion. Nothing has done so

---

[1] Bel Geddes was not a Scotchman, though his great-great-grandfather had left Scotland for Pennsylvania in 1790. See Bel Geddes, *Miracle*, 9.

[2] Edward Gordon Craig (1872–1966), illegitimate son of the celebrated actress Ellen Terry (1847–1928), had become famous for his modernist stage designs based on a symbolist aesthetic. His stage work broke decisively with nineteenth-century realism.

more effectively than the report about the principal people being in a state of friction. None of this was evident at the performance, which went with rare smoothness with the composer as conductor making his initial appearance as leader of an orchestra.

Montemezzi Well Fitted For Task

And well did the composer of 'The Love of Three Kings' and 'La Nave' prove himself fitted for the work he had undertaken. A youngish man, slim, lithe, and yet with compelling personality, he carried the performance through to a brilliant success and won for himself a distinguished place. His opera may not live, but it will have a certain number of performances, and every one should see it at least once, for the music is beautiful. It is a symphonic piece of writing with characters and pictoral illustration. One rather senses the fact that the music and drama could be produced separately with a better chance of prolonged existence. One might just as well try to make an opera of Tennyson's 'Cup'[1] as to put d'Annunzio's great drama to musical accompaniment.

Montemezzi's music is that of the modern orchestra writer and of a school almost his own, for he cannot be said to be influenced by any other. Vocally the composer has treated his characters with scant consideration, for each of the principal singers is asked to accomplish the almost impossible.

Raisa's Magnificent Performance

Rosa Raisa, the dominant figure and the only woman in the cast, surpassed even her previous magnificent efforts, and there was no need to wonder why leading critics had proclaimed her supremacy of voice. She was absolutely marvelous. With this

---

1 *The Cup*, Alfred Tennyson's richly poetic tragedy of Roman times, first performed in 1881. It has not been adapted as an opera.

remarkable voice is allied an intelligence equally as great. The role of Basiliola cannot be entirely sympathetic, for it does not permit the exercise of all her many talents. There is continuous declamation on the high notes, and as a tax on strength Montemezzi has Wagner far outclassed. Only such a voice as Rosa Raisa's, with its power and volume and endurance, could stand the terrific strain. No other singer, surely, would want to sing this particular role. Emotionally, dramatically and vocally Rosa Raisa is the embodiment of the three noted stage women of our time.[1] Never has she looked more beautiful, and never has she dominated a performance so completely. Montemezzi was indeed fortunate in having this remarkable artist to present the hapless heroine of 'La Nave.' She had a triumph which superseded any formerly achieved, and her achievements have been great.

Alexander [sic] Dolci revealed again the heroic quality in his voice and brought to the part a finely dramatic interpretation. He shared in the triumphs of the evening and was one of the big factors of its success. Virgilio Lazzari is always a tower of strength in any performance in which he takes part, for there is a certainty and authority about his art which make him one of the most valuable members of the company. Giacomo Rimini did some extremely fine work; he is gaining all along the line, as actor and singer, and he had a big share in the glories of the evening. Mr. Arimondi was, as always, an artist whose noble

---

1 It is not clear who is referred to here. If 'stage women' is meant as an umbrella term for both actresses and opera singers, then my guess would be that the actresses Sarah Bernhardt (1844–1923) and Eleonora Duse (1858–1924) and the opera singer Mary Garden (1874–1967) are evoked – the last being particularly celebrated in Chicago, where she had been singing since 1910. If the reference is simply to actresses, then the third might be Ellen Terry (1847–1928), or if simply to opera singers the other two might be Nellie Melba (1861–1931) and Geraldine Farrar (1882–1967).

voice enhanced the performance. The orchestra gave sincerest support to the composer and his work, contributing to one of the most extraordinary performances ever given by the Chicago Opera Company. Whether one agrees with the scene designer, or sides with the composer and his supporters and publishers, it must be acknowledged that in new design and color the various scenes offered much to interest.

Montemezzi leans heavily towards the weirdly dramatic with a tendency to dark color and but little of the melody for which his countrymen are noted. From the opening until the closing phrases it is one great symphonic illustration to blank verse, with only occasional splashes of rhythmic cadence and melody.

Mr. Montemezzi made an individual, personal success with his conducting, and if, as has been claimed, he has never before conducted an orchestra, he is recommended to continue in his new vocation. The composer, who first came to American notice in 'The Love of Three Kings,' has long been awaited here, and his first appearance confirmed the good reports that had come of his charm of manner, his modesty and genius. He has complete control of the men, the orchestra and the forces on the stage, and it is doubtful if the most seasoned conductor could have given a more brilliant and finished performance. Whether 'La Nave' (The Ship) will rival or surpass 'The Love of Three Kings' only time will tell; the latter opera seemed to reach the apex of skilful writing and dramatic intensity.

Montemezzi in Chicago, January 1920,
with Mary Garden (*L*) and Rosa Raisa (*R*)

Front page photograph from the
Chicago Daily Tribune, 19 January 1920

6. Unsigned review attributed to Jeannette Cox,
Musical Courier, 20 November 1919.

Chicago Hears American Premiere of 'La Nave'

CHICAGO, NOVEMBER 19, 1919. – Years succeed years and generally they seem alike. This state of things was true before 1914. The opening of an operatic season was yearly similar in brilliancy before 1914, but during the years of war a sort of gloom over the public mind was reflected in the more sombre vestments worn by the fashionable ladies of this city. After the rain, sunshine – after gloom, happiness; and the opening of the 1919–1920 season at the Auditorium was glorious. The society editor of the Musical Courier informed the writer that the gowns, furs and jewels displayed at the Auditorium on Tuesday evening, November 18, were the most magnificent ever seen in the home of opera in Chicago. More pleasant to record was that among the many auditors were recognized most of Chicago's leading musicians, who showed by their presence that money was plentiful among the tonal fraternity, as not only had they bought seats, but their garments and jewels compared most favorably with those worn by society leaders. For the opening night, General Manager Maestro Campanini decided to present a novelty composed by one of Italy's best known musicians – Italo Montemezzi, who at the conductor's desk presided over the destinies of 'La Nave' ('The Ship'), which had its world première at La Scala, Milan, last November.

The Plot

'La Nave' is a lyric drama in three episodes and a prologue. It is based on a drama in blank verse by Gabrielle [sic] D'Annunzio, Italy's greatest poet of the present day. In preparing the libretto for Montemezzi's music, Tito Ricordi was forced to sacrifice three thousand lines, but it seems that by so doing he still thought he was able to maintain the action and the proper developments of the tragedy. 'The Ship' symbolizes the early struggles and the early successes of the Venetian state. In its properly dramatic circumference it deals with the passion of the two brothers Gratici for a woman, Basiliola, who remembers that her four brothers have had their eyes plucked out because of their surreptitious dealings with the Greeks. She swears bitter vengeance against the two brothers who are enemies of her house and succeeds in playing havoc by means of her own beauty and charm. Sacrilege, sin, and fratricide follow in the wake of her passion; but in the end righteousness wins over lust, and the woman pays the penalty of sin, while Venice continues once again on her way towards greatness, opulence and happiness. Those who believe that no musical drama could hold in itself any political significance would have only to hear 'La Nave' to think differently, as D'Annunzio, the propagandist, most assuredly had visions of Fiume when he wrote 'La Nave.'[1] Yet so well covered is the plot that only by minute inspection can it be realized that such dramas are conceived upon political inspiration.

The brothers, Marco and Sergio Gratico, are Venice in the allegory, and Basiliola is the woman who represents all the ills that may kill Venice in its birth. Listen to the last lines of the chorus:

> Our country is on the ship!
> O Lord our God, redeem the Adriatic!
> Restore the Adriatic to Thy people!
> Give the Adriatic to the Venetians!

---

[1] This is true only in the most general sense. D'Annunzio had long believed in the rights of Italy to the former Venetian possessions, but had shown no specific interest in Fiume before August 1919. John Woodhouse points out that 'he had not harped upon the name of Fiume as he had in the case of other "lost" cities' (*Gabriele D'Annunzio: Defiant Archangel* [Oxford: Clarendon Press, 1998], 317).

Hallelujah! Christ shall reign!
Christ and San Marco!
Christ and Santo Ermagora![1]

With that final chorus the ship, boarded by Marco Gratico and his chosen comrades[,] glides into the water amid the exultation of the whole populace while the curtain falls and leaves the public amazed, not quite understanding the ambiguous plot; but those who had read the libretto carefully understood, and found behind 'La Nave' not only D'Annunzio the poet, but D'Annunzio the Italian patriot.

[An extended summary of the plot.]

This lengthy story of the plot was necessary as, even with it, those who do not understand Italian will have great difficulty in following the story. D'Annunzio is the Shakespeare of the day. He coins words, and indeed, it has been reported that there is today in Italy a D'Annunzio dictionary,[2] so no wonder the Auditorium audience was somewhat bewildered as to what was taking place on the stage.

The Music

Italo Montemezzi, best known in America by his 'L'Amore dei tre Re,' has written several other operas and symphonic works, and if, as prophesied here, 'La Nave' should have a short life on the operatic stage, the fault will not be with the composer but with the librettist, as Montemezzi has written a masterpiece in this new opera. Probably a great admirer of Richard Wagner and Richard Strauss, Montemezzi, the great Italian composer, speaks Teutonically

---

[1] The quotation is from R. H. Elkin's translation of the libretto, slightly adapted.

[2] The scholar Giuseppe Lando Passerini (1862–1932) had indeed published *Il Vocabolario della Poesia Dannunziana* (1912) and *Il Vocabolario della Prosa Dannunziana* (1913).

musically. He has written themes for every chorus. For instance, there is a carpenter theme, a sail maker's, and particularly one given to the millers – all combined in tremendous action. Then there is a seductive theme given to Basiliola, which on close examination resembles greatly that given to Salome in Richard Strauss's opera of that name, and there are many pages given to the tenor that demonstrates Montemezzi a fervent admirer of the man that made Bayreuth famous. A master musician, Montemezzi's orchestration is stupendous. Closely woven is his music. At times a stray melodious phrase is given to the singers or to the woodwind or strings, but more generally following the modern ideas in writing, Montemezzi is scrupulously symphonic in his treatment of the score. To him the singers are only part of his orchestra. He virtually sacrifices them, using them to add color to his tonal scheme. His musical palette is tinged with rainbow colors, mostly brilliant but at times sombre, and then his music is uninspired and even tedious. There isn't a single passage in the opera that will in the common term of the word become popular. There isn't a phrase that will be whistled. There isn't an excerpt from the opera that will ever be sung on the concert platform. There is nothing in it to popularize the opera, but there is a great deal that will make the musicians happy, as in it they will find many puzzles and problems well worth discovering. By his 'La Nave,' which is far inferior in the mind of this humble writer to his 'L'Amore dei tre Re,' Montemezzi has won added fame as an ultra-modern composer.

The Cast

'The days of the giants have gone by,' so they say, but giants are demanded by Montemezzi to sing his new work. It takes a Raisa for the role of Basiliola. She won, with the composer-conductor, first honors of the evening. The role is stupendous in its demand on the vocal chords. Written extremely high for the voice, Miss Raisa encompassed all the difficulties with the greatest ease. Her stentorian voice dominated over the orchestra even in climaxes which succeed repeatedly one another, testing the full vocal faculties of the singer, but Miss Raisa never flinched. She sang gloriously all through the opera, pouring out her golden tones with as great volubility at the close of the evening as she did at the beginning – a remarkable feat indeed when one is acquainted with the score. Dressed gorgeously, she made an alluring and seductive Basiliola, and histrionically she did admirable things. If the role of Basiliola demands a powerful voice, the same is true of the role of Marco, given to the tenor Dolci, one of the most popular tenors who have graced the Auditorium stage, an excellent musician who found the part of Marco Gratico a little too heavy for him, as it requires a Tamagno[1] to sustain the burden placed on the tenor by Montemezzi. That Dolci did as well as he did by the role is indeed a great credit to him, and it may be stated that no tenor of the day heard by this writer could have done better than he did, yet truly his voice sounded too light, as it is a lyric organ of great beauty, while a robusto tenor voice would make the role stand out in better light.

Sergio Gratico was capitally represented in the hands of Giacomo Rimini. He made the part live in the minds of the public, and vocally Mr. Rimini had seldom been heard to such advantage. His voice since last year has taken on much volume and he made the role stand out big in the episodes in which he figured.

Especially words of praise are due the work of Virgilio Lazzari as the Monk, although the part is not a big one. It was so effectively done as to make a great impression on the hearers, and the same may well be said of Orso Faledro, given to Vittorio Arimondi, who as ever made his presence felt. The other roles are

---

1 Francesco Tamagno (1850–1905), the Italian tenor who created the part of Verdi's Otello. His heroic voice was extremely powerful in its upper registers.

so small as to necessitate no comment, yet they were entrusted to many popular singers of the company, including Constantin Nicolay, Vittorio Trevisan, Desire Defrere and Emma Noe.[1]

Italo Montemezzi, contrary to the general rule of composers being poor conductors, is quite efficient with the stick, and he made a stunning picture in the orchestral pit, conducting with great authority, elasticity and decision. After each episode, as well as after the prologue, he and the principal artists were recalled many times before the curtain.

Words of praise are due the chorus and orchestra, who were excellent, and they too should receive more attention from the reviewer, but space forbids giving them their due outside of stating once more that they were up to the high standard demanded from this opera company.

The only black spot in the opera was the scenery arranged by Norman-Bel Geddes. Even with a stretch of imagination it was impossible to understand what Mr. Geddes devised as the arsenal, for instance.[2] That scene, already difficult to understand for those who do not comprehend Italian, was made even more so by the picture presented by Mr. Geddes. Other scenes likewise were blurred in the minds of the people, due to scenic effects which hardly were in accord with the book. The launching of the ship was the best effect of the evening, but retrieved only in part the bad impression produced by previous scenes. The stage management, however, was not at fault and under prevailing conditions did itself proud.

---

[1] These singers sang the parts, respectively, of Lucio Polo the pilot, Simon D'Armario, the Boatswain's Voice, and 'The Voice.'

[2] This is a puzzling comment for D'Annunzio nowhere refers to an arsenal. It is most likely to refer to a misunderstanding of the scene with the pit in the First Episode.

7. William L. Hubbard, *Chicago Sunday Tribune*, 23 November 1919.

Music and the Musicians

THE FIRST presentation in America of Montemezzi's 'The Ship' last Tuesday evening at the Auditorium brought to the attention of the Chicago public an opera of distinct interest and of no inconsiderable musical beauty. Repeated hearings later in the season will make possible more definite and exact estimates of its inherent and lasting worth than could be formed from listening to the first performance and the preceding dress rehearsal.

Until such decision has been reached, opinion as to the Montemezzi music may justly be held in abeyance, save perhaps to state that the score is one which every musician will enjoy hearing and should hear, and is one which contains much that will appeal more or less unconsciously to the lay music lover. There is virtually nothing of the long-spun, sustained melody and tunefulness which make the older Italian operas immediate in the power and charm they exert.

Montemezzi fashions melodies which are attractive and which have individuality, but they are short melodies, and he uses them orchestrally and vocally in symphonic manner, interweaving them as does the purely instrumental writer. The result is a constant shifting of shade and line, and the resultant music is less easy of grasp than is the more frankly tuneful. Yet such is the composer's skill in handling his material that he produces tonal waves and masses, the power, color, or sensuous quality of which is such that even the indifferent listener is impressed and moved.

There seemed from the superficial hearing thus far had that the score is not the equal in beauty and potency of the one which first made Montemezzi known to us – that of 'The Love of the

Three Kings,' but something of this impression may be due to the difference in the quality of the dramas used as basis for the two operas. Sem Benelli's gripping tragedy of the invasion of mythical Alturia moves with so much more swiftness, clarity and directness than does Gabriele D'Annunzio's symbolic drama of the building of old time Venice that its accompanying musical score naturally takes on a compactness and vividness that are not possible in the later one.

The chief shortcoming of 'The Ship' as a grand opera will be found to lie, it is believed, in the libretto that Tito Ricordi has fashioned from the D'Annunzio tragedy. Italians familiar with the tragedy in its integrity claim that as a drama enacted on the stage, it is of exceptional beauty and of compelling forcefulness. The claim can easily be credited for the skill of the Italian poet in the handling of his native language is well known and is masterly. And even from the skeletonized drama which the opera brings us, it is readily believed he would fashion a play rich in color and movement, strong in character drawing, and not only fine in its symbolism, but appealing in its immediate human interest.

It is therefore no belittling of the D'Annunzio skill or creation to say that 'The Ship' is not suited to grand opera libretto use. The fault lies not in the work itself but in its quality. Symbolism may be all right in the spoken drama, but it is virtually lost and useless in grand opera.

No one thinks, for example, of the symbolism that is contained in 'The Love of Three Kings' and yet it is there, and its poet wished the tragedy considered as an allegory of Italy. But it is the human interest and the swift moving drama that make the libretto so valuable for grand opera purposes and it is these alone that appeal to the opera patron.

'The Ship' in libretto form is ambiguous and confusing. There are big holes in the drama which may have been well filled for the minds of Mr. Ricordi and Mr. Montemezzi, but which the person unfamiliar with the original drama of D'Annunzio has no way of leveling up.

We know that the Faledro family had been punished by the Gratici brothers, the father having been blinded and his four sons not only blinded but having had their tongues cut out. Just why the daughter, Basiliola, should have escaped is not made clear. It is comprehensible, however, that Basiliola, realizing the cruel punishment that was meted out to her father and brothers, should plan the using of her beauty as means for avenging herself on the Gratici brothers when they arrive from their campaign against the barbarians.

The prologue, therefore, while wanting in the obvious action that is desirable for grand opera, is still understandable. But the first act which follows is mystifying even to a person who has studied the libretto and is a complete blank to any one who merely views the performance.

What are the men who cry for bread from behind the pile of things that obstructs the center of the stage? They are supposed to have insulted Basiliola, but when and why and where? Why does she come there? Why does she hesitate about killing them? Why does she finally do so? And in the next act when we see her reveling with Sergio instead of with Marco, when and how did she gain her influence over him after vamping Marco throughout the preceding acts? And when the time comes for her to die does she go willingly to her death or should she resist?

These and many other points are unclear and remain so throughout the performance. The result is confusion, lessening of interest, and final apathy or irritation on the part of the opera patron. In the spoken drama it would be easy to keep before the spectator the fact that Basiliola's fascinating of the Gratici brothers is purely vengeful, and that even in the midst of the exerting of her powers, she gloats over the downfall she is bringing to them. But in the opera she seems doing it solely for the pleasure she derives from the fascinating. The result is complete loss of sympathy to her as a woman and a character.

And to this ambiguity and confusion which the shortening of the drama has created, the settings and costuming supplied by Norman-Bel Geddes for the American production furnish further obstacles. Mr. Geddes has fashioned stage pictures and costumes that are undeniably beautiful, and viewed solely as pictures and costumes are certainly effective. But they hinder rather than help understanding of the story and with a libretto as confusing as is this one and with opera sung to us in foreign tongue, all the help that scenery and clothes can lend needs to be utilized.

Mr. Geddes possibly might argue that it is not the province of stage enframement to further comprehension of the drama presented. This may be true, but the American operatic stage, held in darkness as it is through lack of understandable language, cannot afford to utilize anything that hampers and prevents that comprehension.

The prologue of 'The Ship' for example should be a picture of almost feverish labor activity. The cathedral is being built, ships are coming and going, the workmen of every kind are plying their craft. The watchman stands announcing the movements of the vessels, and Venice is being taken by force from the sea and is being builded.

What of all this activity is suggested by Mr. Geddes' beautiful back drop of yellow sail, against which a figure clad in green stands on a pedestal, and when he is not saying something unintelligible poses there in ineffective attitude? And what do the two reddish curtains, which inclose this yellow glory and which are seen in all the succeeding acts, have to do with such a scene of labor? The symbolism may be there, but it conveys nothing whatever to the opera spectator.

And the same misapplied beauty which is found in the settings is discoverable also in the costumes. An Adonis could not be anything other than ludicrous in the tin-plated costume that has been supplied for Mr. Dolci in the opening act, and the double blanket robe which he has to wear in the second scene surely has nothing of beauty to it, and its shade of red may be futuristically correct when placed side by side with the pink of Miss Raisa's gown in the same scene, but it is not pleasing to old fashioned eyes.

And the Raisa gowns are in themselves interesting and beautiful, but seem wholly out of keeping with the demands of the drama. As the drama reads Basiliola charms the Gratici brothers by using the same means that have been employed since female first exerted her wiles on male – by revealing her physical beauty rather than by hiding it. Mr. Geddes has Basiliola constantly more solidly and heavily clothed than is the average woman on the street or in the home today, and whenever she makes up her mind to vamp either of the men, he has her take off a veil and show her substantial gown worn under it, instead of arranging for her to remove a cloak and show veil-like garments as the poet clearly wishes.

The costumes kill the whole effect and significance of the act and inasmuch as Mr. Montemezzi has compelled his heroine to sing most of the time when she should be dancing, and since Miss Raisa has not mastered the art of dancing any more than she has the method of shooting an arrow, the scenes fail where they might by judicious use of dress and training be made clear and reasonably convincing.

Maurice Rosenfeld, 1914
Rosenfeld reviewed *La Nave* for the
Chicago Daily News and *Musical America*

8. Maurice Rosenfeld, *Musical America*, 29 November 1919.

Premiere of 'La Nave' Marks Brilliant Opening of Chicago's Opera Season

Montemezzi Himself Conducts His Work, Which Proves One of Tremendous Strength – Raisa, Dolci and Rimini, Stars of Performance

CHICAGO'S NINTH opera season began last Tuesday evening with the American première of 'La Nave,' the latest opus from the pen of the gifted composer Italo Montemezzi, at the Auditorium Theater, conducted by the composer himself.

As a matter of record it may be stated here, that the Auditorium presented a brilliant spectacle. Every seat in the big opera house was occupied.

'La Nave' is a tragic music drama in a prologue and three episodes written to a text taken originally from a poem in blank verse by Gabriele D'Annunzio.

[Summary of the plot.]

This tragic tale has been transmuted into a music drama which is thickly and heavily scored. The symphonic partiture is rich in tone, turbulent in movement and for the most part, somber of theme.

There are no moments of relief, either in the action or in the music. There are of course many melodic passages of great beauty. There are tremendous climaxes. The orchestra depicts and illumines the text admirably, but through it all, a manner of labor rather than inspiration is patent, and the composer of 'La Nave' has fallen short in his later work when compared to his masterpiece 'L'Amore Dei Tre Re.'

There is a long list of characters in the opera, but the three principal rôles are those of Marco and Sergio Gratico and Basiliola. Faldero and the Monk also have short episodes of song and the other twenty-odd personages add little to the action and not more to the musical interest. In fact 'La Nave' is a symphony with chorus, soloists and scenery as accessories, for one might almost dispense with the soloists, so ponderous is the orchestration.

Montemezzi, who conducted, got every ounce of music from the opera company. The chorus, whose parts are most trying, was always in tune, and only occasionally uncertain in attack. The scenery especially designed and painted by Norman Bel-Geddes, an American artist, was imaginative and the second episode, 'The Atrium of the Basilica,' particularly beautiful.

As for the principals, the most arduous work of them all, was allotted to Rosa Raisa, who accomplished wonders with the enormously difficult music of her rôle. Her luscious, deep-throated dramatic soprano rang through the theater with ringing power, with tonal beauty and with dramatic fire. She was given a great reception at the hands of the public.

Alessandro Dolci as Marco also sang with warmth and musical style. He has improved vocally, in that he has begun to shade his music, adding a certain refinement to his singing. He had a very trying rôle, often the music lies very high for him, but he sang with certainty and with assurance.

Sergio in Giacomo Rimini's hands was adequately impersonated and also sung with robust and powerful tone.

Arimondi's Faldero and Virgilio Lazzari's Monk, deserve commendatory mention.

Part Four

Third Production

Verona, Teatro Filarmonico, 8 March 1923

Cast:
Basiliola .... Maria Carena
Marco Gratico .... Ulisse Lappas
Sergio Gratico......... Apollo Granforte
Orso Faledro......... Oreste Carozzi
Traba, the monk ...... Nino Marotta

Director: Pasquale La Rotella
Stage and Costume Design: Guido Marussig
Conductor: Pasquale La Rotella

8 performances

The Teatro Filarmonico, Verona, Early 1900s

Introduction

THE PRODUCTION of *La Nave* at the Teatro Filarmonico, Verona, in March 1923, is much the least documented of the five productions of Montemezzi's opera. As Montemezzi had grown up in Vigasio, a village eight miles from Verona, had attended school in Verona, and moved there after the great success of *L'Amore dei Tre Re*, the production was in part at least a tribute – a delayed tribute – to a local worthy. In March 1906 the Filarmonico had staged Montemezzi's *Giovanni Gallurese*, and it had hoped to stage *L'Amore dei Tre Re* in March 1913, though the delayed La Scala premiere prevented this.[1] Strangely enough, no further attempt to stage Montemezzi's most successful opera had been made in Verona. When the Verona Arena reopened in 1919, there was a body of local opinion that said it should be with *La Nave*, but in the end Ponchielli's *Il Figliolo Prodigo* was chosen instead, and to this day the Arena has not attempted *La Nave*. This decision led Zandonai, Montemezzi's main commercial rival in the field of the Italian *Literaturoper*, to give his not wholly impartial verdict on the matter: 'For Zandonai the reasons impresarios did not want to perform *La [N]ave* were obvious: He believed the opera was not liked at La Scala, and that it cost an enormous amount to mount, with revenues that were not certain.'[2] The Filarmonico also considered staging *La Nave* in 1919, but eventually selected Zandonai's own *Francesca da Rimini* instead, to Montemezzi's annoyance.[3] Given Montemezzi's later attempts

---

1 In a letter of 22 February 1913 to Uberto Visconti di Modrone, in the possession of the present writer, Montemezzi writes: 'I ... had to give up a series of performances of *L'Amore dei tre re* during the Fair season in my Verona from 8th March onwards, performances that were subject to the possible success of my opera [at La Scala].'

2 Konrad Dryden, *Riccardo Zandonai: A Biography* (Frankfurt: Peter Lang, 1999), 202. See page

3 See below, p. 314.

to lobby support for *La Nave*, discussed below in relation to the Rome production, it is quite possible that he influenced the Filarmonico's decision to produce the opera in 1923. He took a strong interest in the production, attending all the rehearsals and offering his advice on how the opera should be presented.

The Verona *Nave*, directed and conducted by Pasquale La Rotella (1880–1963), himself an opera composer, offered no fundamental novelties, for it reused the set and costume designs by Guido Marussig which had been well received at La Scala (meaning that over three-quarters of the performances of *La Nave* to date have employed Marussig's designs). This, in combination with the fact that the opera had been widely reviewed in 1918, was doubtless the main reason why the revival, despite a strong cast and an impressive run of eight performances, received very little attention in the national press. Even *Musica d'Oggi*, Casa Ricordi's new house journal, devoted just a single paragraph to the production, merely listing the cast, reporting that the opera had 'completely conquered' the audience, and noting that Montemezzi himself had been ecstatically applauded.[1] The local press gave the production appreciative notices, but I have traced only one review of real substance, and it is this that is included here. It appeared in *L'Arena*, Verona's leading newspaper, and was authored by Montemezzi's close contemporary, Giovanni (Gino) Bertolaso (1876–1957). The two men almost certainly knew each other, for Bertolaso was a prominent figure in Verona's musical life for decades, and for over thirty years the music critic for *L'Arena*.[2] In his review he writes affectionately of Montemezzi and suggests that he had personally made efforts to get *La Nave* performed in Verona. Around 1923 he was in fact venturing into

---

[1] *Musica d'Oggi* 5:3 (March 1923), 90.

[2] For Bertolaso, see the brief account in *Dizionario Biografico dei Veronesi: Secolo 20*, ed. Giuseppe Franco Viviani (Verona: Fondazione Cassa di Risparmio di Verona, Vicenza, Belluno e Ancona, 2006).

a career as an impresario, and he managed the Arena summer festival between 1923 and 1926, a period most remarkable for a spectacular production of Boito's *Nerone* (an opera offering several comparisons with *La Nave*) in 1926.

Bertolaso's review of *La Nave* placed Montemezzi's work in the context of the general decline of the international popularity of Italian opera, and the efforts of Italian composers to 'renovate' the genre. Bertolaso argued, against the doubts of many of the 1918 critics, that Montemezzi is more 'genuinely Italian' than his immediate rivals, and generously praised his melodic inspiration and technical prowess. On the other hand, he considered *La Nave* not 'best suited' to Montemezzi's artistic character, and welcomed his choice of the very different subject of *Paolo e Virginia* for his next – later abandoned – opera.[1]

---

1 For *Paolo e Virginia*, see above, pp. 24–25.

Maria Carena, 1924
The Third Basiliola

(Photograph inscribed to the Turin chorus master, Giulio Moglioti)

1. Giovanni Bertolaso, *L'Arena*, 9 March 1923.

The Premiere of 'La Nave' by Italo Montemezzi at the Teatro Filarmonico

IN AN age like the present, of literary tiredness and artistic decline in general, there are few authentic forces, sprung from the blood of our healthy youth, that are sensitive to a modern movement of restoration, forces directed to the reconquest of musical awareness, dispelling the gloomy atmosphere of diffidence created around our theatrical environment. The Italian melodramatic production offers an astonishing statistic as to quantity: in 1921 there were about a hundred new operas, but the eloquence of the number is in strong contrast with that of the quality.

It is a distressing observation that in our homeland, and especially abroad, where we used to have an unquestionable primacy, the Italian repertoire is gradually yielding to the foreign: the works that still stand up are 'The Barber of Seville,' the comic operas of Donizetti, 'Mefistofele,' three or four operas by Verdi, one or two by Mascagni, and two or three by Puccini; our very latest productions sometimes get accepted more as novelties than for their artistic interest.

Within the weariness of this disheartened era, is there really the fecund activity for a revival, for a new spring for Italian music? We believe we are not wrong in thinking that Italo Montemezzi has always held great promise, and that our confidence is rightly placed in our fellow-citizen, who has given us very serious proofs of possessing an extremely marked and lofty purpose as a modern composer.

Indeed, among the bold energies (*energie*) who reject the past in order to renovate Italian art by revolutionising it from its foundations, such as Pizzetti, Alfano[1] and company – still without solving, in our opinion, the problem raised – and among the still fresh energies (we exclude Mascagni and Puccini who have by now completed their cycle) who cling to the past but feel the need of modernizing themselves without considering the question of a new melodramatic ideal, adopting, instead, harmonic and instrumental roughness and asperities from the likes of Strauss, Debussy, Stravinsky, Scriabin etc., such as Zandonai, who is more than anything else a good force of thought (*forza di pensiero*), we think that Montemezzi sticks to a way that is more correct, and more in keeping with the voice that is in the soul of our people.

In 'L'Amore dei tre re' and in 'La Nave' we seem to notice, better than in other operas, the exact and definite signs that make Montemezzi approach closer our national modern taste and feeling. Although his works emerge from the Wagnerian spirit and form, his expressions are almost always personal, always noble and admirable, and in all his productions a sacred enthusiasm shows through, the manifestation of an exquisite sincerity.

In fact, when the libretto offers him the opportunity to feel a delicate note, he produces pages of great humanity, pages whose sentimental content can compete with the best composers of our glorious past. Then his beautiful figure as a composer is revealed, genuinely Italian, wide-ranging, with a new and significant melodic expression that deeply touches and moves us. Because, it's no use hiding the fact, the highest aspirations of our music are and always will be expressed in melodic singing, even

---

[1] Franco Alfano (1875–1954), mainly remembered for *Risurrezione* (1904) and for completing Puccini's *Turandot*, was not very obviously part of the same trend as Pizzetti, and not obviously as revolutionary as he is represented here. Bertolaso was perhaps thinking mainly of the artistic innovations found in Alfano's recent *La Leggenda di Sakùntala* (1921), one of the first Italian operas with a prose libretto.

if regulated in an austere and modern way.

So we see how, in the final duet of the first episode of 'La Nave,' the sentence '*Tu m'odii e m'abbandoni...*' (You hate me and abandon me)[1] and the ending of the episode express human passion with an absolute emphasis, giving us an intuition of the truth through the mystery of the melody. In the Prologue, the scene of Basiliola's meeting with her blinded brothers has the same emotional power; it is a page full of virgin inspiration and a sweetness that touches our hearts. When a composer can write that way, he can have the consciousness of communicating with people through a definite form of art, with neat contours and a firm character, expressing all his soul in his own sorrows, aspirations and faith.

Furthermore, in 'La Nave' Montemezzi is strong and confident technically; with an intuitive feeling for theatre, he treats the instrumental aspect as an experienced and consummate maestro, taking care of everything with a very modern sensitivity, although there are connections with and interpositions from the Wagnerian style, which he quite rightly chose as his model.

Really praiseworthy in the score of 'La Nave' are the choruses, and Montemezzi has the great merit of having been able to develop this important element in an original way. In the Prologue, and particularly in the second and third Episodes, the choruses achieve a singular reality, so that we have the impression that the crowd is a living and necessary character, an indispensable essence of the drama.

We don't think that the broad and complex D'Annunzian tragedy was best suited to Montemezzi's musical temperament, and we, who love him, will eagerly wait for his next work, which he seems to have already definitely chosen.[2] In that work, among

---

1 Marco Gratico's words to Basiliola, slightly misquoted.

2 The subsequently abandoned *Paolo e Virginia*, for which see above, pp. 24–25.

delicate and elegiac tones, he will be able to feel free from every academic and tiring practice, freely and comprehensively sweeping through the field of his imagination, letting his sweet and tender passion well up. This is something that we all wish, as also for the need that is in the air for a return to simplicity and clarity.

Last night the cream of Verona flocked to the Teatro Filarmonico to do justice to their valiant fellow-citizen, and there was the most animated admiration for the reconsecration of his latest powerful work, performed five years ago at La Scala. And we were the first to rejoice at last night's splendid manifestation, since we had long been attempting to ensure that Verona would hasten to pay this deserved homage to its fellow-citizen, a due tribute after his great success in Milan.

We hope that the triumph of this new production of 'La Nave' at the Teatro Filarmonico marks the true dawn of the opera, so that we can, in the end, see it gloriously dock on the stages of the Italian opera houses, a good wish that we heartily express to the dear artist.

On the whole, the performance was most praiseworthy; the composer had followed all the rehearsals and this greatly contributed to the very happy result last night. But the composer also had a precious collaborator, Maestro La Rotella, who was able to perfectly render his will with uncommon intelligence and fervour. The blending of the orchestra with the events on stage was always laudable, which is a considerable feat, if we consider the dimensions of the opera. The difficulties, particularly serious in the second episode, were overcome happily, and it goes without saying that on Saturday night,[1] after the success of this crucial test, everything will proceed with absolute perfection.

---

1 The first performance was on a Thursday.

The orchestra, composed of very good elements, always responded to the animating baton of La Rotella faultlessly, playing with precision and emphasizing every detail with great artistic expression. Therefore, we are very happy to render the first honour for the performance to this orchestral conductor, new in Verona, who already occupies an eminent place in the operatic world. In addition to him, we give our applause to the maestro who instructed the chorus, Milani,[1] who, ably assisted by his substitutes, was able to get them to overcome the difficulties scattered in profusion throughout the score.

The vocal parts were given to first-rate artists like Carena, Lappas and Granforte. Basiliola couldn't have had a more worthy and exquisite interpreter than Carena. Her voice is well suited to express this difficult part in respect to both intonation and register (*tessitura*), and the capable artist maintained the highest level throughout the performance, showing no sign of tiredness in her vocal efforts. The spirit of the complex figure of this peculiar character was understood by the select interpreter, and the audience followed her with keen interest, especially in the most salient moments, such as the scene with the blinded men in the finale of the prologue, and in the duet in the first episode.

The tenor Lappas, too, was very much appreciated by the audience: he possesses indeed indubitable stamina. He impressed precisely because of his excellent vocal means, obtaining a great success.

Granforte took the role of the bishop Sergio Gratico, who is a curious part of the colossal tragedy. We already knew this excellent artist, having heard him recently in 'Boris' in Mantua,[2] where we admired his uncommon qualities as an expert and intelligent actor, as well as a singer. It goes without saying that

---

1 Ferruccio Milani (dates unknown).

2 Granforte had sung the title role in the production of *Boris Godunov* which opened in Mantua on 17 January 1923.

last night, too, he was a perfect bishop, if not in the austerity wished for by the church, then certainly in the way conceived of by D'Annunzio, and his beautiful voice expanded pleasantly amid the most animated satisfaction of the audience.

The other innumerable characters did very well in their various parts and I mention their names: Oreste Carozzi, Alfredo Mattioli, Giovanni Novelli, Gino Treves, G. Ballardin, Mazza Aurelio and Millo Marucci.

The ballet in the second episode was performed well by the dancers of the small *corps de ballet* perfectly instructed by Signora Sciantarelli. The light effects were entrusted to the skilful hands of our Ghirotto, who excelled in his task. The stage was directed by the good Carotini,[1] who did his complicated duty perfectly. The scenery was excellent, and the costumes fairly good.

---

1   Napoleone Carotini (dates unknown).

Part Five

Fourth Production

Rome, Teatro Reale dell'Opera, 14 December 1938

Cast:
Basiliola . . . . Gina Cigna
Marco Gratico . . . . Paolo Civil
                         (Pau Civil)
Sergio Gratico. . . . . Mario Basiola
Orso Faledro . . . . Filippo Romito
Traba, the monk . . . . . . Augusto Beuf

Director: Carlo Piccinato
Stage and Costume Design: Cipriano E. Oppo
Conductor: Tullio Serafin

3 performances

The Teatro Reale, Rome, 1937

Introduction

THROUGHOUT THE 1920s Montemezzi lobbied hard to get *La Nave* performed. On 11 September 1931 he wrote:

> For years and years I requested the revival of my *Nave* that had the good fortune to be performed at La Scala in 1918 for ten consecutive evenings, achieving a great success.
>
> This opera, whose meaning is known to all, applauded, approved, considered among the most significant of the last thirty years, has always been rejected without explanation.[1]

The 1923 Verona production may represent a successful response to such lobbying, but it was to prove the only one of the decade. It is unlikely, however, that the growing pile of rejection letters were all 'without explanation': the biggest objection was doubtless that the opera would be very expensive to put on, therefore exceedingly likely to make a loss, and this at a time when the economics of opera had become strained by the loss to cinema of a good proportion of the popular audience. Opera houses preferred to stage works that were either completely new or proven crowd pleasers. Montemezzi experienced an increasing sense of injustice, apparently only exacerbated by the fact that *L'Amore dei Tre Re* was being played all around the world, and at the end of the decade he determined to take his case to the highest authority in the land: Mussolini.

In March 1930 Montemezzi sent a copy of *La Nave* to the Duce, with a request that he be allowed to meet him; he was, accordingly, granted an audience with Mussolini on 29 May the same year.[2]

---

[1] Letter to Mussolini. See Fiamma Nicolodi, *Musica e Musicisti nel Ventennio Fascista* (Fiesole: Discanto, 1984), 418.

[2] Ibid. 413 and n. 5.

On that occasion he clearly made a strong case for the importance of *La Nave*, and, given his knowledge of the man he was talking to, probably put considerable emphasis on the patriotism and politics of the opera. Montemezzi expressed the view that such an epic Italian opera deserved to be produced at the Teatro Reale dell' Opera, Rome. The Teatro Reale, a grand Fascist project which had seen the old Teatro Costanzi transformed almost beyond recognition, had opened on 28 February 1928, and was meant to be a showpiece national opera house. Mussolini was convinced, or at least sufficiently convinced to promise to help. The Fascist bureaucracy then took up the case, the governor of Rome, Francesco Boncompagni Ludovisi, was applied to, and he passed the matter to his deputy, Paolo d'Ancora, who happened to be the head of the committee which ran the Teatro Reale. The response from the theatre committee was not encouraging, however, and the message got passed back up the chain that the opera was considered 'very expensive [to produce] – but heavy and not well received. … [d'Ancora did] not think the Teatro Reale should perform an opera that would represent a sure and unjustified loss.'[1]

Montemezzi responded to this rebuff with a long, pleading letter to Mussolini of 18 July, representing the decision as part of a general culture discouraging new operas, and passionately urging the claims of *La Nave* to be heard:

> *La Nave* … is my major work.
> I insist: my major work. I shout it to the rooftops so that I may be heard.
> I would really like to be understood before I die! I'm shouting because in the artist's creed, which considers art from the point of view of beauty and beauty alone, I'm sure I deserve that my *Nave* be looked upon in good faith.

---

1 Ibid. 414–15.

It was composed at a moment when everyone was looking to the other side of the Adriatic, with eyes full of tears and hope, and a heart swollen with sublime love. It was my greatest dream: to provide Italy with an opera solely and characteristically Italian which had no precedent, such as to be a modest contribution from a faithful and doting artist.[1]

Given the universal consensus of Italian critics that *La Nave* was particularly Germanic in its musical language, it is difficult to know what Montemezzi meant by calling it 'solely and characteristically Italian,' and his assertion of the claims of 'pure' beauty sits awkwardly beside the emphasis on the opera's patriotic significance. By this juncture, however, it appears he was prepared to make almost any claim for his work to help secure a new production. On 11 September 1931 he took up the cause again, arguing that *La Nave* would be an appropriate opera to mark 'the tenth anniversary of fascism [1932]. ... Certainly no other opera can be more suitable than *La Nave* to exalt the power of our race. And no other moment could be more opportune than the tenth anniversary of fascism.'[2]

Such statements are embarrassing now, and their publication in 1984 probably worked against the possibility of a modern revival of *La Nave*. They sharply raise the question of Montemezzi's attitude to the Fascist regime. There is no space here to consider the matter in depth, and until more of his private correspondence becomes accessible it would be impossible to make a definitive statement in any case. He was, like most of his musical contemporaries, prepared to write obsequious letters and telegrams to Mussolini (who thrived on obsequiousness, and sometimes rewarded it). On the other hand, Montemezzi signed no mani-

---

1 Ibid. 416.
2 Ibid. 418.

festos and neither accepted, nor sought, any position from the regime. Later, when living in America, he defined himself as an anti-Fascist, and in 1933 he started work on his final opera, *L'Incantesimo*, in which I read an unmistakably anti-Fascist message. Perhaps the worst that can be said of him is that in his great eagerness to have *La Nave* performed he was prepared to ingratiate himself with a regime from which, in other respects, he preferred to keep his distance.

Montemezzi's 1931 letters led to a second official approach being made to the Teatro Reale, but again the theatre committee rejected *La Nave* on financial grounds. Montemezzi did not give up, however, and more letters were written, and in July 1934 the tide finally began to turn in his favour when his old friend Tullio Serafin was appointed artistic director of the Teatro Reale. Serafin initially proposed *La Nave* for the 1935–36 season, when he was unable to get the committee to accept it,[1] but pressure was mounting and finally *La Nave* was chosen to open the 1938–39 season. It had been a painfully long wait. Political factors almost certainly played their part in the decision to revive the opera. After Italy's post-First World War disappointments, and a focus on domestic politics in the early Fascist years, by the late 1920s there was much talk of creating an Italian Empire. The popular Second Italo-Abyssinian War of 1935–36 led to an enormous expansion of Italian power in Africa and Mussolini's declaration on 9 May 1936 (words that were then carved into marble):

> Italy has her empire at last – a Fascist empire because it bears the indestructible symbols of the will and power of the Roman lictors, because this is the goal that for fourteen years spurred on the exuberant and disciplined energies of the young and the dashing generations of Italy.

---

[1] Ibid. 425.

... That is in the tradition of Rome, which, after victory, associated the different peoples with her own destiny.[1]

Mussolini's announcement was enthusiastically received by the majority of the Italian people, and he found himself at the zenith of his personal popularity. In such a context, the political narrative of *La Nave* began to have real relevance again. The death of D'Annunzio on 1 March 1938, though probably too late to influence the selection of the opera for the following season, can only have added to the sense that its time had come. It is worth noting that a spectacular open-air revival of the original spoken play was put on in Venice by the city authorities in September 1938; the minister of popular culture announced that this production was made possible by 'the will of the regime.'[2]

Montemezzi's *La Nave* was meant to open the Teatro Reale season on 8 December (see illustration overleaf) and it was scheduled, like the other operas being presented, to run for four performances. Unfortunately Gina Cigna, who was singing the part of Basiliola, fell ill, so the first performance had to be cancelled and replaced with *Tannhäuser*, leading to an odd conspiracy theory that the Vatican had proscribed the production.[3] Fortunately Cigna recovered quickly, and the second performance on 14 December went ahead on schedule. Despite the claims of excessive expense which had regularly been used to reject the opera, *La Nave* received a lavish production in Rome with new set and costume designs by the prominent artist Cipriano

---

[1] For the full speech, as it was afterwards memorialized, see: <http://www.hist.uib.no/antikk/eftertid/foroitalicoL.htm>. I have slightly altered the translation given there.

[2] Mary Ann Frese Witt, *The Search for Modern Tragedy: Aesthetic Fascism in Italy and France* (Ithaca, NY: Cornell UP, 2001), 71–3.

[3] See 'Vatican Protest? Banned Play Withdrawn,' *Catholic Herald*, 16 December 1938, p. 7.

PROGRAMMA-CALENDARIO

ESECUTORI PRINCIPALI

LA NAVE
di I. Montemezzi
su Poema di G. D'Annunzio
Nuova per Roma
8 Dicembre

Gina Cigna - Paolo Civil - Mario Basiola - Augusto Beuf - Filippo Romito - Adelio Zagonara.
M° Direttore: TULLIO SERAFIN

TANNHAEUSER
di R. Wagner
Nuovo allestimento
10 Dicembre

Gabriella Gatti - Anna Reali - Fiorenza Tasso - Armando Borgioli - Giacomo Vaghi
M° Direttore: TULLIO SERAFIN

L'ARLESIANA
di F. Cilea

Gianna Pederzini - Licia Albanese - Tito Schipa - Gino Bechi - Tito Gobbi - Giulio Neri

IL CAPPELLO A TRE PUNTE
(Ballo)
(El sombrero de tres picos)
di M. De Falla
Nuova per Roma
11 Dicembre

Attilia Radice (prima ballerina assoluta)
Alexander Von Swaine - Aurel M. Millos (primi ballerini)
Coreografia di Aurel M. Millos
M°. Direttore: OLIVIERO DE FABRITIIS

OBERON
di C. M. Weber
Nuova per Roma
15 Dicembre

Gina Cigna - Ebe Stignani - Gida Alfano - Giulietta Simionato - Bruno Landi - Emilio Ghirardini
M° Direttore: TULLIO SERAFIN

TOSCA
di G. Puccini
21 Dicembre

Iva Pacetti - Giuseppe Lugo - Mariano Stabile
M°. Direttore: VINCENZO BELLEZZA

LA FIGLIA DEL RE
di A. Lualdi
Nuova per Roma
26 Dicembre

Giuseppina Cobelli - Oscar Vidal - Benvenuto Franci - Filippo Romito
M° Direttore: TULLIO SERAFIN

TRISTANO E ISOTTA
di R. Wagner
nella edizione tedesca e col complesso artistico di Bayreuth
4 Gennaio

Gertrud Rünger - Margarete Klose - Max Lorenz - Paul Schoffler - Ludwig Weber - Martin Kremer
M°. Direttore: VICTOR DE SABATA

RISURREZIONE
di F. Alfano
11 Gennaio

Giuseppina Cobelli - Alessandro Granda - Gino Bechi
M°. Direttore: OLIVIERO DE FABRITIIS

The First Page of the Teatro Reale Calendar, 1938–39

E. Oppo (1891–1962) that were faithful to the general spirit of Marussig's, but more spacious in conception. Montemezzi, who was present, saw much in the result to vindicate his faith in his most ambitious work. The audience response was positive; even Pizzetti, much the harshest of the critics, accepted that the opera had been received 'very favourably.'[1] And the six or seven curtain calls at the end, as opposed to the two at La Scala in 1918, suggests that *La Nave* was able to hold the interest of the spectators throughout. The difficulties of the opera appear to have been embraced more readily in 1938 than in 1918, a result, it would seem, of altered expectations concerning new opera in general and the fact that *La Nave* no longer seemed a threat to an existing tradition of more accessible musical theatre.

Having courted the Fascist party to get *La Nave* produced, Montemezzi was in no position to complain that the critical reception of the opera he considered his masterpiece would be significantly shaped by card-carrying Fascist critics and overtly Fascist publications. This was not such a simple matter as it might sound, however, for, as Harvey Sachs has shown, the Fascists never produced a coherent, consensual policy regarding music beyond a determination to control its institutions.[2] And while it is tempting to try and separate clearly Fascist from non-Fascist criticism, this is not always easy. Nevertheless, though the dividing line is often unclear, the seven critics featured here can be roughly divided into two groups. In the first, Alceo Toni and Adriano Lualdi were both among the most senior figures in the Fascist musical bureaucracy, while Augusto Righetti was writing for *Il Tevere*, an extreme Fascist newspaper serving as Mussolini's

---

1 See below, p. 264.

2 See Harvey Sachs, *Music in Fascist Italy* (London: Weidenfeld and Nicolson, 1987).

unofficial mouthpiece. In the second group, Bruno Barilli and Ildebrando Pizzetti, though they both signed the Manifesto of Fascist Intellectuals in 1925 and personally benefitted from the prizes on offer under Fascism, were not representative of the regime in the same way: indeed Barilli, notably, was writing for a publication soon afterwards closed down by the Fascist authorities. The unidentified critic who reviewed *La Nave* for *La Stampa* appears, from his concluding comments, to have been sympathetic to the Fascists, but it is unlikely that he represented the party as such. Matteo Incagliati, the oldest critic included in this section, was probably the most politically innocent.

Among the Fascist critics, Toni and Lualdi almost certainly knew of Montemezzi's long campaign to get *La Nave* revived and that official efforts had been made on his behalf. They both gave the production generous advance publicity, Toni in *Il Popolo d'Italia* and *La Rivista Illustra del Popolo d'Italia* and Lualdi in *Il Giornale d'Italia*. Both sharply questioned why the opera had gone so long unheard and clearly considered themselves empowered to set matters straight for the Italian people.

Alceo Toni (1884–1969) was a thorough-going Fascist bureaucrat. Sachs introduces him in the following terms:

> Music critic for the fascists' *Il popolo d'Italia* throughout the regime's existence and president of the Milan Conservatory from 1936 to 1940, Toni was also a conductor, arranger and composer of retrograde tastes and great pretensions. His political functions under fascism included a period as secretary of the Province of Milan's Musicians' Union and, later, membership in the National Directorate of the Fascist Union of Musicians.[1]

---

1 Ibid. 23.

Toni is most famous, or notorious, for drawing up the 'Manifesto of Italian Musicians for the Tradition of Nineteenth-Century Romantic Art' ('Manifesto di musicisti italiani per la tradizione dell'arte romantic dell'ottocento'), published in 1932 over the signatures of several notable musicians, including, notably, Pizzetti and Zandonai. As the title of this manifesto suggests, Toni was exceptionally conservative in his musical views and harshly opposed to all modernist tendencies. Yet he was no mean scholar, and Tullio Serafin, Montemezzi's friend, thought highly enough of him to subsequently collaborate on the two-volume *Style, Traditions and Conventions of Italian Opera in the Eighteenth and Nineteenth Centuries* (*Stile, Tradizioni e Convenzioni del Melodramma Italiano del Settecento e dell'Ottocento*) (1958, 1964). Toni's review of *La Nave*, like many of his reviews, contains a great deal of gratuitous axe grinding. This was his roundabout way of praising Montemezzi, who is essentially given a clean bill of health and declared devoid of modernist perversions. Indeed Toni co-opts *La Nave* for his beloved Romantic tradition, declaring, in an attractive formula, that 'in the spirit of the romanticized chronicle,' *La Nave* 'draws ... on the confluence of the two big streams of Verdian and Wagnerian romanticism.' Yet though Toni was largely positive about Montemezzi's opera, praising the choral element especially, he did feel, like some of the earlier critics, that it was composed less from the heart than from the head, thus 'the architecture surpasses the inspiration.' He blamed this on the excessive Wagnerian influence, though this is lightly touched on compared to many of the 1918 critics. Altogether, Toni considered the revival of *La Nave* a cause for celebration.

Adriano Lualdi (1885–1971), much more talented than Toni both as a musician and a critic, was also of greater importance in the Fascist bureaucracy. Sachs introduces him as follows:

Lualdi, a solidly trained composer of decidedly conservative stamp as well as a conductor and writer on musical subjects, ardently supported the regime from its early years and, in 1929, entered the completely fascisticized, evirated Chamber of Deputies as representative of the Fascist Union of Musicians. His official activities later extended to representing the artistic and professional category on the governing board of the Corporation of the Performing Arts, which entitled him to serve as a national councilor in the Chamber of Fasces and Corporations. These high-ranking political positions gave him a great deal of clout within the Italian musical world: he founded and organized government-subsidized festivals, and he participated – or interfered – in the administration of many cultural organizations and enterprises. Lualdi directed the Naples Conservatory from 1936 to 1944, arranged important national and foreign tours for himself and managed to have his works performed by the most important ensembles in the country.[1]

Whereas Toni had composed one opera, which proved completely unsuccessful, the prolific Lualdi had composed half a dozen, three of which enjoyed moderate acclaim. *La Figlia del Re* was actually included in the same 1938 Teatro Reale season as *La Nave*. He was known to Montemezzi,[2] and it is reasonable to suppose that they had discussed their views on opera. Lualdi's greater practical experience of composition combined with less dogmatic views – he did not sign the 1932 manifesto – made him

---

1 Ibid. 21.

2 See above, p. 52, n. 1.

a much more perceptive and objective critic than Toni, and were it not for his strong association with Fascism his critical writings would probably have had a more enduring impact.

Lualdi devoted a good part of his review to extolling the musical qualities of D'Annunzio himself, whose musical attitudes, especially his championship of Monteverdi and early Italian music, he found highly praiseworthy. After this, his emphasis was on the difficulty, rather than the inadvisability, of setting *La Nave* to music, and his central assertion was that 'Italo Montemezzi tackled and solved such a difficult problem with admirable confidence and skill.' While many earlier critics had fretted about the obscurities and incompleteness of the story the opera tells, Lualdi praised the picturesque approach which had distilled the dramatic essence in 'a series of large frescoes' (a pictorial counterpart to Toni's 'romanticized chronicle'). Like earlier critics, he highly valued the choral and orchestral aspects of *La Nave*, and rather than condemning Montemezzi's Wagnerianism he represented the opera as at once the summit and the conclusion of Italian music's attempts to learn from the great German composer. *La Nave* was to be understood as a great end-of-an-era work, and by this stage in the review the reader realizes that Lualdi's initial praise of D'Annunzio had a deeper motive: just as the great writer, a onetime devotee of Wagner, had come to believe in the superiority of Monteverdi, so should Montemezzi. Though the latter would never significantly change his musical bearings, one imagines that Lualdi's sympathetic review of *La Nave* would have meant a great deal to him. Of all the reviews, it perhaps comes closest to establishing the terms on which Montemezzi would have wanted his opera to be judged.

Toni was writing for *Il Popolo d'Italia*, the newspaper founded by Mussolini in 1914 that served as the official mouthpiece of the regime. Lualdi was writing for *Il Giornale d'Italia*, a more respectable and very influential paper which had served the cause of

Building the Ship for the Rome Production

Stage Set for the Third Episode
Cipriano E. Oppo

liberalism before becoming to all intents and purposes a regime publication in the hands of Virginio Gayda, the editor from 1926. Gayda was a friend of Mussolini and offered the dictator all the advantages of a trustworthy newspaper not too obviously controlled by the Fascist party. A striking demonstration of how important *Il Giornale* had become for Mussolini by 1938 is that it was this paper, rather than *Il Popolo d'Italia*, that he allowed to first print his 'Manifesto degli scienziati razzisti' ('Manifesto of the Racial Scientists') on 15 July. This was essentially a statement of the regime's new antisemitism, following Hitler's visit to Italy in May that year, and it presumably appalled Montemezzi, whose wife was Jewish. If *Il Popolo d'Italia* was the recognized voice of the regime, and *Il Giornale d'Italia* its favourite indirect means of communication with the Italian people and the outside world – *Il Giornale* was the Italian paper most cited by the international press – *Il Tevere*, the third publication featured here, was a down-market, ultra-Fascist paper answering only to Mussolini himself.[1] The dictator had founded it in 1924 and handpicked its editor, Telesio Interlandi. Initially it attracted a number of illustrious contributors, but Interlandi's fierce editorials, love of abuse and muckraking, and the difficulty those connected with the paper had in getting paid (with the exception of the editor), soon set it on an irreversibly downward course. Mussolini, the only person Interlandi considered untouchable, seems to have genuinely enjoyed it, and he shielded his editor from his many enemies, describing him as 'a personal whim of mine, which, unlike an eternal passion, can also endure.'[2] *Il Tevere* was a throwback to the earlier, cruder and more violent political culture from which

---

[1] For a detailed and fascinating study of *Il Tevere* see Meir Michaelis, 'Mussolini's unofficial mouthpiece: Telesio Interlandi – *Il Tevere* and the evolution of Mussolini's anti-Semitism,' *Journal of Modern Italian Studies* 3 (1998), 217–40.

[2] Quoted in ibid. 237.

Fascism sprung, and it offered Mussolini a chance to disseminate wilder and more personal views than those deemed appropriate for the now much more respectable *Il Popolo d'Italia*.

Augusto Righetti became the music critic of *Il Tevere* in 1935. Very little is known about him, but he died in 1942 at the age of fifty-seven, so was presumably born in 1885 or 1886. Righetti had none of the academic standing of Toni or Lualdi, neither of whom, one suspects, would have condescended to write for *Il Tevere*, and his only substantial publication appears to have been a short, popular, critical biography of Verdi published in Rome in 1910. This reveals him to have been an old-fashioned populist for whom *Rigoletto*, *Il Trovatore* and *La Traviata* had fixed the standard in matters operatic. In particular, he judged that Verdi had 'written no work that surpasses *Rigoletto*,'[1] and the several pages he devotes to this opera contrast remarkably with his very brief mentions of *Otello* and *Falstaff*. Such a man was hardly likely to have much appetite for *La Nave*, and his biggest criticism was that Montemezzi's opera was not popular enough – it had not genuinely stirred the masses. It is probable that Righetti was relied upon to make such judgements, which represent one side of Fascist musical endeavour (comparable to attempts to promote 'healthy' popular music in other totalitarian regimes), and which kept everyone one on their toes, including critics like Toni and Lualdi whose own commitment to composition, if nothing else, would have made them shy of appealing to such democratic standards. In some ways, of course, such standards worked to Montemezzi's advantage, as he had written an opera more popular than almost all those of his Italian contemporaries, and Righetti's patriotism perhaps partly overcame his personal taste when he allowed that *L'Amore dei Tre Re* had 'victoriously established [Montemezzi] among the great composers of our generation.' In any case, a final point to make about Righetti's noteworthy review is that, despite

---

1 *Giuseppe Verdi* (Rome: Carra, 1910), 39.

his reactionary attitudes, he managed to be as positive about *La Nave* as most of the 1918 critics.

Of the critics writing in non-Fascist publications, the first featured here is Matteo Incagliati (1873–1941), who reviewed *La Nave* for *Il Messagero*, one of Italy's leading half dozen newspapers. He was a veteran opera critic. Having published brief studies of Mascagni's *Iris* and Puccini's *Tosca* in 1899 and 1900 respectively, he established his scholarly credentials with a well-received monograph, *Il Teatro Costanzi: 1880–1907* (1907). He corresponded with Puccini, and his personal taste in opera appears to have been for the popular works of the Puccini-Mascagni generation. He wrote on musical topics for various newspapers and periodicals until his death, clearly well respected as a critic even though he was never a leader in the field. His review of *La Nave* came closest to those of 1918, and his terminology suggests that he may have been influenced by Podrecca's approach to the opera (note, in particular, the emphasis on 'synthesis' and how D'Annunzio's play made this virtually impossible). The basic unsuitability of the play and the excessively Wagnerian style were again found fault with (though the latter aspect was only lightly touched on), and Incagliati considered the first half of the opera much less impressive than the second. Nevertheless, his review as a whole comes across as positive; nothing is said of *La Nave* being unmelodic; on the contrary, indeed, Incagliati judged the opera rich in inspired melody. Similarly, he praised the choral and orchestral aspects, as well as the 'genuine singing quality' of the score – something not appreciated by the 1918 critics.

Bruno Barilli (1880–1952), the second critic in this second group, was a celebrity in the world of music criticism. He studied music at the Parma Conservatory, then went to Germany in 1901 to pursue his studies further at the Munich Conservatory. He returned to Italy in 1910, initially hoping to become an opera composer, but his two operas, *Medusa* (completed 1914) and *Emiral* (1915), though they both won competitions, did not get performed until much later (*Emiral* in 1924, *Medusa* in 1938). Meanwhile, in the early 1910s, Barilli discovered that his real vocation was for writing about music. He disliked the conventional formulas and jargon used in Italian criticism, and set out to develop a new kind of impressionistic writing which sought to convey in highly poetic language something of the experience of listening to music. By 1938 he had developed his style in hundreds of reviews and articles and several books, and was equally admired and derided. Barilli signed the Manifesto of Fascist Intellectuals in 1925, as did Pizzetti, and he was subsequently funded by the regime.[1] But Barilli appears to have been officially supported, not because he wanted to politicize art, but because he was very good at maintaining the illusion that art was a wonderful thing that had nothing to do with politics. In fact, his review of *La Nave* appeared in *Omnibus*, the short-lived weekly news magazine, edited by Leo Longanesi (1905–1957), which regularly encountered censorship issues and was closed down by the regime in 1939. Barilli's brief review is very different from the others collected in this book, and in places reads like an appreciative prose poem. The only argument he really advanced is that Montemezzi, despite the claims of other critics, had thoroughly assimilated his foreign influences. Barilli judged *La Nave* an organic and unified work of art, and Montemezzi a calm, powerful and original composer, capable of handling enormous musical forces with great authority. He recognized that some passages in the score were less inspired than others, but nevertheless excused these poetically as 'shadows that serve the light.'

Whereas Incagliati and Barilli were among the most positive critics of *La Nave*, Ildebrando Pizzetti was much the most severe, and Montemezzi must have found his harsh dismissal in *La Tribuna*, another leading Roman paper, painful reading. There

---

[1] Sachs, *Music*, 119. Sachs emphasizes that it is wrong to 'automatically' assume that everyone subsidised by the regime was 'a fascist sympathizer.'

is no need for a general introduction to Pizzetti (1880–1968) here as he remains one of the best known Italian composers of the twentieth century. On the other hand, it is important to establish the personal motivation behind his attack on Montemezzi. The two men, though rivals in the field of Italian opera, had very different notions of their vocation. Montemezzi aspired simply to write operas, and, like Puccini and many earlier Italian composers, to live off the profits they generated. Very different, Pizzetti fitted the now more recognizable model of the academic composer who combines creativity with a teaching position. He was a careerist whose artistic purism existed alongside a political opportunism, and he flourished in the Fascist era, holding a series of prestigious academic posts while continuing to produce a great deal of music in many different genres. In marked contrast, since the premiere of *La Nave* in 1918 Montemezzi had only made public two new works, a one-act opera and a symphonic poem, and he lived a leisurely and retired existence funded by his income from *L'Amore dei Tre Re* and that acquired by his marriage to a wealthy American woman. There was, then, unlikely to be much personal sympathy between the two composers, but the same could be said of Montemezzi and Lualdi, so this is not enough to explain active hostility. In Pizzetti's case, there were deeper factors concerning territory and musical procedure. His career as a composer had commenced with the incidental music to the original spoken play version of *La Nave* (1908), giving him a personal investment in D'Annunzio's tragedy not shared by Montemezzi's other critics. Pizzetti's work on *La Nave* drew him into D'Annunzio's orbit, something that affected him personally, for he came to hero-worship the writer, and professionally, for he was soon at work on a series of D'Annunzio projects, most notably a setting of *Fedra* as a *Literaturoper*, as discussed in the general introduction. *Fedra*, though beautifully composed according to the exacting artistic standards Pizzetti consistently set himself, had to wait on the much greater commercial success that Montemezzi's *L'Amore dei Tre Re* and Zandonai's *Francesca da Rimini* enjoyed before it could be produced. Looking back on his and Montemezzi's respective careers, Pizzetti almost certainly thought that *L'Amore dei Tre Re* had been unfairly successful, and his own *Fedra*, indeed most of his operas, unfairly neglected; he doubtless thought, too, that his own music for *La Nave* had better captured the spirit of the play than Montemezzi's. Altogether, it was hardly a recipe for neutral criticism.

In his review of *La Nave*, Pizzetti began by carefully praising every aspect of the production apart from the opera itself. He then attacked the libretto, incorporating as it did the 'deformations' of Tito Ricordi, and having dealt with that asserted, in rather devastating fashion: '*La Nave* by maestro Montemezzi is … one of those operas about which the critics can say very little.' The reason Pizzetti gave for this astonishing claim was that the music lacks character or individuality, despite its 'technical correctness.' Pizzetti then went on to make an attack on Montemezzi's notion of the *Literaturoper*, leaving his informed readers to infer that he himself knew much better how to write such an opera. The Montemezzian *Literaturoper*, according to Pizzetti, is neither one thing nor another, neither a proper melodrama nor a proper drama; moreover, Montemezzi's music is an unworthy accompaniment to D'Annunzio's sublime poetry. Pizzetti concluded his review with a series of attacks on Montemezzi's melody, prosody, interpretative powers, formulaic approach to composition and old-fashioned 'romanticism.' His determination to be displeased is so obvious that his accusations lose force; one hopes that contemporary readers were put on their guard.

The final review in this section appeared in *La Stampa*, then as now one of Italy's leading newspapers. As this paper's head office was in Turin, and as Montemezzi's first two operas to reach the stage – *Giovanni Gallurese* and *Héllera* – were brought out there, *La Stampa* had played a very significant role in commenting on his career from the beginning. The review is signed 's.s.,' and I have been unable to identify the reviewer. The chief music critic for the paper was Andrea Della Corte (1883–1968), who sometimes reviewed Teatro Reale productions, but on this occasion *La Nave* was clearly entrusted to another hand. The review is most useful for including a lengthy statement that Montemezzi himself made about his opera: a statement which goes over much the same ground as his 1938 *Scenario* essay, but changes certain details and emphases. The review is, like most of the 1938 reviews, largely positive, judging *La Nave* a successful translation of D'Annunzio's play into musical terms, an intelligent synthesis of the 'last Verdi' and Wagner (comparable here to Toni's review), an opera with masterly orchestral and choral elements, and a work 'of high artistic dignity.'

Altogether, despite Righetti's doubts about the degree of public enthusiasm and Pizzetti's embittered attack, there can be no doubt that *La Nave* was considerably better received in 1938 than in 1918. Montemezzi's magnum opus now seemed much more accessible; none of the 1918 critics had come close to declaring, as 's.s.' did in *La Stampa*, that '[i]t is an opera of certain and immediate popular comprehensibility.' The reviewers, too, were now much less concerned about the Wagnerianism of the score and the compositional constraints imposed by the *Literaturoper* form. If history had been different, *La Nave* might, one suspects, have established itself: not exactly as a regular repertoire piece, but as a respected epic work worth occasional and prestigious revival. Montemezzi probably hoped for no more. As it was, the outbreak of war the following year, and the destruction of the performance materials by allied bombing in 1943, put an end to the opera's stage career.

1. Alceo Toni, *Il Popolo d'Italia*, 15 December 1938.

'La Nave' by Italo Montemezzi at the Reale dell'Opera

Rome, 14 December

PERHAPS WE don't know the Roman audience of the Teatro Reale dell'Opera well enough, but it seems to us that the displays of affection it abandoned itself to at tonight's performance were not the usual stereotyped ones that for some time we have had to take notice of at 'premiere' nights.

This audience is usually described as prone to applause and yet, at the same time, indifferent and sceptical; however, when confronted with the new score, it didn't remain inert and passive, with an air of indulgence and, worse, of condescension. That is, it didn't maintain the usual demeanour – yes, let's say it openly! – of all our audiences toward new operas and new composers.

'La Nave,' it's true, doesn't offer us abysmal aesthetic enigmas, nor does it force us to make Herculean efforts to follow and understand that part of its being that can be called its most constitutional: music. There will be something to be said about this opera, with some critical reservations, which we will hint at.

Yet tonight, we all felt that 'La Nave' is an opera, a true opera, according to the meaning of theatre in music, not only in so far as it is traditional, but also according to the character and fundamental needs, immutable and indisputable, of said theatre in music.

It was clear that it hadn't grown up anaemic, sclerotic and rickety with the help of medications and injections, like many operas we have seen lately. It is not the child of exclusively cerebral little concepts; it is not the fruit of a bastard mind, half philosophic and half artistic, half literary and half musical.

The hand that composed it knew, and knows, how to bend the notes to its will, with the experience and the awareness of its own masterly command.

Its musicality is not forced, deliberate and convoluted (*voluta e involuta*), spurted out and distilled, less than you'd get out of a dropper, from a poor and arid imagination.

Its architectonic lines are not impoverished into becoming short and contorted strokes, they are not reduced to sharp and formless stumps.

Strange, therefore: why did 'La Nave' take so long to find its way back to the stage, after its distant and successful first appearance? Given all the dwarfs and freaks that have been tumbling on the stage, and that tumble on it continually, making it seem that there is nothing else that can and will delight us? Given all the resits that have been granted, with up to two, three and four examination sessions, to all the scores that flopped in the last twenty years? Why did we have to be difficult with this opera in particular?

Undoubtedly there is a destiny, that less abstractly can be identified with our own conscious or unconscious wickedness (*cattiveria*) or lack of understanding, that bars the way to those who have the strength and the right to proceed, and this needs to be corrected. It is not the task of the critic, some may observe, to go into these kinds of facts, but given the dangers and the damage that derive from them, by who else should they be exposed?

It is true, we are not here to launch a loud outcry over this unappreciated and underestimated masterpiece. We believe we know what Montemezzi's 'La Nave' is, and we will say it: it is an opera in which the architecture surpasses the inspiration. The frame, in other words, is worth the picture, even if it shouldn't be said – as it shouldn't – that it nullifies it or, less forcefully, that it includes the picture within itself. Indeed, this architecture is not detrimental to inspiration: it doesn't stifle it, nor overwhelm it. And inspiration is not always absent, nor does it fail to fly, or fly so low, that it can be said, for this reason, that it has no virtue whatsoever.

Italo Montemezzi is a musician and an opera composer of congenital and acquired virtues, of instinct and of learning. He has already demonstrated this in more than one opera, indisputably, and hence 'La Nave' shows this too, even though it is not worth as much as 'L'Amore dei Tre Re,' where it was possible to see, and where can still be found, the best of him.

'La Nave' is an opera grasped and expressed with a great breadth of concept. One could not possibly have thought of writing it without feeling full of musical lymph. It was not composed, in fact, by an artist short of breath. It is what would once have been called an *operone*,[1] with grandiose dramatization, a dramatic weaving of tragic and epic surges and flashings: it is a score typical of the grand spectacle of the nineteenth century.

Created at the height of the flourishing of verismo opera, during the triumphal period of the most sentimental melodrama, 'La Nave,' entirely in the spirit of the romanticized chronicle, draws instead on the confluence of the two big streams of Verdian and Wagnerian romanticism. It feeds on their waters, it swells and rises with their foamy waves. There is some Verdi in 'La Nave,' for there is that which is full-blooded and muscular dramatic vehemence and that which is *illustrative* vastness against a dramatic background; and there is some Wagner in a certain mythical appearance and in some dramatic shading (*tratteggi*) and deepening. There is much more Wagner, certainly.

This, of course, is on the outside or, to put it better, in the opera's generic dramatic values and characteristics, not in its inner, specific, expressive substantiality, both dramatic (in a broad sense) and musical (strictly speaking). If there is a part of this opera, and there is, that is all its own, it can be found in

---

[1] I.e. a grand opera.

the chorus, indeed in the choral nature that pervades the whole, which is the best and the largest part of the total entity.

In 'La Nave,' Montemezzi didn't just see a conflict of individual passions. Basiliola and Marco Gratico are not the only driving forces of the action, and the action is neither focussed nor exhausted solely in them. Basiliola is not made simply a sister or a half-sister of Salomé. The lust and the domination of a perverted viperish femininity here form only one episode, they have the value of an episode.

The drama is in the fervour and the seething of primitive forces and instincts at the point of the highest and hardest conflict: in the inevitable tragedy which determines the destiny of a heroic race. Given this, was the music unequal to its task and was this inevitable? Does the tragedy exceed the possibilities of successful musical expression? Was the composer not allowed to claim priority and take the place of the Poet? Can D'Annunzio not be recreated or redone in music?

The libretto of 'La Nave' certainly sacrifices many among the most beautiful literary pages of our last great Poet, restricting and impoverishing some of their necessary dramatic development. We can agree on this. But if a melodrama doesn't manage to be one thing, music and drama at the same time, what sort of melodrama is it? Or, putting this better, if the music in an opera doesn't make one forget the libretto, doesn't absorb it and recreate on its own the characters and scenic atmosphere, what task does it accomplish? What is its raison d'etre?

Well, then, at this point it is possible to talk about 'La Nave' as music. It is there in armfuls. It is music of very clear speech, excellently arranged in broad structures, in closed forms or constructed symphonically (*squadrature sinfoniche*); also very well orchestrated; mainly melodic and adhering to the characters and to every detail of the scenic action. Therefore, it is varied and fast, fragmented when necessary, sometimes with soft, sometimes with strong, coloristic hues, with impressionistic strokes and outbursts (*tratti e scatti*) meant to emphasize the entrance of a character, to isolate and highlight, in a Verdian way, a 'scenic word,' to make a 'scene' out of a particular, essential dramatic situation.

This is theatrical material and art par excellence, in which Montemezzi's operatic skill exercises and asserts itself with a confident, strong instinct. However, what degree of expressive potentiality does it reach? And is it possible to speak of an unmistakable originality of its own if, precisely, originality itself is always the determining element and sign of a share of artistic potentiality?

We cannot but repeat that it is all sort of steeped in Vagner [sic] and the Vagner is not always absorbed and assimilated as, on the contrary, it is to a better and greater extent in 'L'Amore dei tre Re.'

The inspiration, consequently, is often not sustained within the scope of pure and fervid emotion. Simple dynamic fervour takes the place of keen spiritual elation. The expansive emphasis stands in for the natural warmth of abandoned passion. What is more lively, more sincere, more in order, emerging in a beautiful expressive coincidence between dramatic spirit and music is, we repeat, the choral passages. Didn't we hint at the prevalence of choral music in Montemezzi's 'La Nave'? And would we say D'Annunzio's has less of it? We who are, for want of a genius who acts as a true leader, both neoclassic, archaizing with Gregorian chant, and revolutionary modernists (!) with the mannered populism of folklore, say Montemezzi was very wrong for not having avoided the atmosphere of his time and having been under the influence of the musical God who dominated him. Yet how wrong shall we ourselves be judged in twenty or thirty years and how many of us then will be as alive as Montemezzi is today?

Let's talk about something else. It is likely that the composer of 'La Nave' worked at his score during the years of the Great

War, just before Caporetto and at the time of Caporetto.[1] What faith and what fervid love of his country animated him so that he could give the high musical tone to the lofty and superb line of verse, 'Arm the prow and sail toward the world,' so that he felt compelled to celebrate the turbid yet heroic commencement of some of our epic deeds with such magnificence of sounds as to serve as a prophetic song?

You will smile at this nationalistic digression. However, one can also smile at, and be suspicious of, that music which doesn't explain anything but itself, not being connected to any circumstance related to the passions of the person who composed it; and similarly be suspicious of those artists who, in this way, wouldn't represent anything but themselves.[2]

The performance was put together with a sumptuous wealth of means, such as an opera house like the Reale must and does have, and as were required by the grand score. Therefore, on stage, there was a magnificence of lights, costumes, furnishings and large crowds; the latter was the most impeccable and effective element.

For the principal roles, 'La Nave' requires the type of voices that, it is said, once used to flourish abundantly. The Reale opera house was able to avail itself of some of the best of those voices available today: Gina Cigna, who had some magnificent

---

[1] The important battle of Caporetto, fought on the Austro-Italian front between October and November 1917, was an overwhelming defeat for the Italian army, and came to represent the nadir of Italy's war effort.

[2] Toni appears to mean that modernist composers, with objective rather than subjective goals in composing, end up producing music that reveals their own small-mindedness and incapacity to be moved by the world around them. Ironically, then, their music is actually more purely representative of themselves than that of romantic composers who were open to external stimuli.

moments as well as lyrical and dramatic tones; Paolo Civil, vibrant and melodious, sparing no effort, as well as the baritones Basiola and Beuf.

The orchestral preparation and conducting by maestro Serafin was careful, accurate and fervid. The choruses, the magnificent crowds we talked about, were instructed by maestro Conca.[1] The direction was by Piccinato, the staging by Pende Ansaldo[2] who succeeded in another of his pieces of magic: a real launch. The scenery, some of which was suggestive and poetic, was painted after sketches by Oppo.

For the record, the audience was worthy of an imperial capital: all the exceptional public of Rome, worldly, political and diplomatic.

The success, expressed in numbers, is as follows: six curtain calls after the prologue, seven after the first act, six after the second and seven after the last.

---

1 Giuseppe Conca (1895–1983), who had become chorus master at the Teatro Reale in 1934.

2 In fact Pericle Ansaldo (1889–1969), the technical stage director at the Teatro Reale; he was the son of Giovanni Ansaldo, who had been in charge of the 1918 staging of *La Nave*.

Three Music Critics at the Rome Premiere of La Nave: (L to R) Pizzetti, Lualdi and Barilli

Cartoon from La Tribuna, 16 December 1938

2. Adriano Lualdi, *Il Giornale d'Italia*, 16 December 1938.

'La Nave' by D'Annunzio and Montemezzi at the Reale

OBSESSED AS he is with music, it's clear that one day Gabriele D'Annunzio, remembering the famous advice given by the oracle to Socrates, wondered 'what music he might have found' if Socrates himself had been his teacher.[1]

Two very different musical models, two different musical geniuses, shared for a long time his stormy and restless soul: that of old Italy, from Palestrina to the eighteenth century, and that of Richard Wagner's modern Germany. Then more loves came, but they didn't surpass, nor even equal, these first ones, until finally they all seemed to be summed up and sublimated in one name: Claudio Monteverdi.

Among all contemporary novels, the *Trionfo della Morte* is certainly the one that most directly emerged from *Tristan and Isolde*.[2] It is wholly impregnated with Wagnerian thought, and the final part contains an analysis of *Tristan* that has no equal elsewhere for intelligence, sensitivity, and accuracy. Even the famous and much too highly extolled musical 'intuitions' of Marcel Proust become

---

1 In Plato's *Phaedo* there is a report of Socrates saying, at the end of his life: 'The same dream came to me often in my past life ... always saying the same thing: "Socrates," it said, "make music and work at it." And I formerly thought it was urging and encouraging me to do what I was doing already ... that is, to make music, because philosophy was the greatest kind of music and I was working at that. But now, after the trial ... I thought, in case the repeated dream really meant to tell me to make this which is ordinarily called music, I ought to do so and not to disobey.' See *Plato* ed. and trans. Harold North Fowler *et al.*, 10 vols (London, William Heinemann, 1914–29), 1:211–13. Lualdi confuses this report with the much better known story in Plato's *Apology* in which the Oracle at Delphi stated that none were wiser than Socrates.

2 *Il Trionfo della Morte* (*The Triumph of Death*) was serialized in 1893, then published in book form the following year.

a very little thing in comparison. However, in another novel, *Il Fuoco*,[1] a different atmosphere makes the air red hot, the atmosphere of Venice; other masterworks exalt the soul of the Poet, those by Giorgione and Carpaccio; other voices move him, those of the bronzes of Saint Mark;[2] another musical genius towers above the former, foreign love: the very Italian genius of Claudio Monteverdi. Only the Latin Monteverdi can weaken, in the deep sensitivity of the Poet, his great admiration for the Germanic Wagner. It is the Poet who speaks through Stelio, when he notices that Monteverdi, through the simplest means, is able to draw on the highest degree of that pure beauty which the foreigner only rarely approached in his confused aspiration to the homeland of Sophocles.[3]

---

1 *Il Fuoco* (*The Fire*) was published in 1900.

2 The famous Horses of Saint Mark that date from classical times.

3 The narrative Lualdi sets out here is substantially correct, and it is given solid scholarly support by Andrew Dell'Antonio, '*Il divino Claudio*: Monteverdi and lyric nostalgia in fascist Italy,' *Cambridge Opera Journal* 8 (1996), 271–84. As Dell'Antonio documents, D'Annunzio was a key figure in 'rediscovering' Monteverdi as the father of opera and the greatest exponent of the form, a nationalist myth that was widely taken up in Fascist musical history. Behind it lay the fear that modern Italian opera was degenerate and that the 'lyric spirit' had passed to Wagner's Germany. Part of the myth was that Monteverdi and the composers of the Florentine Camerata were much closer to the principles of ancient Greek dramaturgy than Wagner. Lualdi quotes D'Annunzio virtually word for word here:

> 'Here ... is an artist of our own race [Monteverdi],' said Stelio Effrena, 'who, by the simplest means, has succeeded in touching the highest degree of that beauty which the German [Wagner] rarely approached in his confused aspirations towards the fatherland of Sophocles.'

(See *The Flame of Life*, trans. Kassandra Vivaria [London: William Heinemann, 1900], 116.) Reflecting further on the difference between Monteverdi and Wagner, Stelio feels 'A kind of instinctive rancour, of obscure hostility which was not of the intellect ... against the tenacious German who had succeeded in inflaming the world' (ibid. 120).

Among all modern tragedies, three or four by D'Annunzio are the richest in musical spirits (*spiriti musicali*); in allusions to, and architecture and pretexts for, music; and *La Nave* can be placed at the head of them. *La Nave*, like *Il Fuoco*, has Venice as its background, a city of which D'Annunzio so deeply felt and understood the musicality and preeminent individual character: that of a melodious city (*città melodiosa*) among all its sister cities.

The time of Marco and Sergio Gratico, and Basiliola, is remote; the island in the estuary, where it is pretended that the tragedy takes place, is nothing more than an embryo of Venice; in more than one episode the language and gestures of the characters are harsh and blunt. However, in the ideal, sublime climate of the play, everything is composed of poetry: the heat of passions, the civil struggles and conflicts, the hatred between the Faledri and the Gratici, and the clash of opposed political conceptions: Byzantium sovereignty or the foundation – amid the mud and lagoons – of a maritime Roman and Venetian power (the first narrators of the chronicles of St. Mark boasted of being 'real Romans') which would launch itself on the conquest of the sea and of the East. Everything is wrapped in the mists of mystery and of a legendary remoteness; but everything, in D'Annunzio's solemn and sublime poetry, is also wrapped in a halo of music, of an implied music.

The music that D'Annunzio might have found, had he been a disciple of Socrates, would certainly not have been more eloquent than the music that he – a disciple of his own genius only, and that of his race – was able to compose in some of his tragedies. They are so musical, in their architecture and in their words, that they can be hardly set to music; so fully do they express the inner movements of the characters that hardly any space is left for that unique way of expressing the ineffable that is music. Yet, on the other hand, they are very worthy of being clad with the only garment worthy of them: music.

Certainly the figure of Basiliola, and her function in the economy of the play, slightly distracts the attention and the thoughts of the audience from the real protagonist of the tragedy, albeit one not always visible: the ship *Totus Mundus*. She diminishes, displaces and sometimes overshadows what was undoubtedly the Poet's initial inspiration: the celebration of the birth of Venice.

Basiliola is humanity, or rather base humanity, in the way she manifests herself: neither good, nor bad; not consistent in her hatred (she hates both brothers, Sergio and Marco, yet she is the concubine of both; and why then, in the duel, does she side with the bishop?); and no more magnanimous in her acts and passions than Marco and Sergio themselves. Of the latter, one is a pagan bishop; the other a tribune who is gratuitously unfaithful to his followers – since it's not amorous passion that makes him entirely dominated by the Faledra[1] – whom he throws in the Fuia pit, together with his enemies in the opposing party. Neither Marco nor Sergio are heroes: therefore, here too there is humanity of a common level, which in many episodes of the tragedy hides the miracle announced in the Adriatic sky almost like a veil, and stands in contrast to the fated greatness of the event being fulfilled: the birth of Venice.

But here too, perhaps, it is the profound wisdom, the sovereign perspicacity of the Poet, that speaks. The grandest affairs and destinies of man.

It is a very arduous task, even for a well-trained (*agguerrito*) artist of superior stature such as Italo Montemezzi, to set to music a poem by D'Annunzio; and in this case, where we are dealing with *La Nave*, it is even more arduous.

---

[1] Lualdi's point seems to be that Marco Gratico is not a strong and virtuous man weakened by love, but rather an intrinsically weak and treacherous man who would be dominated by a stronger personality with or without 'amorous passion.'

Carlo Piccinato, 1938
Director of the Rome Production of *La Nave*

On one hand, considering D'Annunzio's poetry in general terms, there is its great musicality, its 'saying everything,' the extreme richness of the images, the rapidity of transitions, the preciousness of the accents. As I mentioned earlier, music, whoever composes it, has nothing to add to this poetry; moreover, it can only be hard to sing if it wants faithfully to follow the swiftness and diversity of the poetry's flights. On the other hand, considering the distinctive characteristics of the tragedy of *La Nave*, we have to say that all those successive scenes with episodes of collective movement, which can be seen especially in the Prologue as well as in a great part of the second and third acts, though certainly very good theatre, are nevertheless as little suited to musical setting as one can imagine, because of the way they are directed and the frequent dialogue between individuals that interrupts the choral dialogue. To this, which is no trifling difficulty, add the fact that amid the vastness and pomp of the scenic event there is an absence of a strong, genuine passion within the action; a passion which, whether suffered by a man or woman or body of people, could offer the composer, with its flame, its power and its weight, enough of the energies (*calorie*) he needs to ensure that the tragedy becomes lyrical in the true sense of the word, and the word becomes song.

Italo Montemezzi tackled and solved such a difficult problem with admirable confidence and skill. He saw D'Annunzio's tragedy as akin to a series of large frescoes; and he took great pains – at least it appears so when considering his work – to render through music the atmosphere of the pictures and the episodes, the great moments of the body of people, as well as the epic accent of many pages of the poem. Being the sensitive artist he is, Montemezzi perfectly understood that only by using the bold manner of the great decorative painters would he be able to accomplish a work not unworthy of the task. In fact, he was able to keep the music of the whole opera at a consistently high level of nobility and austerity, and with uncommon breadth of thought and vigour of tones, especially in the choral parts, which are unquestionably effective. Indeed, in my opinion the choral parts and symphonic writing are the excellent qualities of Montemezzi's *La Nave*.

The chorus has a role of great importance and serious responsibility in this opera. It participates, it can be said, in all the most important episodes, contributing to them both musically and scenically in a far from inconsequential way. It is treated with mastery; especially in moments of agitation, when it is split into several voices, it constitutes an element with very considerable dramatic power and vigour. One among the many choral pages deserves to be highlighted for its breadth of thought and expression: the one preceding the launch of *Totus Mundus*, although it is a little spoilt by its too obvious derivation from a celebrated passage in *Die Meistersinger*. As to the symphonic life (*vita sinfonica*) of the opera, this is rich also, always active, and always appropriate to the various scenic episodes. Montemezzi's large ensemble musical scenes respond perfectly, in the culminating moments, to the large scenes conceived by D'Annunzio. The solo parts, those of Basiliola, of Sergio, of Marco, of Orso Faledro and Traba, are treated with religious respect to the poetic text and a taste nearly always flawless, except for some vocal and instrumental phrasing which is slightly too much in the style of the 'verist melodrama' (given the prevailing atmosphere, which is far from it), and except for a short motif (*disegno*) repeated by the small brass (*piccoli ottoni*) that, with its banality, really spoils the finale of the second act.

In short, this is a work of a vigorous and generous composer; it is indeed worthy – this opera which has been buried in the archives for exactly twenty years – of being at least as fortunate as the many others, far less deserving than this one, that nevertheless managed to achieve much greater success for various reasons, but not artistic ones.

Originality of spirit and attitude, of concept and of form, cannot be found in *La Nave*. It doesn't yet *feel* the Italian musical Renovation that in 1917 and 1918 had already been taking place for some years.[1] But of a particular trend (the one that looked to the North) of the late 1800s, of the most informed and cultivated trend that summarizes and stylizes with great skill and taste, it must be said that this *Nave* offers all the best and all that (in the matter of procedures, architecture, modes of expression that, here too, generically speaking, reflect the composer's predilection for Wagner, although attenuated in comparison to *L'Amore dei tre re*) deserves to be saved of the old inheritance, doing timely justice to all the baggage of the past (*bagaglio del passato*) that really belongs to the past.

The performance and interpretation of *La Nave* were superb for dignity and loftiness. If the management of the Teatro Reale is to be highly praised for choosing this most noble and worthy opera for the inauguration of the season for the year XVII,[2] it is Tullio Serafin who should be recognized as taking the greatest credit for a presentation in which the splendid and already solid traditions of the Teatro Reale are not only confirmed but even surpassed. The whole spectacle, from the fundamental musical part – to which the orchestra, chorus and individual artists all admirably contributed – to the spectacular scenery, created by the great talent of C. E. Oppo, the costumes, the direction by Carlo Piccinato, and the

---

1 This is a complex and not wholly fair accusation. In the 1910s a group of younger Italian composers loosely led by Alfredo Casella (1883–1947) and Gian Francesco Malipiero (1882–1973), and to some extent Pizzetti, revolted against the long domination of Italian musical life by popular opera and sought to revive the native tradition of instrumental composition (though this did not necessarily stop them writing operas, especially in Pizzetti's case). This movement was, in part, concerned with reviving and taking inspiration from the Italian music of the past, but it was also strongly influenced by modernist music in other countries, especially France. Lualdi associated himself with this movement in its more conservative aspects. Montemezzi did not differ from the younger composers by seeking inspiration abroad, but by still seeking it primarily in Germany, and specifically German opera.

2 I.e. year 17 of the Fascist era, 1938.

lights, all had a stamp of extraordinary perfection, absolute confidence and flawless harmony. Tullio Serafin was clearly moved by his work, and under his inspired, fervid and enthusiastic direction everybody gave the most one could wish for, producing a first-rate artistic performance.

I have little space remaining to say something about the individual artists, but it's enough to acknowledge that they all proved themselves equal to the tasks entrusted to them. Gina Cigna, with a splendid voice, a very confident stage presence and penetrating accents, was an excellent Basiliola. The tenor Civil, for his part, conveyed the impression of being undoubtedly on an ascending artistic path; should he manage to control some high notes better, he will be a singer and actor of the highest quality. Basiola, too, showed himself totally satisfactory, with his rich vocal resources, his diction and his stage presence. Romito, in his short part, was able to draw attention to himself and win very favourable appreciation; the same can be said of Beuf, very good in all respects, as well as the always excellent Zagonara, and everybody else.

The chorus, in its difficult part, was magnificent in its confidence, its accents and its sonority, and the greatest praise for this should go to the chorus master, Giovanni Conca.

I mentioned the scenery and the direction; for the final scene, the launch of the ship *Totus Mundus*, which was very successful, with a striking grandiosity, much of the merit goes to Ansaldo, a seaman.[1]

La Nave received a very warm welcome. Each act provoked keen manifestations of approval and applause, expressed with seven curtain calls at every drop of the curtain for Maestro Montemezzi, Maestro Serafin, as well as all the artists, and Piccinato and Ansaldo.

---

1 For Pericle Ansaldo, see above, p. 231, n. 2.

Gina Cigna, 1937
The Fourth Basiliola

3. Augusto Righetti, *Il Tevere*, 15–16 December 1938.

The success of 'La Nave' by Montemezzi and D'Annunzio at the Reale dell'Opera

LET'S FIX two dates: 3 November 1918, the first performance of *La Nave* at La Scala, Milan; 14 December 1938, the revival in Rome of the same opera by Montemezzi. Twenty years is far too long to cover the distance between Rome and Milan; or rather it *would be* too long if the opera's getting stranded in the shallows of public indifference didn't justify the huge delay. Perhaps this delay would have turned into definitive oblivion if celebratory circumstances had not suggested an attempt at re-launching Montemezzi's vessel at the Teatro Reale. Well, having attended two consecutive rehearsals and the first performance of the opera, in which no details pertaining to its artistic dignity have been neglected, we can affirm that the audience's disinterest and coldness are mostly based on an instinctive judgement from which the technical and considered assessment by the critics cannot depart much.

It is a serious, a very serious, trial to place notes under the lines of one of D'Annunzio's poems, already so sonorous and musically complete. We had already felt this danger, one best expressed in the words 'to carry out a uselessly redundant (*pleonastica*) task,' on the occasion of such melodramas as *Cirano* [sic] *di Bergerac*, *Cena delle beffe* and similar ones,[1] in which the composer risks ending up like the proverbial earthenware pots

---

[1] *Cyrano de Bergerac*, Franco Alfano's opera based on Edmond Rostand's play, had been premiered at the Teatro Reale on 22 January 1936; *La cena delle beffe*, Umberto Giordano's 1924 opera based on Sem Benelli's play, had been revived at the Teatro Reale in 1934.

in contact with iron pots[1] unless he has the fibre of a lion and the flight of an eagle.

First of all, the indispensable work of lightening the original, weighty poem, achieved through the suppression of a few thousand lines of verses, caused a remarkable impoverishment both of the logical concatenation of facts and the personality of the characters – an impoverishment that Montemezzi's music did not manage to make us forget. Then, going into the details, we wonder: what specific enhancement were the notes, the keys and the musical signs capable of, in short, in comparison with the poetic charm of such lines of verse as the most celebrated 'Arm the prow and sail toward the world' or 'Make of all the oceans our own sea'? These examples could be multiplied ten or a hundred times and the critical study could end here.

Maestro Montemezzi chose the form of *declamato* for the voices and a definitely Wagnerian symphonic orchestral background to create a musical environment matching the feelings that drive and move the persons of the story. We are not criticising the system chosen; it is just that the results achieved through the various moments of the score don't seem to us the happiest. We believe that Montemezzi's music, which never rises to a true individuality of artistic style, most of the time ends up taking a background role in a too generic and almost interchangeable manner which only superficially adheres to the *animus* of the protagonists and the *climax* of the places and the action. Almost all the time, the music of *La Nave* could be, roughly, adapted to any other event having a dramatic style, whatever the time and

---

1 A reference, ultimately, to Aesop's fable of 'The Two Pots.' When an earthenware pot and iron pot are being swept along a river, the iron pot wants them to travel together, while the earthenware pot wants to keep its distance, recognizing that if they are knocked together it will be the victim.

the place where it was set, apart from the peculiar passions that stir *Basiliola*, the two *Gratico* brothers, the Faledro *Orso* and the *Traba* monk. See, for example, the few pages of the score which are supposed to prepare, with the curtain lowered, the tragic scene of the Fuia pit: it is a succession of routine notes that neither in melodic content, nor in rhythmic incisiveness, nor in evocative strength of harmony or timbre manage to effectively prelude what is brewing on stage. There is no disguising the fact that the terribly sadistic episode of *Basiliola* running her lovers through with arrows presented almost insurmountable difficulties for the composer. On the other hand, though, we must point out that the whole of the second act, that of the profane Agape, thanks to the recurrence of the danced episodes, as well as the clash of both the two brothers and the two factions, and the variety of feelings expressed by both sides, could have offered the composer a wonderful opportunity for a musical commentary of extraordinary pictorial and empowering strength. On the contrary, this scene especially, despite the technical ability shown in the construction, the even excessive and sometimes superstructural intervention of the timbric element, as well as the variety and accentuation of the rhythmic life, cannot be considered one of the happiest ones in the opera.

Let's get this straight: the overall effect is achieved, but it is achieved thanks to a complex of factors among which music is certainly not what predominates.

Having thus briefly reviewed that part of the score we shall call negative, and for which the judgement cannot be such as to give *La Nave* the chance of a definitive, profitable permanence within the current opera repertoire, let's see, as cursorily as the usual space constraints impose, what the elements are that attract our consideration and even our admiration. And this because we must not forget that we are talking about a composer of the power, the probity and the nobility of Italo Montemezzi, composer, among other works, of that *Amore dei tre Re* which so victoriously established him among the great composers of our generation.

Basiliola, though a musically manqué character with regard to the complexity of her feelings, inspired in Montemezzi two moments of lyrical abandon that need to be remembered as among the best things of the score: the invocation to her brother *Marino* in the prologue and, even finer, the love duet in the first act which is really a superb thing thanks to the happy concurrence of the melodic invention with the harmonic and timbric elements that frame it effectively. This page is a huge honour to Montemezzi and it doesn't cut a poor figure in comparison with the best ones in *L'Amore dei tre Re*.

Then we shall mention the grand scene of the procession, still in the prologue, constructed with a wealth of means, and the following scene that takes place in front of the church, equally effective thanks also to the contribution of some skilfully introduced rests which are beneficial to the dramatic power of the action and interrupt, at the right moment, the overall turgid sonority of the act.

Likewise, we should notice the power of almost all the choral interventions and, generally speaking, the dignified nobility of the whole score, the composer's intelligent command of his expressive means, his talents as a masterly builder, his dosing of the outward effects, always meant to achieve a conclusive *crescendo* that, theatrically, attains remarkable results, as also noticed in the finale of the opera, organically conceived and concluded over a very well-made, magniloquent sonority.

The realization of *La Nave* on the stage of our Teatro Reale was such as to justify the word 'event.' The animating and harmonizing centre for every detail, even those not strictly musical, was maestro Tullio Serafin, who, having conducted the opera twenty years ago at La Scala, seemed the most entitled among the eminent conductors to preside authoritatively over today's performance. The fervid and passionate work of Serafin, regulated by a happy marriage between profound technical knowledge and the sensibility of a true artist's soul, achieved such effective results that, within the limits of the music conceived by Montemezzi, it is hardly possible to imagine anything more complete and definitive. The orchestra, well trained and valiant, obeyed in an excellent way the authoritative baton, and, similarly, the choral forces, entrusted with a big and difficult task, were an honour to their instructor, maestro Conca.[1] The exhausting and tricky part of *Basiliola* was entrusted to Gina Cigna, who, having recently recovered from a serious indisposition, was able to give the character a fair share of her magnificent voice and eminent artistry. The Spanish tenor Paolo Civil was admired with good reason for the dignity of his scenic play (*giuoco scenico*) and even more for his clear and proper accentuation and his power in sustaining the high register where the part of Marco Gratico mostly likes to linger. The baritone Mario Basiola (*Sergio Gratico*) was a very effective actor and singer; at his side, Filippo Romito and Augusto Beuf cut fine figures. As usual, Adelio Zagonara, Mazziotti, Gobbi, Taddei and the many others did well with minor parts that were sung in tune and harmonically blended.

The direction by Carlo Piccinato proved very happy in the ensemble scenes, rich in particularly well-chosen moments and details. The scenery made by Ettore Polidori after sketches by C. E. Oppo aroused general approval thanks to the harmonious propriety of lines and colours as well as the due respect shown for D'Annunzio's stage directions. Lights, costumes, staging and choreography were up to the event: in particular, the scene of the *Agape* aroused unanimous admiration, as well as, in the

---

[1] See above, p. 231, n. 1

finale, the launch of the ship *Tuttoilmondo* [sic] which confirmed the technical excellence achieved by Ansaldo[1] and his closest collaborators. The only fault we will remark is the constant immobility of the sails occupying almost the whole backcloth in the prologue. Yet would this have been easy to remedy?

For the record, there were about 25 curtain calls, in many of which the composer took part and was given a hearty welcome. However, to determine the true success, the large number of curtain calls is not enough (we know the easy mechanism); it is necessary to take into account the tone and the provenance of the applause which inspires those calls. Last night's applause, rather tired and distracted, seemed to us motivated more by an act of deference to the composer than by enthusiasm for the work of art. Some may say this always happens with subscription *premières*. Let's wait for the people's performance then or, better, the *people's performances* that we'd like to see numerous and all received with great success.[2] It doesn't matter if our judgement has to suffer one more setback; what matters is the success of works of art. These remain, the critic's judgement will fade.

---

1 See above, p. 231, n. 2

2 Righetti makes a distinction between a premiere, with many regular subscribers to the opera house present, and subsequent performances dependent more on ticket sales to a less exclusive class of non-subscribers.

4. Matteo Incagliati, *Il Messaggero*, 15 December 1938.

At the Teatro Reale dell'Opera 'LA NAVE' by Montemezzi and D'Annunzio earned the most brilliant success

Is *La Nave* by Italo Montemezzi, who twenty years ago became infatuated with the dark, picturesque tragedy by Gabriele D'Annunzio, and clad it with music, a new, pure, fresh source of life for the Italian stage? Even though there were some faults and errors, mainly a result of the spirit and format of the event, it deserved the favourable welcome that the magnificent audience, gathered at the call of this exceptional theatrical occurrence, bestowed upon it last night. The reception of the opera a few hours ago was a just, serene acknowledgment in favour of a cultured and passionate composer, and one who is genuinely theatrical, as we ought to recognize that Montemezzi is.

The new opera did not move the audience deeply, nor did it arouse fits of irresistible enthusiasm. Instead, it produced an impression of admiration with a bit of help from the eye and the mental faculties. The heart, for that matter, is absent from the innermost core of the D'Annunzian tragedy, bare as it is and not pervaded with any sense of humanity. Its characters become restless and come into conflict with each other within the atmosphere of an unreal world. The passions that develop in it are remote from the ardour of real life and human speculation. Basiliola herself, even though she is the best drawn character, shows – obscurely here but clearly there – some affinities, some analogies with Strauss's *Salome*. This is a sin of origin of which Montemezzi's opera carries the weight, though he overcame it as much as he could, with the help of his ingenuity and his own theatrical spirit.

When confronted with D'Annunzio's tragedy, was the composer in the happy frame of mind necessary to attempt, musically, that process of synthesis through which he could have renounced everything that is literary, historical, archaeological, the fruit of an aestheticism by its very nature so subjective? In the adaptation made by Tito Ricordi all this background remained there almost unchanged to encumber, to stop the flight of the composer's imagination, forcing him to linger over and clothe with notes the descriptive, illustrative, pleonastic details.

What is certain is that Montemezzi, trusting to a tragedy which has its life outside this world, proceeded through impulses of intuition, especially in those places where his spirit urged him to beat the path of sentiment, such as in the finale of the first episode. And it is here that his melody flows clear, fantastic and flexuous, directed to seize and favour the voice of what 'speaks inside' and in doing so indicating the true intervention of fresh, genuine inspiration. Thus the expressiveness of the verses intertwines with the inner impulse that is moved and expanded.

The orchestral atmosphere, which was supposed to reflect the architecture of the work of art, projects itself in two different aspects: in the prologue and in the first episode a hue for the most part, as it were, slightly grey, hangs over the action, produced by Montemezzi's insistence on basing his instrumentation on the quartet, of which the orchestra seems a prisoner; in the two following episodes, the metre changes. The action is now all animated with flashes and flickering illuminating the stage. The chorus, which has the function of a real character, shouts, bursts into invectives, cries like lunatics; it riots, predominates and fills the scene with its presence. The last episode broadens the sphere of the new conception, through which the composer gathers within himself so much power and courage as to stamp the impressive scene of the launch of the shining ship with the mark of powerful musical energy. Consequently, the rhythmic interest does not languish for a moment, and a dynamic, although fast and overpowering, comments with an irresistible and uncontainable vigour of sound on the intervention of Basiliola, 'tied up with ropes, like a lioness caught in the snare.'

Compared to these pages of accomplished beauty of sound, in the previous episodes we lament that we have to notice a prevailing theme (*tematica*) lacking in incisiveness, inventiveness and warm musical effusion. Yet, to say the truth, here and there some melodic proceedings denote and acquire such a plastic importance as to give value and ardour to certain specific moods, even if some Wagnerian proceedings intervene to obscure them fleetingly, almost as though to indicate the inclination of Montemezzi to idolize the music of the Leipzig genius. But, on the other hand, the music is often enlivened by that genuine singing quality (*cantabilità*) that in *L'Amore dei tre re* reached such a remarkable and effective prominence.

The opera attests, unquestionably, to the talent and imagination of a vigorously theatrical temperament. Therefore, Montemezzi can be satisfied with the favourable welcome bestowed upon *La Nave*, which we can reasonably regard as a mostly choral opera. And as a *choral* opera, it is a proof of the strong fibre of the composer, of the character of a fervent and well-trained (*agguerrito*) musician. An opera of this type and this aspect, when it appeared for the first time on stage at La Scala twenty years ago, made a profound impression. Now, after the numerous performances of *Boris Godunov*, the element of surprise is greatly lessened.[1] Yet *La Nave* still remains a title showing a lofty and noble dream of the imagination, realized through the vigour of the composer's talent and with his inspiration participating in its full emotion.

---

1 The Italian premiere of *Boris Godunov* took place at La Scala in 1909 (under Toscanini), but Mussorgsky's 'choral opera' was still little known in Italy in 1918.

But what and how many sonic emotions, meaning musical ones, were attributable to the interpretation of Maestro Tullio Serafin, who is due the credit of having baptized all the operas of Montemezzi,[1] as well as the *Cantata* composed to celebrate Ponchielli![2] Serafin did everything he could in his conducting, employing all the heat, the mastery and the ingenuousness of his intellect and energies. He transfused into the orchestra, with youthful ardour, all the vehement élan that characterizes the score, with the help of the magnificent and eloquent choruses, and brought out all the signs of the noble and austere musical conception, especially in those places where a wave of lyricism emerges, as in the first episode. He firmly grasped the spectacle, in which predominate no inconsiderable difficulties, many and varied, of which he managed to overcome the great tangle.

Gina Cigna, fully restored to health, delineated the character of Basiliola with traits of wickedness and voluptuousness, and her singing expressed the beauty of tones with good timbre and prodigious blaring (*squilli*). Her voice, showing that she was moved by the role, spread generously through the exultance, the joy of the privileged organ that she possesses. The tenor Paolo Civil was a welcome acquaintance of our audience. His voice is full of warm effusiveness in the middle register and blaring (*squillante*) sonority in the high notes. He sang the duet in the first episode with suggestive modulations and the last part of the tragedy with such a heat and impetus as to be appreciated and applauded.

---

[1] This is not completely true: the premieres of *Giovanni Gallurere*, *Héllera*, *L'Amore dei Tre Re* and *La Nave* had all been conducted by Serafin, but not that of *La Notte di Zoraima* (1931), conducted by Montemezzi himself. Serafin had, though, conducted the American production of *La Notte di Zoraima* later in 1931.

[2] Montemezzi was commissioned by the Cremona City Council to compose a *Cantata* for choir and orchestra in commemoration of the 25th anniversary of Annibale Ponchielli's death. This was performed in Cremona, under Serafin's baton, on 23 May 1911.

Also received favourably were the baritone Mario Basiola, with broad and resonant singing and a warmth that animates his whole person; the bass Augusto Beuf, who emphasized his role with a nice and mellow voice; and the bass Filippo Romito, who sang with art and a vigorous tone. Everyone excelled.

Zagonara, Mazziotti, Masini Sparti, Bartolazzi, Tito Gobbi, Taddei, Bianchi, Conti, Marucci, Daddi and Giusti contributed to the success.

The chorus, that has an imposing role in the opera, sang under the direction of Maestro Giuseppe Conca[1] with a precision, a diligence and a fervour that were admirable indeed. Last night the chorus was one of the elements that contributed, together with the soloists, to the success of *La Nave*.

The staging by Carlo Piccinato was informed with such a discipline in the movement of the masses of people, even though very arduous, and to such a freedom of changes of position as to convey the illusion of an animated crowd. Pericle Ansaldo[2] surpassed himself with the launch of the ship, creating such a scenic veracity as to make it seem we were watching the marriage of the large vessel with the sea in La Spezia.[3] It was a prodigy of technique. The same can be said of the lighting, arranged by Ettore Salani, who dominated it with his spirit, which manages to turn a technical effect into an artistic one; the lighting spectacle was sometimes of a rare splendour. Maestro Luigi Ricci,[4] with all his substitute maestros, encouraged discipline in the singing and the various aspects of the stage with all his steely and vivid intelligence.

---

1 See above, p. 231, n. 1.

2 See above, p. 231, n. 2.

3 Incagliati offers a remarkably 'updated' interpretation of the significance of the spectacle: La Spezia was the main base of the modern Italian navy.

4 Luigi Ricci (1893–1981) was the stage musical director (*direttore musicale del palcoscenico*).

The stage designs by Oppo received unanimous admiration, both for their marked pictorial sense, the artistry with which they were drawn, and their broad perspective. The scene of the first episode was suggestive, all framed with centuries-old pine trees, and that of the launch was imposing. The scenery was realized with taste and art by Polidori.[1]

The success was marked by six curtain calls after the Prologue, seven after the first episode, six after the second, and six or seven at the end of the opera; the composer joined Serafin and the vocal interpreters on the stage, and was met with warm manifestations of unanimous approval.

---

[1] Ettore Polidori, the scenographer.

5. Bruno Barilli, *Omnibus*, 24 December 1938.

La Nave

LAST NIGHT, apropos this opera, we heard Wagner and Strauss mentioned, as if *La Nave* was nothing but a pile of stuff acquired illegally and placed in liquidation.

True, in many cases of new operas the circumstances are like this, but this time the situation strikes us as different, and we are not at all inclined to confiscate Montemezzi's music. We listened with the greatest attention to this opera composed thirty years ago,[1] wherein it seems to us that we have to do with the authorized and convinced assimilation that already means power.

Many maestros who are very popular did as much, sometimes, even, with more eclecticism and a more marked indiscretion.

Montemezzi is a composer and a man of the theatre – is that nothing? His music filled our lungs, and we won't be unappreciative. The qualities typical of those who dominate theatrical horizons belong to him. His instrumentation ripples (*ondeggia*) calmly and regularly within a basin (*bacino*) that is broad, capacious and deep; the furious foam of the string instruments[2] agitates its surface; in this *Nave* there is some Wagnerian titanism, yes, but it is inherent in the nature of our composer. And his order is full of space.

His harmony unfolds in a chain, broad and magnificent, around the drama. Everything is musical in this organism, from

---

1 Barilli is obviously exaggerating, or in error.
2 Literally it is the furious foam of the *archi*, or bows, used by the musicians.

beginning to end. Montemezzi knows how to turn off (*spegnere*) the instrumental clamours and raise to the light the singing human voice; he knows how to make a tangle of dissonances, and he knows how to undo it without confusion in timely respites in the sound. He builds and expands (*dilaga*) in the orchestra and on the choral scene, an arbitrator with a long arm. Montemezzi writes what he feels: and he feels on a large scale, with justice and truth.

His thematic material is slightly generic, yet industriously connected. The outline of his motives appears when necessary. In his opera there is hardly anything disjoined, his fervour has fused every element together. This is the sure sign of a personality who combines practice with intelligence.

Sometimes his music has a symmetry that is a little tired, a little mechanized; but these are shadows that serve the light.

Some dull passages pass by without hurting the general architecture: very soon the orchestral accompaniment flows back abundantly around the voices, which are its core.

Montemezzi creates love scenes excellently: a good sign. The tone then plays, in a slightly overdone (*sfatta*) atmosphere, its bewitching ace: the prostration of voluptuousness, the tiredness of the body, the moment when mouths can be no longer separated, astonished and sudden awakenings, when eyes cannot see straight, and nature and things have the appearance of a mutant theatre (*un teatro mutante*), when our imagination, crawling over the silk of night skies, becomes red hot and throws out sparks.

The entire finales of the first and second acts could not have been written by anyone lacking talent. And throughout the rest of the opera the music stands on its feet, thanks to the great skill of the Veronese composer.

At present we don't have time to enter into a calmer examination of the performance of this *Nave*, which had, in every respect, faithful and intelligent interpreters.

The pillar of this successful production was undoubtedly Maestro Tullio Serafin, who always throws himself with passion, body and soul, into his theatre; he is always equal to the demands of first-rate works. He found in *La Nave* his own perfect place, and was superior to any possible praise.

It can be said that Serafin, last night, struck his best blow for Montemezzi: may God reward him. In this undisputed success he had valiant companions: Gina Cigna, the magnificent tenor Civil, the bass Beuf, with his acrid and powerful tone, the baritone Basiola, and all the others who were at least worth the trouble of remembrance.

The chorus did well too, and the scenery and costumes by Oppo were worthy of the great spectacle. The orchestra worked wonders, and the conclusion of the night was very happy; the imposing opera house, packed out by a large audience, wanted solemnly to confer upon Italo Montemezzi and his interpreters a firm, full and solid (*quadrato*) success of Roman acclamation.

Ildebrando Pizzetti, c.1940
Montemezzi's harshest critic

6. Ildebrando Pizzetti, *La Tribuna*, 16 December 1938.

La Nave by Montemezzi at the Reale

NOW THAT Signora Gina Cigna has recovered from the serious illness she suddenly contracted a week ago, following which the Teatro Reale had to change its opening performance of the season, it was finally possible for *La Nave* by maestro Montemezzi to be performed last night. It is an opera composed, as is well known, on a libretto drawn by Tito Ricordi from the tragedy of Gabriele D'Annunzio, and it was first performed twenty years ago, on the glorious and memorable night when the first announcement rang out over Italy of the great victory won by the Italian army, crowning the greatest war in which it had fought.

And once again, as twenty years ago, the performance of the opera last night, clearly studied and rehearsed with the utmost care, was conducted by Tullio Serafin. It was conducted wonderfully, with the very fervent affection of a friend[1] and the profound abnegation of an artist, so as to make every rhythmic and melodic pattern of the score stand out with incisive vigour, and skilfully controlling the work's sonorities, from the most complex and intense to the softest and most delicate. Just as the orchestra played in a way worthy of the conductor, so the chorus, perfectly instructed by maestro Giuseppe Conca, as well as all the performing artists on stage, with no exceptions, marvellously matched and obeyed, respectively, his fervour as an interpreter and his authority as a commander. Two of them demand special mention, first of all for the great importance and difficulty of their parts: the tenor Paolo Civil, a really magnificent Marco Gratico, for the manly beauty of his voice, for the incisiveness of his dramatic tone, for his intelligent and very effective acting, and for the fine appearance of his person; and Signora Cigna,

---

1 Serafin was a close friend of Montemezzi: see above, p. 55.

who used all her best qualities as a singer and her experience as an artist to render the character of Basiliola. The other characters are less important. Yet Filippo Romito gave the character of Orso Faledro a wonderful stage presence, and all possible musical emphasis. Mario Basiola, too, was a great Sergio Gratico, and the bass Augusto Beuf was excellent as Traba.

[Pizzetti lists and praises the singers of the minor parts.]

The scenic movement was very well regulated by Piccinato, in accordance with the spirit of the opera. And the stage apparatus was very rich and spectacular: the imaginative scenery (the pinewood had a beautiful effect) and the costumes, designed and made after sketches and fashion-plates by Cipriano E. Oppo, as well as the lights, the tools, the smoke from the incense and fragrances, and finally the great ship, which went into the sea with such verisimilitude that it drew a big applause from the audience for Pericle Ansaldo[1] and his collaborators and machinists.

It is known how troublesome D'Annunzio found it to return to works which had already been finished. Therefore, as we cannot know how much his tolerance would have excused the cuts and deformations that the original tragedy underwent, becoming a libretto according to the mediocre theatrical sense of Tito Ricordi, we won't talk of it.

However, to us, one of those deformations is especially difficult to accept, even if it was hypothetically accepted by the Poet: it is the one concerning Basiliola's death.[2] In the original tragedy it is a resplendent death, willed and heroic, while in the libretto it is only atrocious and degrading. In the original tragedy, in

---

1 For Ansaldo, see above, p. 231, n. 2.

2 It is noteworthy that Pizzetti was the only critic to complain about this change. For more on Tito Ricordi's 'deformation' here, see below, pp. 321–22.

fact, Basiliola, as everybody knows, rather than letting herself be killed by the enemies she was unable to defeat, and against whom she has vainly employed all the powers of her soul and arts of her beauty, throws herself on the altar of the sea warriors (*Naumachi*), where the fire is blazing to bring the executioner's sword to red-heat, and in the fire she plunges her head: thus Basiliola gives herself the 'beautiful death' (*'bella morte'*):

> ... *If I couldn't mint my face*
> *in the gold of Rome, well, watch,*
> *I imprint it in the fire.*[1]

This is such a heroic act that Marco Gratico himself orders the shield bearers (*clipeati*) to honour the heroine for him, by forming around her, with large shields raised, the square *testudo*.

In the libretto, there is nothing of all this. Basiliola is treated like a base slave and nailed to the bow of the ship ready for its launch.

Some will say that she, a lustful woman and sacrilegious sinner, thus gets the punishment she deserves. But the character imagined and created by D'Annunzio merited something better. (Last night Basiliola was indeed bound to the ship, but nobody wanted to take the trouble of nailing her to it.)

Though the work of a composer stocked with the fruits of a good education and remarkably skilled in the technique of orchestration, and who possesses a certain theatrical sense of his own, *La Nave* by maestro Montemezzi is nevertheless one of those operas about which the critics can say very little.

Accurately composed and orchestrated as the opera is, it would be unfair to censure it from the point of view of technical correctness. On the other hand, though, it seems to me that

---

[1] These are Basiliola's last words in *La Nave*.

it presents no aesthetic character of its own, nor any boldness, nor any innovation – in its fundamental conception or its architectural form or language – which the critics can approve or disapprove of after some discussion.

I wouldn't say *La Nave* can be considered a melodrama, as it lacks what is most typical and distinctive in the melodrama: that is, the predominance of strophic melic forms. Nor can it certainly be defined as a drama, since the poetry, that is to say the drama, is constantly kept subject to the musical effusions and to a constant intention and the most insistent effort of wanting to sing. In short, as a musical theatrical work it is a *quid medium* between the melodrama and the so-called lyrical drama: similar, therefore, to several other operas composed in the last fifty years. And it would be difficult to say more.

It would be difficult, too, I believe, to prove and maintain the correspondence of the music to the special tragic atmosphere of D'Annunzio's *Nave* and the poetry of D'Annunzio in general. Because if in D'Annunzio's poetry there are, here and there, passages of emphatic magniloquence, as there are very frequently, almost one after the other, in maestro Montemezzi's music, the difference is nevertheless great: the poetry of D'Annunzio always has a stony solidity in its foundations, an iron-like solidity in its structure, that the music of maestro Montemezzi lacks. Similarly, and to an even greater extent – and notwithstanding that it possesses certain traits of communicative sentimental warmth and effective scenic suggestion – the music lacks, it seems to me, that stupendous power and variety of tones, now arising from deep human divinations, now emerging unexpected and very powerfully from a clash of passions, that give to the best and most genuine of D'Annunzio's poetry the lofty lyric and epic effectiveness that we all know and admire.

In the *Nave* by maestro Montemezzi the musical intonation of the verse – it not even being possible to call it a proper melody – is either melodramatic and stentorian or of a conversational nature that I would define as fat yet flaccid (*adiposa ma floscia*), regulated by the progression of the underlying musical fabric arranged according to the approximate temporal requirements of the text. I say this not from the point of view of prosody, which maestro Montemezzi treats with perceptible carelessness or contempt, but in the sense that music can exteriorize the lyrical throb of the verse (the *cantus obscurior*), intensifying and enhancing its psychological and dramatic meaning.

Omitting special consideration of the thematic material and its harmonic construction – the latter with six-four chords inserted at every moment, giving it a continuous, exasperating, cadenza-like character – and omitting other considerations of maestro Montemezzi's skillfulness as an orchestrator and his choral technique – which can approach that of Ponchielli[1] – it is possible to say, I believe, that if in the more sweetly affectionate and idyllic episodes maestro Montemezzi's music, always very accurately composed yet scholastic, is of a romanticism that can recall the fine and amiable romanticism of Zandonai, in the more dramatic and excited episodes, and to an even greater extent in the more complex and animated scenes, it is of a romanticism that comes from the so-called pseudo-historic 'grand opera' (there is no need to name the most representative authors of those works), or that which is clearly derived from Strauss. It is understandable that this could happen to a composer who, by writing at a more juvenile age that very noteworthy opera which is *L'Amore dei tre re* (the most important of his operas), had the status in Italy of being the most Wagnerian among the most renowned opera composers of his generation.

---

[1] Pizzetti's point is that Montemezzi's choral technique has old-fashioned elements; by the 1930s Amilcare Ponchielli (1834–86) was remembered almost entirely for *La Gioconda* (1876).

The very elegant audience at the Teatro Reale received Maestro Montemezzi's opera and its performance very favourably.

Special applause greeted Signora Cigna on her first appearance; it was heard again, very strongly, when the tenor Civil hit one of his blaring high notes; and it burst out a third time at the beginning of the final scene, when the ship is revealed ready for launching.

The curtain calls at the end of the four acts, for the performers, Maestro Serafin, and the director, Piccinato, numbered twenty-four or twenty-five altogether; in half of them they were joined, amid particularly celebratory manifestations, by the composer of the opera.

7. Unattributed review signed 's. s.,' *La Stampa*, 15 December 1938.

'La Nave' by Montemezzi at the Teatro Reale dell'Opera

Rome, 14 December

AT THE Teatro Reale dell'Opera tonight was staged 'La Nave' by Italo Montemezzi with a libretto by Tito Ricordi based on the D'Annunzian tragedy. The opera was meant to inaugurate the season, but it was not possible to perform it then due to the sudden indisposition suffered by Signora Cigna; it was very eagerly awaited and let's say that its success, twenty years after its first performance at La Scala, was memorable.

La Nave, rehearsed and conducted by the same maestro Serafin who rehearsed and conducted it again in this second edition – and strangely enough all of Montemezzi's operas have been godfathered by Serafin[1] – first appeared at La Scala on 3 November 1918. It was exactly twenty years ago. Since then, it has not been performed again in any opera house.[2]

'It was a tormenting love – maestro Montemezzi declared some time ago – the one that seized me for this magnificent poem by Gabriele D'Annunzio. For almost two years it was all an alternation of enthusiasms and discouragements. I would think about it. I would study it for months, but then I would abandon it, feeling my strength failing before the vastness, the breadth and the greatness of the picture. After the outbreak of the war in '14, I thought of *La Nave* again, and it seemed to me almost my duty to contribute to the diffusion of that

---

1 This is not completely true: see p.252, n. 1.

2 This is, of course, erroneous, but it does demonstrate how the Verona performances had gone largely unnoticed.

atmosphere of Adriatic propaganda which is the inner and profound D'Annunzian meaning. Taking my courage in both hands, I went to see Tito Ricordi to state my intention to him. Ricordi immediately seemed enthusiastic about the idea and, without delay, set about the difficult task of adapting the poem to the needs of the lyric theatre. He completed the adaptation and submitted it to the Poet for his approval; the latter did not hesitate to grant his full consent. Then my own work started. It was feverish, intense work that depressed and exalted me at the same time. On *La Nave*, which I consider the best of my operas, I worked for three years and three months.'[1]

On the night of 3 November, during the performance of the first act of the new opera, the news arrived at the opera house that the Italian troops had entered Trieste. The telegram was read during the interval amid great demonstrations of joy.

Then Montemezzi's *La Nave* fell into obscurity.

Now, twenty years later, here is *La Nave* again starting to sail toward the world. It is to be wished that it will have greater fortune this time because, first of all, the performance is beautiful and also because, let's tell the truth, even though the opera shows traces of the depressions and exaltations that filled the author during the period of its composition, and even though it is not possible to speak of a clear personality, neither of style nor of character, on the whole the music succeeds in emphasizing the dramatic panic (*panico drammatico*) of the D'Annunzian

---

[1] If this was taken from a printed source, I have been unable to identify that source. On the other hand, it may represent a first-hand report of what Montemezzi had said. There are some correspondences with the article Montemezzi had published on his opera in April 1938 (see above, pp. 45–52), but the differences are sufficient to suggest that this statement is not a paraphrase of that essay. The statement is revealing in its increased emphasis on the long period of consideration and study preceding the composition of the opera: something that Montemezzi made no mention of in 1918. See above, p. 18.

poem and in conferring on it something profound and vigorous. It also manages to envelop it in an emotional atmosphere of real effectiveness. And this is no little merit if one considers the difficulty of the D'Annunzian *declamato* that is already music in itself, even though made of air, and the irresistible force of certain feelings that, mixed up as they are, reveal their affectedness even though they happily overflow in the lofty realms of poetry. With regard to the music of *La Nave*, it would not be totally wrong to talk of a Verdian (of the last Verdi) and Wagnerian epigone. However, is it not preferable to allow oneself to be influenced by the greats rather than getting lost in the vain pursuit of originality at any cost through arbitrary and extravagant proceedings that betray not only the artist's nature but the very rationale of art? When Montemezzi sings, in the Italian sense of the word, he sings nobly, with a sincere tone, although sometimes with an inadequate correspondence to the feeling that he expresses. And when passion urges, the orchestral peroration always achieves powerful and overwhelming effects. *Marco Gratico*, the character who is musically best defined and expressed, takes on concrete form spiritually, especially in the second and third acts, thanks to the emotional contribution of the music which supports and generously expresses the feelings and the nature of his character. Also it cannot be denied that the chorus, thanks to which the *Graticos*' tragedy finds its place within the larger tragedy of the people, has in this opera a fundamental task and accomplishes it with perfect dignity and undeniable success. This is the sign that the composer was able to build it firmly with a masterly variety of motifs and with rhythms that can be easily and quickly remembered; he was also able to keep it within a noble line that satisfies and interests even the most intelligent musician.

On the whole, it is an opera of high artistic dignity which, although it doesn't present anything exceptional, testifies to the sound and honest artistic integrity of its composer. His melodramatic talent, coupled with an inspired imagination, a good

Pau Civil (1899–1987)
The Fourth Marco Gratico

taste and his possession of a technique that, although it doesn't seem ingenious is certainly intelligent, cannot be questioned. *La Nave* is an accomplished opera, a complex and on the whole well-organized opera honouring that trend that was called the young Italian school,[1] though it is already old by now. It is an opera of certain and immediate popular comprehensibility. It could be lamented that it was growing old for twenty years in Casa Ricordi's archives, but today's revenge will reward its illustrious composer for the injustice suffered.

What rightly contributed to increase the success of this new edition of Montemezzi's opera was the good performance prepared by maestro Tullio Serafin. With assiduous and intelligent care for all the orchestral and vocal details, he conferred on the opera an incisiveness and vibration (*vibrazione*) that at times were really dynamic (*scattante*) and gripping. Gina Cigna, who was the perfidious *Basiliola*, acted with insinuating cunning, showing off her full and gripping *cantabile* skill every time the part offered her the opportunity. It was the same thing with Bassiola [sic], very forceful in his acting and his singing, but the singer who impressed above all others was the tenor Paolo Civil. No one could have given life to the character of *Marco Gratico* better than he did. His powerful and confident voice unfolded in the middle and high registers as he sang in a full-throated manner with great ease and conferred on his wish to express himself an even too generous naturalness that surprised and amazed. *Marco Gratico*'s role is suited to him. The whole body of minor roles was very good, from Boeuf to Romito, Taddei, Mazziotti, Gobbi and Zagonara. The very large chorus, diligently prepared by maestro Conca, sang with admirable force. The scenery, realized by Parravicini[2] after

---

1 I.e. the young composers, led by Catalani, who began to emerge from Verdi's shadow in the 1880s.

2 A mistake for (Ettore) Polidori. The author was confusing him with Camillo Parravicini (1902–78), the scenographer at La Scala.

sketches by Oppo, framed the performance beautifully. The first act scenery especially, vivid and airy, earned the audience's keenest approbation. This was the audience of the great occasions, with big names in politics, the aristocracy, great minds, and of high society, diplomats and party officials (*gerarchi*); with ladies wearing low-necked dresses and bejewelled according to the latest fashion, supplying a harmony of delicate colours besides the smart uniforms of the Army and the Party and the tailcoats. It was a show that only Rome has the ability to offer.

We have spoken of the success. The composer was called out, on his own and with the other artists, uncountable times amid general acclamations.

Part Six

Fifth Production

New York, Rose Theater, 31 October 2012

Cast:
Basiliola . . . . Tiffany Abban
Marco Gratico . . . . Robert Brubaker
Sergio Gratico. . . . . Daniel Ihn-Kyu Lee
Orso Faledro. . . . . Ashraf Sewailam
Traba, the monk . . . . . . Joseph Flaxman

Director: Duane D. Printz
Conductor: Israel Gursky

1 performance

The Rose Theater (upper left) is part of the vast Time Warner Center (opened 2003)

Introduction

By the beginning of the twenty-first century the chance of a revival of *La Nave* must have appeared almost non-existent, even though *L'Amore dei Tre Re* was still being occasionally produced. That it was revived is entirely due to the can-do attitude of Teatro Grattacielo of New York and its director Duane D. Printz. Teatro Grattacielo was founded in 1994 with a view to reviving neglected operas of the verismo era in concert performances. The first of these concert performances was devoted to *L'Amore dei Tre Re*.

Printz, a particular admirer of Montemezzi, first became interested in *La Nave* in 2010 when she noted that, somewhat surprisingly, it was listed in Ricordi's catalogue of rental materials. An enquiry confirmed that no parts were actually available; nevertheless, Ricordi said they would, free of charge, reproduce the parts from Montemezzi's manuscript full score if Teatro Grattacielo could guarantee a performance. This would take two years. Printz accepted this generous offer, and the performance originally loosely planned for 2011 was put off until 2012.

Teatro Grattacielo's revival of *La Nave* was scheduled for 29 October at the Rose Theater, Lincoln Center. Unfortunately the havoc caused by Hurricane Sandy, which struck the New York area on that very day, forced the postponement of the concert to 31 October. It took place with slightly depleted forces and a general sense of relief that it was taking place at all. Sadly, many of those with tickets were unable to get to the Lincoln Center. More details concerning the background to this performance can be found in the foreword to the present volume.

The 2012 *La Nave* was different in kind from the earlier productions, not just in being a concert performance, but in being understood, in essence, as the resuscitation of a completely unknown opera. Reviewers accordingly devoted a good deal of space not only to the extraordinary circumstances of the postponement, but to the earlier history of the opera and details of the plot. Nevertheless, the nature of a concert performance foregrounds purely musical qualities, and Montemezzi's score attracted a good deal of commentary, nearly all positive, and some really enthusiastic. His skill in orchestration and descriptive detail was highly praised, as was the extraordinary care with which the score was constructed and the overall grandeur it conveyed. Altogether the Teatro Grattacielo performance made a strong case for what was clearly a major opera and Montemezzi's admirers can reasonably hope for a fully staged revival now the performance materials are available once more.

Two reviews are included here, both originally published in online publications. The first is by Peter G. Davis (b. 1936), a Harvard graduate who obtained his master's degree in composition from Columbia University where he studied with Jack Beeson and Otto Luening. In a long career as a music critic, he has served as the music editor of *High Fidelity Magazine*, and as a critic for the *New York Times* and editor of their Arts & Leisure section. He wrote a weekly arts column for *New York Magazine* for 26 years and has also written for *Opera News*, *Opera Magazine* and *Musical America*. His book, *The American Opera Singer: The Lives and Adventures of America's Great Singers in Opera and In Concert From 1825 to the Present*, was published in 1997. The second critic featured in this section is Dan Foley (b. 1970), who graduated from Ohio University in 1993 with bachelor's degrees in philosophy and mathematics. A keen musician and music critic, he is the United States representative for the London-based Donizetti Society, and the founder of Ottocento Opera, a New York company dedicated to reviving works by contemporaries of Verdi. He has a particular enthusiasm for the composer Giovanni Pacini, and has maintained two websites devoted to Pacini's work. He has reviewed for the *Donizetti Society Newsletter*, *Musicalcriticism.com*, *Opera Today* and *Opera Quarterly*, and written liner notes for Opera Rara.

1. Peter G. Davis, *MusicalAmerica.com*, 5 November 2012.

Hurricane Sandy could easily have shipwrecked Teatro Grattacielo's one-time-only concert presentation of Italo Montemezzi's rarely heard opera *La Nave* (The Ship), originally scheduled to take place on Monday, Oct. 29 in Lincoln Center's Rose Theater. With New York City still badly crippled by the storm, the performance had to be postponed until Oct. 31, and luckily the theater, musicians, and a small but enthusiastic audience were available to save the occasion.

Aficionados of early 20th-century Italian opera, which is Teatro Grattacielo's specialty and a corner of the repertory still underappreciated, could only rejoice. Senior opera-goers may be familiar with Montemezzi's *L'Amore dei Tre Re* (The Love of Three Kings), a huge hit after its premiere at La Scala in 1913 and frequently seen at the Met until it fell out of fashion in the 1950s. In his classic text-book history of opera, published in 1947, Donald Jay Grout calls the work 'without doubt the greatest Italian tragic opera since Verdi's *Otello*,'[1] a judgment that may well still stand.

La Nave, first performed in 1918, also at La Scala, was to be the triumphant sequel, but the piece never caught on. Since the premiere there have only been three productions, including one in Chicago in 1919. Despite the lukewarm initial reception, fans of *L'Amore dei Tre Re* have always been curious to hear the grandly scaled *La Nave*, based on a typically florid verse play by the Italian poet-dramatist-patriot Gabriele D'Annunzio.

Perhaps no other Italian composer of his generation embraced the stylistic advances of Wagner and Debussy more warmly than Montemezzi, and few synthesized these polar influences more smoothly or with such technical assurance. Both *L'Amore dei Tre Re* and *La Nave* are notable for detailed orchestral textures of

---

[1] *A Short History of Opera*, 2 vols (New York: Columbia UP, 1947), 2:444.

extraordinary clarity despite their harmonic density and splashy instrumental coloring. It was probably the sheer gorgeous sound of these scores that first seduced audiences. Even at that, the declamatory vocal writing primarily dictates the dramatic flavor of each opera, and for better or worse Montemezzi responded faithfully to texts drawn directly from two contemporary Italian plays that could hardly be more different in tone and language.

The earlier opera is based on a drama by the now obscure Sem Benelli, a trim tragedy of crossed love and terrible vengeance that never wastes a word – a play, like Maeterlinck's *Pelléas et Mélisande*, that seemed to be waiting for a composer to set it to music. *La Nave*, on the other hand, is hobbled by the extravagant verbal posturing and erotic excesses of D'Annunzio, whose plays also defeated the musical talents of Pizzetti, Mascagni, Franchetti, and even Debussy (Zandonai had better luck with *Francesca da Rimini*, one of the poet's earliest and comparatively restrained efforts).

As told in a prologue and three 'episodes,' the plot concerns the struggles between the Faledro and Gràtico families in Venice 'during the years of the bountiful incarnation of the Son of God 552.' The offspring of the two dueling clans, Basiliola and Marco, conduct a love-hate relationship of unprecedented sensuality and brutality, even for opera, until she pleads to be granted 'a beautiful death.' Marco obliges by having Basiliola nailed to the prow of his ship *Totus Mundus*, which sets sail to conquer the Adriatic and, by extension, oceans all over the globe – a dangerous policy of irredentism that would soon poison Italian politics, D'Annunzio's reputation, and possibly the fate of *La Nave*.

In the end Montemezzi may have lavished his talents on a libretto that did his career no favors, but at least its poetic imagery and longer scenic spans gave him an opportunity to luxuriate as a composer in ways that the terser *L'Amore dei Tre Re* did not. It would be impossible to catalog all the beauties of this absorbing score, one suffused with caloric orchestral warmth as well as the poised, aristocratic nobility so characteristic of Montemezzi's musical nature. From that first gently murmuring seascape to the spectacular ceremonial conclusion, the piece is virtually without a dead spot or a carelessly written passage – compliments that few opera composers of any era can readily earn.

Teatro Grattacielo once again delivered a performance of quality – quite an accomplishment considering the challenges of the work, not to mention the difficult logistics of the occasion. The orchestra, perhaps the most important ingredient of *La Nave*, played with both skill and expressive flair for conductor Israel Gursky, who also deftly coordinated the chorus and a variety of antiphonal instrumental effects located about the theater.

The two leading roles require the sort of lung power and vocal stamina that make so many Italian operas of this period difficult to cast. Tiffany Abban tore into Basiliola's music with abandon, sounding sumptuous in nearly all of it and raising hopes that she will ration such strenuous parts in the future, lest she damage what is clearly an important voice. Robert Brubaker's burly tenor may have tired a bit toward the end, but he attacked all of Marco Gràtico's trumpeting passages with fearless authority. The rest of the large cast consisted mostly of cameo roles, all of them more than capably performed.

One wonders if Montemezzi's *La Nave* will ever be heard or seen again after this heroic performance. At least we happy few, thanks to Teatro Grattacielo, can say we were there.

The cast and conductor of the New York *Nave*

2. Dan Foley, *MusicalCriticism.com*, 9 December 2012.

FORTUNE HAS been unkind to the opera Italo Montemezzi considered his masterpiece, the 1918 epic *La Nave*. At its successful *prima* in Milan, where Tullio Serafin conducted, critics gushed over it and audiences identified strongly with its nationalist message.[1] It received a much-publicized American debut in Chicago the following year, starring Rosa Raisa and conducted by the composer himself. There, despite the craze for the composer's *L'Amore di Tre Re* in the States, *La Nave*'s reception was more measured. Critics from the windy city were less than knowledgeable (one complained there were no tunes one could whistle); American audiences enjoyed the two performances, but didn't quite connect with a symbolic, mythical tale whose intended audience was Italian.

Montemezzi fought for the rest of his career to have *La Nave* produced elsewhere, but with depressing results: after Italian productions in 1923 and 1938, a hush of nearly seventy-five years settled on the score. Then the visionary Duane Printz, Artistic Director of Teatro Grattacielo – a New York-based concert opera company specializing in unfamiliar Italian verismo works – took an interest. Wowed by the vocal score, Printz learned to her dismay that the orchestral score and parts had been destroyed by bombing in World War II. But Casa Ricordi generously offered to reconstruct the materials from Montemezzi's autograph score, provided she guaranteed a performance. Printz began assembling the massive orchestral and choral forces required, along with a cast capable of rising to the considerable demands of the principal parts.

---

1 Several online sources convey the misleading impression that *La Nave* was a great popular and critical success in 1918. The source of this error appears to be a statement Tullio Serafin made in *Opera News* in 1953: '*La nave* was received as well as – perhaps better than – *L'Amore*. ... it was received with warm enthusiasm by the critics of all the Milan papers ...'. See 'Italo Montemezzi – an appreciation,' *Opera News* 19 January 1953, 10–11, 31, p. 31.

It began to seem as if, finally, *La Nave* would be christened anew, but once again, disaster threatened, this time in the form of Hurricane Sandy. Originally scheduled for October 29, the one-off concert performance fell squarely on the eve of mass evacuations and the unprecedented shutdown of public transit systems, and had to be called off. Oddly, what Sandy took away, she just as capriciously gave back: because local airports were closed, the singers couldn't leave the area. Rescheduled for Halloween night, *La Nave* finally set sail again before a small but appreciative audience.

[Summary of the plot.]

After hearing the opera (and once, mind you, is hardly enough to render judgment on such an unfamiliar and monumental work), it would be hard to argue that the quality of the score had anything to do with the composer's difficulty selling it to impresarios. Partial blame falls on the libretto, whose text is culled directly from Gabriele D'Annunzio's play of the same title. The story-line was tailored specifically to an Italian audience living in particular historical circumstances (the end of World War I, when there was great popular support for reclaiming lands once belonging to Italy). But taken at face value by a modern audience, the plot is a series of gruesome and debaucherous scenes fused together. The characters are unsympathetic, the exact motivation for their outlandish acts of aggression often obscure. But perhaps the most important factors mitigating against revival are the vast stagecraft and musical forces required. Spectacular sets and costumes, a huge, working ship onstage, ballet dancers, duelling choruses (I counted around seventy chorus members), and an enormous orchestra including offstage buccine, an ancient form of trumpet. The opera is positively Meyerbeerian in scope, a prohibitively expensive prospect for all but the most well-heeled companies.

But the music – oh, what music! – is rapturously beautiful. It is reminiscent of the perfumed, soaring orchestrations of Wagner,

Programme for the New York *Nave*

Strauss, and Debussy, with perhaps some Massenet thrown in. Yet its Italian DNA is equally obvious in the impassioned melodic inspiration, and the over-the-top, Puccinian vocal outbursts of the principals. Unlike *Salome* or *Elektra*, despite the bloodshed, the music rarely speaks the language of savagery; it conjures up great, mythic, noble deeds of passion, love. The score almost manages to make it feel plausible that a whole crowd would cheer someone for committing fratricide; that they might instantly agree that crucifying someone on the front of a boat was sheer inspiration. It is all highly melodic, but declamatory. There are no set pieces, nothing that could really be divorced from the matrix of the score and used in a recital context. Perhaps that, too, has made it difficult for the opera to have a lasting legacy. The best parts of the score are a gorgeous, gently rocking barcarola-like prelude that splendidly evokes the maritime setting; the huge choral passages; and most of all, a long, intensely dramatic love/hate dialog in which Basiliola, employing her beauty and wiles, reduces the proud Tribune Marco to kneeling before her. The entire score, though, is very pleasing and accessible to the listener, whether an aficionado or a novice.

Printz assembled a cast that was more than equal to the task. The two principal roles, Basiliola and Marco, were tackled by soprano Tiffany Abban, and tenor Robert Brubaker. I predict we will hear a lot more from Tiffany Abban, perhaps (I hope) as a Verdi soprano. Blessed with a dark, powerful instrument of varied color and great expressive power, she not only impressed, but greatly moved her audience. The opera is a vocal marathon for the soprano, with Basiliola prominent for almost its entire duration (well over two hours). The combination of the tiringly high tessitura, the wide range of feeling required, and the huge orchestral forces that had to be mastered for her to be heard, made Abban's performance a very worthy accomplishment, particularly in a time when the voices that can do this sort of role are in short supply. The ovations she received from the audience were richly deserved.

Brubaker sang valiantly with what appeared to be a bad cold, still managing to deliver a very satisfying reading of this role – something not many tenors could do even in the best of health. Like that of Basiliola, Marco's music calls for sustained and forceful singing in the upper reaches of his range, again in direct conflict with a blaring orchestra and chorus. Brubaker has a hefty heroic tenor voice with the size and control that make this role an excellent fit. He sang with real feeling, breathing vivid life into a rather unlikable character.

Though musically less prominent than those of Basiliola and Marco, the role of Sergio still required big emotions – particularly in the orgy/duel scene. Baritone Daniel Ihn-Kyu Lee has a solid and pleasant enough voice, but didn't quite deliver the heart-on-the-sleeve singing required. This work is, despite all its Teutonic influence, still an Italian opera! As the blinded former tribune Orso Faledro, bass Ashraf Sewailam, a veteran of other Grattacielo performances, gave a performance several sizes larger than the role he was assigned. From his first utterance, he projected the kind of authority and confidence that commanded rapt attention. Equally worthy was Kirk Dougherty, who sang several of the seventeen(!) other male roles with a pleasantly ringing lyric tenor voice. As the Monk Traba, bass Joseph Flaxman was vocally uneven but also very promising, and seems fated for bigger parts. There is only one other female role – that of an unidentified voice – and she sings but a single line during the prologue. Though it is difficult to judge fairly based on such a small sampling, Suzanne Stadler (the cover for Abban) declaimed that single line with such a big, luscious sound that I at first assumed she was the heroine!

The orchestra, confidently led by conductor Israel Gursky, played beautifully and with very few mishaps of intonation, even in the strings. The gorgeous sonorities Montemezzi provided proved one of the major highlights of the evening. The massive chorus, too, was most impressive – especially given the complexity and difficulty of their music. The ballet dancers during the orgy scene – arguably an unnecessary distraction in a concert performance – were for me a guilty pleasure, a small taste of the Meyerbeerian extravagance necessarily lacking in a performance without a set and costumes.

Finally, I must again mention Artistic Director, Duane Printz, whose efforts bring us these fascinating operas, and whose ability to cast them with the right voices means we are always treated to not just a work of great musicological interest, but to an evening of opera that leaves us feeling fulfilled. And though I suspect I will have a long wait, I would love to see *La Nave* back on stage in all its blood-soaked splendor.

Part Seven

Other Criticism 1924–2008

Montemezzi in 1938

Introduction

MOST OF the critical writing on *La Nave* has been in the form of reviews of, and anticipatory features on, specific productions, especially those in Milan, Chicago and Rome. Alongside these reviews, however, a small body of other, more academically-orientated criticism slowly built up, most of it inspired not so much by Montemezzi having composed the opera as the fact that he was setting a D'Annunzio text. The majority of this criticism has been insistently negative and remarkably unsympathetic to Montemezzi's artistic aims. The first two selections in this section are perhaps the most important examples of this sort of negative criticism, for the first was written by the very influential critic Guido M. Gatti, while the second, by Luciano Tomelleri, appeared in what was, for a long time, the most thorough exploration of the subject of D'Annunzio and music. They are included here, not because they are especially insightful, but because they led to the development of a critical orthodoxy and had a considerable and generally lamentable impact on Montemezzi's overall critical standing (both are included in the bibliographies of Montemezzi given in the various *Grove* dictionaries and *Die Musik in Geschichte und Gegenwart*, listed there in preference to the many very positive accounts of *L'Amore dei Tre Re* available).

In part five of the present book, Pizzetti stood out as the fiercest reviewer of *La Nave* for a combination of personal and professional reasons. Gatti and Tomelleri were, unfortunately for Montemezzi, both more or less Pizzettians, both judging *Fedra* the most successful of the D'Annunzio operas and subscribing to a Pizzettian aesthetic. This is particularly true of Gatti (1892–1973). His career as a prolific scholar, critic and editor of music commenced in 1914, when he became the editor of *La Riforma musicale*, and he was from this time an important champion of the the *generazione dell'ottanta* ('generation of '80') composers: the modernists and neoclassicists who reacted against the popular aesthetic of Puccini, Mascagni and other, older composers. Among this group, he had a particular attachment to Pizzetti, with whom he became friends; convinced that Pizzetti was the greatest living Italian composer, Gatti undertook to promote his friend's music abroad at every opportunity. His devotion eventually led him to write the first full critical biography, *Ildebrando Pizzetti* (1934), an updated revision of which, translated by David Moore (1951), was for long the major source of information on Pizzetti outside Italy. It confidently proposed that Pizzetti could be for the twentieth century what Verdi had been for the nineteenth.

Gatti's article, 'Gabriele D'Annunzio and the Italian Opera-Composers,' featured here, was published in the specialized American music journal, *Musical Quarterly*, in 1924.[1] It appeared in a translation by the American musicologist Theodore Baker (1851–1934), now remembered mainly for *Baker's Biographical Dictionary of Musicians*, and since its first publication has been the most readily accessible piece of *La Nave* criticism in most libraries, especially outside Italy. Gatti gave a brief sketch of the earlier history of the Italian libretto, and the changing balance between the words and the music in opera, then discussed the recent rash of D'Annunzio *Literaturopern* in some detail. He deplored their popularity in no uncertain terms:

> An influence more harmful [to opera] than that of D'Annunzio cannot be imagined, when one takes into consideration that the poet's collaboration was like the passive weight of a cope of lead, never changing into active and fruitful coöperation.[2]

---

[1] This was apparently its first appearance anywhere: I have found no record of the essay being published in Italian.

[2] 'Gabriele D'Annunzio and the Italian Opera-Composers,' *Musical Quarterly* 10 (1924), 263–88, p. 287.

The only composer judged to have in some part overcome the harmful influence was, predictably, Gatti's hero:

> Pizzetti alone succeeded in creating an opera dramatically vital, because, as an artist, he was able to impose his will on the material offered him, and to stamp it with his strong personality, so that I might call *Fedra*, as a musical drama, possibly the most 'anti-D'Annunzian' opera that I know. The other composers, at best, were not sensible of the deficiencies of the poems as opera-libretti, and were content to follow the text with more or less adequacy, but always subserviently.[1]

Gatti was obviously aware of Pizzetti's earlier involvement with *La Nave*, and had very likely been appraised of his friend's opinions regarding Montemezzi's making an opera from the same play. Indeed, his 1924 article may reflect Pizzetti's judgement. Certainly Gatti's comments on Montemezzi's *Nave* demonstrate a remarkable critical antipathy. He repeats some of the criticisms made in 1918: that the play was not suited to musical setting, that the various characters did not come to life, and that the vocal writing was strained, unnatural and declamatory. To these alleged faults, however, he adds an attack on those qualities of the opera which had been most admired: the choral scenes and orchestration. And if this were not enough, he includes a gratuitous assault on *L'Amore dei Tre Re*, perhaps because he knew that it had been extremely successful in the United States. The positive reference to *Giovanni Gallurese* (1905), Montemezzi's early opera, supplies a useful clue to the source of Gatti's very obvious prejudice. He thought that Montemezzi should have accepted a relatively modest position in the Italian musical economy as a

---

1 Ibid.

composer of popular opera. He could not abide Montemezzi's more ambitious efforts to advance Italian opera in a direction clearly at odds with Pizzetti's ideas.

It is not clear whether Gatti had actually witnessed a performance of *La Nave*. Tomelleri, who was born in Vicenza in 1913, had almost certainly not seen it at the time he wrote about it in 1936. A good deal of his attitude to the opera is captured in his insistence on retaining the judgement '*La Nave* could no longer be staged' even though this had been firmly disproven by the revival in 1938 that preceded the publication of his essay in *Gabriele D'Annunzio and Music* (*Gabriele D'Annunzio e la Musica*) in 1939.[1] Tomelleri's determination to treat the opera as 'dead,' though a far from objective position, nevertheless has its own significance, for his essay marks the point at which a tradition of critical writing in the form of reviews gave way to one of academic comment based partly on the vocal score and partly on earlier criticism. Remarkably, given its subsequent influence, the essay was derived from Tomelleri's student research: in 1936 he graduated from the faculty of letters at the University of Padua with a master's degree for his thesis on D'Annunzio's influence on musicians. His criticism comes across as jaundiced and rather superficial today, but it appears to have been admired by his peers, for in 1939 Tomelleri obtained the post of chair of poetry and drama at the Milan Conservatory. In Italy, his dismissal of *La Nave* has probably had more long-term influence than any other single piece of critical writing on the opera. It appeared in a volume, notably, in which Pizzetti allowed one of his own essays, devoted to *his* music for *La Nave*, to be reprinted.

Tomelleri, like earlier critics, begins by criticising D'Annunzio's *Nave*, which he finds 'grand,' but cold and unmoving: an essentially pictorial idea inadequately realised in language. When he moves on to Tito Ricordi's libretto, however, he is surprisingly

---

1 See below, p. 306

positive, judging it an improvement on the original play and 'all in all the most likely "libretto" of D'Annunzio's tragedies.' This was a clear departure from Pizzetti, but one suspects that it was to some extent strategic: Tomelleri did not want to allow the possibility that Montemezzi was hopelessly disadvantaged by his libretto. Unlike Gatti, too, he has words of praise for *L'Amore dei Tre Re*, but considers *La Nave* as marking a clear and irreversible decline in Montemezzi's art. *La Nave* is judged as too studied, lacking in personality, and too dependent on formulas: no attempt is made to locate any positive qualities.

Tomelleri was a young critic with the overconfident audacity that finds it much easier to fault than praise. Yet his account of *La Nave* has extended a long shadow over subsequent critical responses to Montemezzi's opera, at least in Italy. The best demonstration of how he fixed the terms of analysis is found in Domenico de Paoli's essay 'Gabriele D'Annunzio: The Music and the Musicians' ('Gabriele D'Annunzio: La Musica e i Musicisti') of 1963. De Paoli (1894–1984) was a major critic, far more important than Tomelleri, yet his brief account of *La Nave* sticks so closely to Tomelleri's that one could almost conclude he had not bothered to examine the opera itself. Again he criticises D'Annunzio's play as spectacular but emotionally hollow, and praises, by contrast, Tito Ricordi's adaptation ('the most successful "libretto" of all D'Annunzio's works'). Of Montemezzi's music he had this to say:

> How did the composer solve the problem with which, even when adapted as a libretto, D'Annunzio's tragedy presented him? By composing music that avoids commonplaces and banalities: clear music, with nobility of purpose, of a simplicity that seeks to be grand, and with good formal mastery. It is music of that type which is habitually referred to as 'noble,' or at

least 'respectable,' but which is useless. All the more useless because the composer has never had much personality; he has always believed in the 'melody' (the traditional one, of course), and with that he has always tried to feed his theatre. Lacking a very broad melodic breath, however, he is often forced to resort to all the means that 'technique' offers him to give the illusion of possessing it. Moreover, at the moment of his composing *La Nave* it would seem that even that meagre melodic vein was about to run out. The musical material forming the fabric of this score is really weak and the composer's skill (quite ingenuous to tell the truth) cannot delude us, not even temporarily, about the quality of his invention and his musical material. He is a noble composer, in the sense that that epithet was commonly applied half a century ago, yet lacking in the strength necessary to create a musical organism having, not only substance, but a life of its own.[1]

Whether De Paoli cribbed this from Tomelleri or not, his brief account of Montemezzi's opera certainly represents the hardening of a critical orthodoxy whereby negative judgements beget negative judgements, gradually reducing the possibility of any fresh reassessment (a process assisted, in the present case, by the unavailability of the opera for performance). The various *Grove* dictionaries and *Die Musik in Geschichte und Gegenwart*, in addition to including Gatti and Tomelleri in their Montemezzi bibliographies, list two unpublished dissertations from the 1970s with a bearing on the subject. The first, by Franco Opice, *Fonti e*

---

[1] 'Gabriele D'Annunzio: La Musica e i Musicisti' in *Nel Centenario di Gabriele D'Annunzio* (Turin: Eri, 1963), 39–118, p. 97.

suggestioni dannunziane nel teatro musicale italiano del Novecento, was submitted to the Catholic University of Milan in 1973;[1] the second, by D. Borghi, '*La Nave' di G. D'Annunzio, musica di I. Montemezzi*, was submitted to the university of Bologna in 1976. Unfortunately neither is available for consultation: the Catholic University can only release dissertations with the permission of the author, with whom they are unable to make contact, while the University of Bologna has no copy of Borghi's dissertation. It is thus impossible to say whether they offered any significant reassessment of *La Nave*, though certainly neither author managed to arrest the general slide of the opera into obscurity.

If *La Nave* is, at the time of writing, better known and better appreciated than at any time since the Second World War, it is above all because of two people: Duane D. Printz, who revived it (as discussed in the previous section), and Raffaele Mellace, who undertook a highly original study and reevaluation of the opera, going back to the sources, including the manuscript full score, to understand Montemezzi's artistic goals rather than simply criticizing the finished product according to largely predetermined conclusions in the Gatti–Tomelleri–De Paoli tradition. Mellace (b. 1969) had made an earlier, broader study of the relationship between Italian literature and twentieth-century music (published as 'Letteratura e musica' in the major reference work *Storia della Letteratura Italiana* in 2001). This included a section on D'Annunzio and music, and led Adriana Guarnieri, who was organizing a conference on the topic, to suggest that Mellace might make a more in depth study of *La Nave*. He accordingly undertook the first detailed historical and archival study of the opera, and presented his findings at the conference, held in Siena in July 2005. A long, detailed and groundbreaking essay subsequently appeared in the conference proceedings, *D'Annunzio musico imaginifico*, edited by Adriana

---

[1] Title and date are given wrongly in the bibliographies.

Guarnieri, Fiamma Nicolodi and Cesare Orselli, and published as volume 48 of *Chigiana* (2008). This was entitled 'Prolegomeni a una lettura della *Nave*. Una collaborazione tra D'Annunzio, Montemezzi e Tito Ricordi.' Professor Mellace has kindly prepared a shortened version of that essay for inclusion in the present volume.

1. Guido M. Gatti, extract from 'Gabriele D'Annunzio and the Italian Opera-Composers,' *Musical Quarterly*, April 1924.[*]

WAS IT the ensemble scenes, the brilliant and pompous finali, that awakened in Italo Montemezzi, and before him in Tito Ricordi,[1] the adapter of the tragedy as an opera-libretto, the belief that they had got hold of a good subject for an opera? It may be so; and thereupon we ask ourselves whether Montemezzi was the fittest musician to illustrate these scenes musically, to build up these finali symphonically and chorally. The actual issue of the opera confirmed the opinion we had held even before we knew the work, by virtue of our acquaintance with the composer's earlier operas.

Italo Montemezzi made his first appearance in the operatic arena with *Giovanni Gallurese* (Turin, 1905), an opera not wanting in dramatic quality; it had good success, and the rosiest hopes were entertained for the young composer's future. *L'Amore dei tre Re* – produced in 1913 – did not wholly bear out these hopes; Montemezzi had fallen off in dash and dramatic energy, with no compensating gain in profundity and originality. True, in *L'Amore dei tre Re* there stand out certain impressionable and impassioned pages 'in minor,' langourous or melancholy, which lent themselves to the *outré* chromaticism of the composer, of a composite style having closest affinity to the Wagnerian; we still distinctly recall the matutinal farewell of Flora[2] to Avito after a clandestine night of love; the beginning of the last act, when Flora is laid out on her bier and the vassals come to view

---

[*] © Oxford University Press. Reprinted by permission.

[1] Gatti makes the erroneous assumption throughout that it was Tito Ricordi who chose the subject. In fact, as Part One of this collection makes clear, it was Montemezzi's choice.

[2] The heroine's name is Fiora.

her, where – excepting an elegiac chorus too reminiscent of Moussorgsky – the musician finds true and adequate expression for the situation. On the other hand, in the dramatic pages – e.g., in the exaggerated contrast between the blind old man and his fair and faithless spouse[1] – Montemezzi vainly sought after pathetic fervor; he remained not only cold, but well-nigh hard and unyielding; in his mode of expression there was something dry and forced; neither the melody nor the harmony dilated to create in their environment a vibrant atmosphere that should irresistibly infect the hearer. An impression is produced that Montemezzi was insensible to the fascination of tone 'as tone,' and therefore incapable of creating beautiful musical forms, [despite] that sumptuously sonorous architecture which commands admiration without in the slightest hastening the heartbeats. This last-named quality – which may occasionally serve to cloak a paucity of feeling – is for us the one which, if magisterially developed, might have kept *La Nave* above water, supposing it to have been set to music in its entirety. Not possessing it, or possessing not enough of it, Montemezzi should have instinctively rejected the book that was offered him. Instead, he could not say *No!* to his publisher, and discounted his weak points, losing much valuable time over a work almost unanimously condemned at its first hearing. The coincidence of the première with the day in which the armistice with Austria was concluded, the day on which the war practically came to an end in our country (just imagine the mood of everybody on that never to be forgotten evening of November the 3d, 1918, after some three and a half years of anxiety and strife!), was certainly unfavorable for the opera, whose mannered patriotism seemed all the more artificial by contrast with the spontaneous and irrepressible feel-

---

[1] Fiora (see previous note) is in fact the wife of the son (Manfredo) of the 'blind old man' (Archibaldo). Gatti was clearly trusting to his unreliable memory of the opera's plot.

ing wherewith every heart was bursting. But a second judgment, equally negative in its totality, was pronounced in 1922 on the revival of the opera at Verona, the natal city of the composer.[1]

A musician who would measure up, at least outwardly, to certain scenes in *La Nave* must above all be a symphonist wielding a broad and sweeping brush, a painter of frescoes who can lay on his colors without stint. Montemezzi's palette is but poorly provided with colors, among which gray, or some other tint that does not 'light up,' predominates – a dull, pasty tint lacking relief; an orchestra that might be called Wagnerian in a sense by reason of its constitution, but of course without the vast polyphonic resources of Wagner. There is such an abuse of 'pedals' (organ-points), especially high ones, as finally to arouse an intolerable distaste; and the mass of strings is always too dense and compact, contributing thereby to rob the orchestral comment of brilliancy and elasticity. When we add that Montemezzi's music does not shine by an excessive variety of rhythmical formulas, or by an extraordinary wealth of harmony and modulation, it will be evident why the great mass-scenes in *La Nave* were not set, by the music, in the light needed to do them justice, if only superficially.

As for the characters of the tragedy, how could they be realistically portrayed by a musician who was not likewise possessed of a capacity to feel their life in himself and to penetrate their psychology – to re-create them, as it were, *ex novo*; one who contented himself with expressing them by music accompanying their verbal sequence, with appreciating them only at the value of their frequent rhetorical perorations? Montemezzi was fairly bewildered by the luxuriant fioritura of the D'Annunzian vocabulary; he did not possess the courage to penetrate through these into the hearts of the characters presented. (But then, had he done so, we fancy that he would quickly have withdrawn from

---

[1] The Verona performances actually took place in March 1923, and were well received. See Part Four of this collection.

the undertaking, recognizing the empty sentimentality hidden beneath all those verbal corruscations.) And he attempted to interpret the insistent gesticulations of all these magniloquent fantasms by equivalent musical gestures; hence the vocal writing is strained, confined to the high registers of the human voice, continuously and vociferously emphatic, every emotion being entrusted to the mechanical effect of shouting, or sobbing, or strident laughter. And even this effect ends in self-immolation, by reason of its frequency; Basiliola herself, after the first act, no longer succeeds in moving us by her vocal paroxysms, now that we are accustomed to see her in this stereotyped attitude of hers as a mænad. And the same might be said of the chorus, which has no expression of its own, as a chorus, but simply gesticulates like all the other characters; as polyphonic writing was designedly excluded – this Montemezzi himself declared in an interview – the composer relied on the efficacy of solo vociferation or vocal unison. He did not consider that the dynamic potentialities of the mass can attain true elevation of expression only when prepared and elaborated according to certain principles in the distribution of the parts, and architectonic levels in the construction, such as all ancient and modern opera composers – down to Verdi, Mussorgsky, and Pizzetti – have carefully borne in mind; that is, each put these principles into practice according to the rôle which he assigned to the chorus – whether for a background or for a dash of color, for lyrical commentary or active dramatic impersonation.

Aided by his personal romantico-idyllic temperament, Montemezzi successfully emerges in pages where heroism – or pseudo-heroism – is absent; he then finds impassioned accents, as in the Prologue, or the scene between Orso Faledro and his blinded sons. But such pages are few and of slight significance in the tragedy, which is a continuous blowing of trumpets and an endless processioning of folk possessed of the demon of oratory; and the composer, ill-advised in grappling with the onerous task, found himself at every step confronted by a phosphorescent, but inert, material, which he was unable to imbue with a life either real and soulful or factitious and adventitious.

If we are not incorrectly informed, he has now (summer of 1923) under advisement a *Paolo e Francesca*, and we should not be surprised but, rather, rejoiced if he succeeded in restoring his reputation with this idyl of Bernardin de St.-Pierre's, in so many respects consonant with what we believe to be the temperamental base of Montemezzi's artistry.[1]

---

[1] Another mistake: the 'idyl' was *Paul et Virginie*. For this abandoned work, see above pp. 24–25.

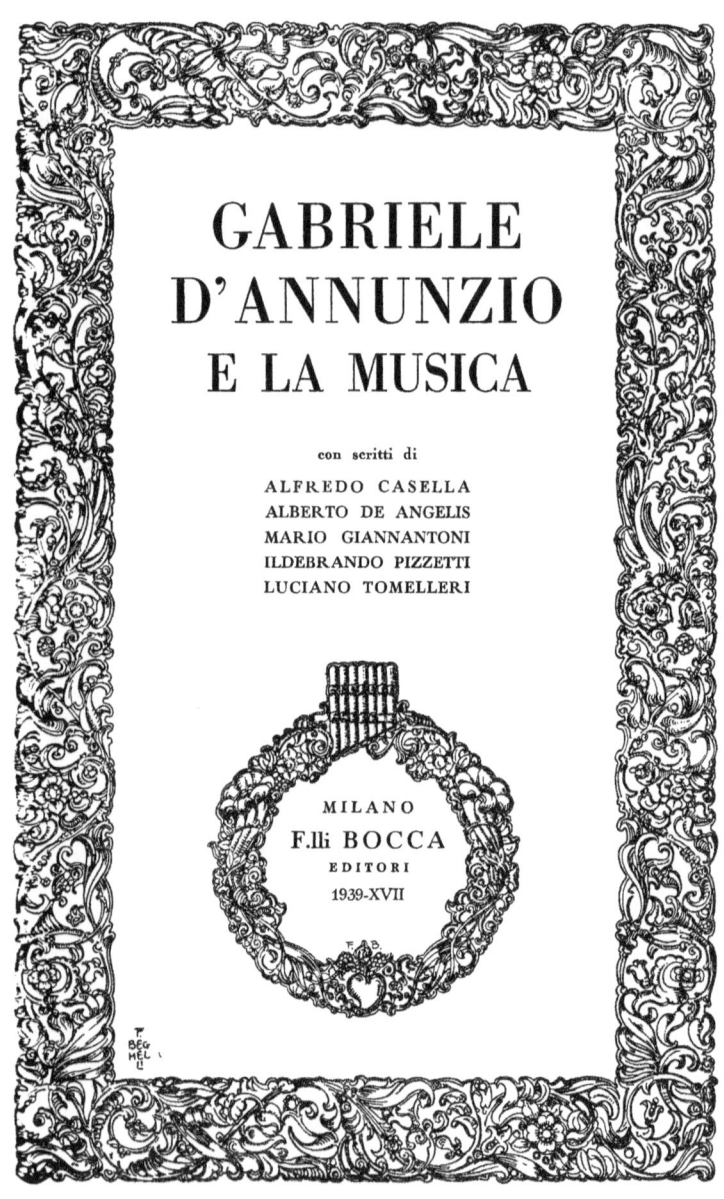

2. Luciano Tomelleri, extract from 'Gabriele D'Annunzio the inspirer of musicians,' in *Gabriele D'Annunzio and Music* (1939).[1]

La Nave (D'Annunzio and Montemezzi)

[D'Annunzio's] *La Nave* conveys pomposity and verbosity as much as it gives the impression of having been written in cold blood, lacking even that emotional tone which many times warms up the words, but the words only. The 'Adriatic tragedy' was created as a consequence of *Francesca*[2] (as a matter of fact, *La Nave* is the first of D'Annunzio's theatrical works in which the author prepares his own material), yet it possesses neither the originality nor the balance of *Francesca*, especially the latter quality: not being spontaneous, every motif gets exacerbated and exasperated, like someone who talks without conviction and yells in order to influence himself first. The sumptuous balance that earlier, in *Francesca*, had been achieved and so well expressed, is spoiled by exaggeration here. A delirium pervades every speaking voice and they are all hoarse.

That this representation of the origins [of Venice] did not have to be written is proved by the verse: it is not a pure expressive form, as in the *Figlia di Iorio*, nor a poetry and harmony of images, as in *Francesca*, but a simple rhythmic pattern, borrowed from the latter play, a vain replica of itself. Thus we can understand well the very appropriate remark by Borgese concerning *La Nave* and similar works being written in verse but thought in prose,[3] so that the verse, instead of being an organic necessity of

---

1 'Gabriele D'Annunzio inspiratore di musicisti' in *Gabriele D'Annunzio e la Musica* (Milan: Bocca, 1939).

2 *Francesca da Rimini* (1902), D'Annunzio's earliest play in verse.

3 Giuseppe A. Borgese, *Gabriele d'Annunzio: con bibliografia, ritratto e autografo* (Naples, 1909), III.

the expression, is a mere garment with which the Poet alternately covers and unveils his matter; therefore the most beautiful lines of verse here, those that are real poetry, are the few quatrains of the dedication to the Adriatic.

Basiliola does not move us, either for good or bad, but what is worse, she is not relived nor recreated, she is not 'objectified'; this is clear, because she is seen through the eyes of the men she has turned into beasts and by the concupiscent Poet himself. It is not us who see her like this: this is how we are made to see her, almost as if a friend described his woman to us and we could know her only in this guise, reflected and changed by the soul of the person who talks of her, not alive and real. The deaconess Ema is not even sketched out as a character, she is nothing but a verbal expression of that insincere and affected religiosity dominating the work: can't you see how little Christian, in his Biblical semblance, is the figure of the Traba Monk? It is the same with the two Graticos; the heroic motifs and Fate theme – how many times does D'Annunzio invoke it? – are, for Marco, only a pretext to justify his physical and sexual violence.

And the spasmodic lechery of those condemned to the Fuia Pit – who is capable of understanding it, even if merely in artistic as opposed to human terms (if there is a separation between humanity and art)? In fact the crowd, in *La Nave*, is purely sensual and its reactions are exclusively of a physical nature.

The motif of the ideal that is supposed to be urgently expressed in the tragedy does not appear to be resolved into poetry, and the necessities that should determine the tragedy are for the Poet only a justification. It would seem, therefore, that we must judge this work negatively and, indeed, *La Nave* is not what best represents the D'Annunzian theatre.

However, our judgement cannot be so hasty and, although the work's major fault is the exaggeration and forced tone, the very exasperation of the exquisitely D'Annunzian motifs and the insistence and the finished effort achieve a magnificence of representation that cannot but impress. Call it outward, choreographic, scenographic – and consistent in this (which I deem a fault) – as much as you like, yet *La Nave* is certainly grand, and if it lacks emotion we still remain dumbfounded in front of such an achievement and such a tension of scenic motifs.

Indeed, nothing moves us here, not even the fratricide, cloaked in a vain heroic and avenger-like appearance, but generated by brute violence and the ferocity of hurt sensuality.

[Tomelleri offers an extended contrast, with examples, between the verse, which is often 'heavy' and fails to take wing, with the poetic and imaginative suggestiveness of many of the stage directions.]

But what am I driving at? I am asked. Nothing, except that this analysis proves the assertion I have maintained so far: the poetic tone is neither created nor resolved and in *La Nave*, indeed, there are many lines of verse but little poetry. However, when the author, as in the stage directions, is placed in front of the subject, then the Poet is delighted, gets fired up and creates. His imagination glows within him, but it is like a fanciful impulse that cannot be communicated. However you interpret it, in the lagoon tragedy one fact is symptomatic: for effectiveness and truthfulness the stage directions very often surpass the verse, verse that remains uncreated as artistic objectification.

To put it in a sentence not new to the D'Annunzian critic, we'll say that D'Annunzio 'suffers' (*patisce*) the subject of his play.

The adaptation of *La Nave* as a libretto is another literary 'labour' of Tito Ricordi, who made use of his previous experience to act with more cleverness and more evident awareness of the goal he was trying to reach. *La Nave*, the way it is set to music, is all in all the most likely 'libretto' of D'Annunzio's tragedies both in terms of the characteristics of the original text and the adapter's work.

To begin with, here there was no danger of spoiling the poetic tone, as there was in *Francesca da Rimini* because of the contraposition of that tragedy's vast scenes. *La Nave* is a vast seething, leavened mass, in which it is possible to pour back in whatever boils over; it is also possible to carve and stir up because the matter doesn't change.

Also, the snare in which the Poet was caught in the *Figlia di Jorio* was absent here, the risk of changing the substance of the poem, perverting its nature. *La Nave* is in fact a vast symphony of choreographic and colouristic motifs, a curious mixture of choral and sexual elements, a sometimes hybrid and sacrilegious mutual contamination of materials of opposite natures: the libretto is the same.

Furthermore, the action is speeded up and made immediate, the tone is further emphasized, the awkward bombastic encumbrance that at times gives the scene a baroque dullness has been removed. Above all, there is a huge advantage: having eliminated that alleged ideal motif of hymning the origins [of Venice] (which is used only as a pretext, as we saw, not resolved in poetry), the tragedy can breathe freed from that premise, which was supposed to determine it and instead was oppressing it, and can progress in a more agile, swift fashion. Actually, in the libretto, there *are* allusions to the origins and to the Fate of lust and violence in those origins, but all this becomes one of the D'Annunzian motifs, equal rather than dominant among the structural motifs of the tragedy.

This could have happened spontaneously when *La Nave* was adapted as a libretto, yet the adapter's merit is noteworthy because of the means he employed.

First, by cutting the few appearances of the figure of Ema, the artificial contrast between her and Basiliola is avoided.[1] This was a useless contrast as neither of the two women rose to an

---

[1] For Ema, and her original significance in the play, see below, pp. 320–21

ideal of human femininity. Then, through the shortening of the characters' speeches, the words acquire a clearer correspondence and even succeed in creating a semblance of those feelings in the souls of those who pronounce them that we were not able to sense before.

The definition of the scenes, as well as their breadth, suits the melodrama well, while the choreographic magnificence, controlled and balanced, lends itself very well to representation in so-called lyric music.

Let's turn to the composer now, Italo Montemezzi. Here is another to whom the title of Wagnerian was rightly applied. This charge could seem justified when *L'Amore dei tre re* appeared, because that opera revealed a remarkable thematic 'liking' for the final (*ultimo*) Wagner, that of *Tristan and Isolde*; certain characteristic orchestral procedures and a generically very similar structuring gave weight to such matching which therefore found its raison d'être. Anyway, in *L'Amore dei tre re* Montemezzi gave us a noteworthy theatrical expression and its success was due not only to the external qualities of the opera, but depended on the intimate atmosphere, quiet and lyrical, of the drama.

With *La Nave* there is a clear decline; here Montemezzi shows he has irremediably started on his way down, having said, in the artistic field, the only word he was allowed to say. And indeed nobody would say, looking at the score, that *La Nave* is later than *L'Amore dei tre re*.

His intentions are serious, yet with good intentions ... Montemezzi tries to express the D'Annunzian phantasmagoria of scenes; however, not having a very strong personality, it is not clear what concept he is following as he attempts to put into practice his integrating function as an artist, and the concept of art alone doesn't support his flight, because there is not much art in *La Nave*.

His conscientiousness (*impegno*) is remarkable, and this quality of his was recognized as early as 1905. 'His music is free from commonplaces, averse to vulgarities, made on the contrary with a constant clarity of views, nobility of intentions and skilful mastery of forms.'[1] After thirty years these words have a far more limited importance, yet they contain a kernel of truth.

It is that this type of music, which critics usually qualify with the generic adjective 'noteworthy' (*notevole*), is already sentenced to death at the moment of its birth. Having been composed before the Great War and structured with substantial lyrical qualities, *L'Amore dei tre re* is still alive; at a distance of only eighteen years[2] from its first appearance, *La Nave* could no longer be staged.

Montemezzi does not possess a very broad melodic breadth, and since he wants to feed on melody, and we mean the traditional opera house melody, he constantly resorts to progressions, especially ascending ones, which seem to confer broadness on the musical discourse, although it is completely artificial. You realise this immediately by analysing the initial pages of the opera and by discovering how meagre (*esigua*) the source is from which the composer attempts to make his creation gush forth and which he uses to create the atmosphere of the Prologue: it is a modest pattern of sextuplets and below that, in syncopation, three chromatic notes. And the limited nature of the 'material' cannot be concealed in the development work. A similar remark ought to be made on each scene, for they all reveal a preoccupation with construction that does not, however, manage to achieve positive results.

Equally, the rhythmical part is very poor: dotted quavers followed by semiquavers, in a progression or repeated on the same

---

1 The quotation is from a review of *Giovanni Gallurese* in *La Stampa*, 29 January 1905. The relevant passage was included in the pamphlet Casa Ricordi published in 1933 to promote interest in Montemezzi's music and it is reasonable to suppose that Tomelleri quoted it from that.

2 This is what we wrote in 1936-XIV

chord, and vaguely alternated patterns of triplets. The recitative then, aiming at bringing out the conclusive accent of the vocal phrase, reverts to an old trick, the descending appoggiatura on the tonic. Certain vocal cadences in this opera are so old-fashioned! However, the adherence to the text (here, too, as a preoccupation and not as an achievement) is remarkable indeed, and there are thus no jarring discords (*stonatura*) between the stage and the orchestral tones.

As you can see, it is really a matter of energy, in the Greek meaning of the word:[1] Montemezzi lacked the force to give life to a musical organism capable of its own and independent life.

---

1 The Greek word *energeia* was used by Aristotle to refer to a state of being in which a thing is actively itself; it is often translated as 'activity.'

Title-page of the First Edition of
D'Annunzio's Play (1908)

3. Raffaele Mellace, *Chigiana*, 2008.[1]

The Art of Seduction: Basiliola (and Montemezzi's Orchestra) on D'Annunzio's *Nave*

THE NAVIGATION of *La Nave* was not easy. At the beginning, a sharp critic, Giannotto Bastianelli, received it with suspicion. On 23 December 1918, reviewing the opera's premiere for the *Nazione*, he acknowledged Montemezzi as 'a seeker of his own ways on the very worn-out floorboards of the Italian music stage,' but complained that the opera

> has not offered me that new formula which for a long time we have been eagerly looking for from Italian composers – by now dissatisfied with the provincial formulae (but still how genuinely national, here and there) of the Mascagnian and Puccinian opera. [...] It is always the now outdated attitude of Wagnerian-Romantic-Germanic derivation, even though, as in the case of Montemezzi, the attitude may have developed in a personal and independent fashion, that is, without him wishing to coincide with the latest manifestations of the radiant attitude of Strauss. Who, when hearing the sadistic tortuosities of the music of the second act of *La Nave* – in my opinion, perhaps the most beautiful of the three – doesn't recall the second movement of *Heldenleben* by Strauss? And it is curious to notice how the poetry of D'Annunzio doesn't disdain this reminiscence.

---

[1] This is a shortened and retitled version of the article, prepared by Professor Mellace.

Indeed, Strauss and D'Annunzio have the same Nietzschean basis as the foundation of their erotic morals, don't they?

Later he will define *La Nave* in trenchant terms as 'a skilful and heavy *ragù* prepared by a cook short of arguments.'[1]

Bastianelli's condemnation, however, does not do justice to a thought out and tenaciously pursued project which led to a wholly musical realization of the tragedy for which Pizzetti had composed, ten years earlier, incidental music.[2] The opera offers numerous interesting aspects in its genesis, in the relationship between the drama and libretto, and in the music conveyed by the imposing autograph score, still unpublished.[3]

1. The launch of the *Nave*

Between 1904 and 1907, Gabriele d'Annunzio, who with Giovanni Pascoli was the leading Italian poet of his generation, wrote the tragedy *La Nave*, which was staged at the Teatro Argentina, Rome, on 11 January 1908. Tito Ricordi, the publisher, who had successfully adapted *Francesca da Rimini*, another D'Annunzian tragedy, for an opera composed by Zandonai (Turin, 19 February 1914), planned to adapt *La Nave* too, and to entrust it to another thoroughbred horse from his stable – the same Montemezzi whose *L'Amore dei tre re* had been brought out at La Scala in 1913, and successfully repeated at the

---

1 Giannotto Bastianelli, *Il nuovo dio della musica*, ed. Marcello De Angelis (Turin: Einaudi, 1978), 163.

2 See Cesare Orselli, 'Primo incontro di Pizzetti con l'estetismo dannunziano: le musiche per "La Nave,"' *Chigiana* 37 (1980), 52–62.

3 The following documents are preserved in the Ricordi Archive in Milan: the autograph score in four volumes, the vocal score by Giuseppe Ramella, the sketches and figurines for the properties and costumes for the La Scala premiere, sixty autograph letters by Montemezzi, as well as the correspondence sent to the latter and to D'Annunzio by Casa Ricordi.

Metropolitan, New York, on 2 January 1914 under Toscanini. Meanwhile, Europe and Italy were entering the Great War: the conflict would strongly condition each phase of the project, culminating in the involuntary mark left by the concomitance of the opera's premiere at La Scala on 3 November 1918 with the Italian victory, announced in the opera house during the performance, amid the jubilation of the audience.[1]

On 14 April 1915 D'Annunzio gave his assent to Tito, who one week later sent him the adaptation of the tragedy:

> [...] first of all, I want to tell you how happy I am that you have accepted the collaboration of Montemezzi: I deeply trust this maestro, and you will see that this time too – my truffle dog nose won't betray me.

On 13 July 1917 the contract with Montemezzi was registered; on 15 December the composer had completed the 'First Episode'; on 13 April 1918 Tito informed Montemezzi of the possibility of a performance at La Scala in the autumn; on 18 April the 'Second Episode' was ready; on 29 May 'it's a matter of a few days'; fifteen days later Montemezzi added at the end of the 'Third Episode' the note: 'The end of La Nave. Vigasio 13 June 1918.' Four days later, it was announced that at La Scala 'they received with great fervour our proposal to stage "La Nave."' Encouraged by this juicy opportunity, on the night of 27 July the composer erupted from Verona with 'I've finished!,' shamelessly exulting in 'having at last taken my Ship into port with an uncommon courage.'

La Nave arrived at her début under the spur of very different motivations for the publisher-librettist and the composer, through

---

[1] It was the last premiere of an opera based on a drama by D'Annunzio to be performed in the poet's lifetime. *La Nave* was staged under the direction of Tullio Serafin (a former classmate of Montemezzi at the Milan Conservatory), who strongly wanted to produce the work. There were ten performances.

a heated dialectics documented in the letters. Montemezzi was motivated by open patriotic exaltation. On 23 June 1917 he wrote:

> <u>The Launch is done!</u> The heroes who go to redeem our Sea carry the echo of a wonderful exaltation. They go confidently, the strong men, to mark the dominion that is due to <u>our great hope</u>. 'The wind has the scent of fortune.' I can smell it. The prophetic Canticle of our victory on the Venetian Sea will spread all over the world, and carry a sign of our new self-assurance.

And again, to D'Annunzio, on 9 October:

> My powers of artistic expression are at their zenith, and in this work I am certainly saying an Italian word that has no precedent. God grants me the fortune of giving to my homeland, in time, a worthy contribution: a new and vigorous breath that will animate this new race; a force that does not desist from willing; a beauty made more beautiful by the love that exalts us, by the pleasure of giving.[1]

On 7 March 1918 he defined the opera as 'almost a rite of the victorious homeland if it is performed after the war.'

These statements do not lack an element of personal interest. The composition was linked to the hope of obtaining an exemption, or at least a long leave, from military service. In the spring of 1917, thanks to D'Annunzio, Montemezzi obtained the longed-for leave, and at its expiration he reminded the poet

---

[1] Adriano Bassi (ed.), *Caro Maestro (D'Annunzio e i Musicisti)* (Genova: De Ferrari, 1918), 103.

of the pressing need for 'a leave in my favour, longer than that I have already enjoyed, which was for three months' in order to devote himself to the 'important work of orchestration.'[1] He would write to D'Annunzio again several times; on 9 October, on the eve of the ruinous rout of Caporetto, he went dramatically beyond his previously expressed requests:

> My dear Maestro, I beg you with all my power to tell me whether I can obtain that exemption that you made me hope for. [...] I ask you one more favour: write to Generale Bompiani and obtain from him my complete freedom, not in the form of an exemption [...], but to be dispensed from the office.[2]

When he had overcome the contingent wartime problem, *La Nave* assumed for Montemezzi an absolute value as the synthesis of patriotic sentiment and desire for personal affirmation. On 18 April 1918:

> We shall transform our opera of propaganda into a ritual celebration for our victorious Homeland. [...] I saw the Costanzi theatre in Rome sold out; a bit of attraction by some good performers was enough. There are a lot of people everywhere and they are not at all averse to withdrawing sometimes from the nightmare of the war. And our work will have a much greater appeal and less scruples for the audience, who will watch an opera pervaded with desire for national claims.

Montemezzi strongly desired a Roman staging; he longs for 'a

---

1 Ibid. 100.

2 Ibid. 103.

big occasion' for its premiere; he was offended when, in 1919, the Teatro Filarmonico in Verona preferred *Francesca* by Zandonai to his opera; the same year he tried to involve D'Annunzio in the project of a 'grand representation' in Venice, 'no less than in Saint Mark's Square';[1] he swallowed the wreck of those projects without surrendering for long to 'an injustice that for 12 years has been taking my breath away,' as he wrote to D'Annunzio as late as 1933.[2] Even the advent of Fascism seemed to him a good opportunity to put *La Nave* back in the water (Montemezzi sent a total of 22 letters to Mussolini and members of the government), and he failed to notice the contradiction between the fascist ideology and the decadentism of his opera.[3]

For publisher-librettist Tito Ricordi, by contrast, *La Nave* was first of all a well-considered entrepreneurial project. Only a week after D'Annunzio had consented to the adaptation, he was ready to send him the libretto, obviously outlined for quite a long time and probably finished with breathless haste:

> And now I must make myself very small and humble [...] to confess to you, with no little trepidation, that the ruin already carried out by me on the divinely beautiful body of your Francesca I dared repeat on the strong and majestic construction of your ship – and that the work I have done is rough-hewn, for I worked worse than a Barbarian, worse than an Iconoclast!! [...] For quite a long time I had been thinking about La Nave as a libretto, but every time I set about the adaptation I

---

1 Ibid. 105.

2 Ibid. 110.

3 See Fiamma Nicolodi, *Musica e Musicisti nel Ventennio Fascista* (Fiesole: Discanto, 1984), 412–426.

was dismayed at the difficulties that appeared before me and abandoned the idea of getting through it. Now, in this hour of hard trial for our homeland, of tension in hearts and nerves all turned to the East, of expectation for the new destinies of Italy, perhaps my enthusiasm made up for my incompetence ... and I have mistreated your great Nave!!

On 9 April he had expressed his opinion about Montemezzi to D'Annunzio in these terms:

> the composer I'm proposing to you for '*La Nave*' won't be an innovator, won't be able to go back to the pure sources of our ancient music (!!) [an allusion, not without irony, to Pizzetti], but he will write good music that will please the audience – quod est in votis.[1]

At that time Montemezzi didn't yet know what the situation was; as late as 27 April he was ignorant of D'Annunzio's response. The very graphics of the libretto drastically reduce the contribution of the composer, with the frontispiece attributing the main responsibility for the opera to D'Annunzio: 'LA NAVE / TRAGEDY IN A PROLOGUE AND THREE EPISODES / BY / GABRIELE D'ANNUNZIO / ADAPTED BY / TITO RICORDI / FOR THE MUSIC BY / ITALO MONTEMEZZI.' The same thing had happened in the case of Zandonai's *Francesca*, and indeed Montemezzi's *L'Amore dei tre re*.

'My dearest Gabriele, I hope and wish that you will still want to entrust this work of yours to my publishing House and to me. You'll see that both of us will make a good deal' – so Tito to D'Annunzio on 9 April. In the foreground here is the relationship between the poet and the publisher / adapter, with a view

---

[1] I.e 'this is exactly what we want' (ed.).

to a commercial success: composer and patriotic aspirations are of secondary importance. Emblematic of this is the resolute snip with which Tito made a clean sweep of the proclamation about Venetian freedom pronounced by Marco Gràtico in the large choral scene that ends the Prologue. Tito must have meant to dampen the patriotic potential of the opera in order to make it independent of its historical contingence and suitable for the international market. Very revealing in this respect is the matter of the dedication of the score, which Montemezzi wrote about in detail on 29 January 1919:

> … the dedication is important with regard to my feelings. La Nave was composed in the atmosphere of war, with the vision of victory; and it was the enthusiasm for my Homeland which armed me with the courage necessary to be able to take upon myself such a big task. It is precisely to my Homeland that La Nave is dedicated. It [the dedication] should be placed on the first page beside the photograph. It should occupy the whole page. The type (in gold, if possible) should be large and bold and with ornaments. It must be an artistic thing. Like this:
>
> TO
MY
HOMELAND
>
> and nothing else. Then, in my opinion, on the page after the photograph I would deem it appropriate to put: <u>Performed for the first time at La Scala on the day of 3 November 1918.</u> The date of the capture of Trieste and Trento deserves this. Communicate this, please, to Signor Tito.

'Signor Tito' totally ignored the fervent wish of the composer.

2. From the tragedy to the opera

Tito Ricordi was responsible for the adaptation of *La Nave* as a libretto, though there were occasional interventions by Montemezzi, from half the verses of a chorus of Sailors in the Prologue to some changes in the agitated finale of the opera, where Montemezzi enlarged the role of Marco Gràtico and rewrote in part some omitted stage directions. The intrusions by the composer provoked tensions that on 4 August 1918 Montemezzi decided to appease, without renouncing his own artistic freedom, in a sorrowful letter to Ricordi:

> Dearest and illustrious Commendatore. [...] I perfectly understood your disappointment. But who ever thought of giving you the awful nuisance of coordinating in hendecasyllables, for example, all those invectives between Zealots and Revellers, of the Prisoners' expressions of glorification of the people, or of a few verses that for musical needs I had to omit or add? I certainly didn't. This bother was my duty and I kept it for myself immediately after finishing the orchestration of the opera in order to send it to you, exactly as I did, together with the last sheets of the score. My composition corresponds almost perfectly to the book [I] sent to you. I'm saying 'almost,' but only in very rare moments is it not identical. But I cannot for this reason be reprimanded as being disrespectful, nor for having little agility as an intellectual. [...] Whoever reads the libretto should notice the accuracy, the harmony and, in short, the

merit of its creator. It is for this reason that I submit to you those things that I have added for my musical needs (that are very few, in relation to the work) and coordinated, so that you, with your skillfulness, can intervene if any metrical stress, or anything else, if there is any, which doesn't work properly, needs to be corrected. But my score must remain unchanged. It was created and thoroughly considered with extraordinary passion and I am fully confident that it is a worthy opera. If some stage directions were, in the score, moved to a different position, there was always a reason for it. Please, look into the score and this will be made clear. Clausetti[1] mentioned some added words that are not in the tragedy. There is not one. He mentioned the absence of the women in the company of the Agape Revellers. This wasn't done without a reason. [...] Please, have a look at the final stage direction that I have added at the end of the 3rd episode when Basiliola is taken onto the Ship; always in relation to the grandiose and solemn musical moment and also to the position of the Ship placed slanting from her stern to her bow. You will find a wonderful new conclusion at the end of the Prologue. [...] [I hope] that this brightens up that atmosphere charged with electricity that had wrongly become thick whereas calmness and serenity of spirit should be the beacons that guide the Sailors to the port.

The adaptation, that the composer liked from the beginning (on 21 October 1916 he exulted: 'I am here in my hermitage

---

1 Carlo Clausetti (1869–1943), the manager of Casa Ricordi (ed.).

totally concentrated on the 2nd episode. It is splendid! Here the concise drama stands out and with extraordinary violence'), was a sophisticated work carried out by means of a skilful rewriting of the text, bold sewing up, and metrical ingeniousness. The massive cuts reveal a precise sense of the subtractive process. The tendency to simplify the text is not a simple shortening, but involves far more profound implications. Some interventions appear indicative:

a) The drastic screening, from the beginning, of historical, political and geographical references. The cuts include the erudite interventions of the Pilot Lucio Polo, who had quoted Belisarius, Justinian, Attila, the Franks, the Goths and the Greeks, and references to the Venetian-Friulian hydrography, from the Isonzo [Soča] to the Tagliamento, from the Anfora Canal to the Livenza.

b) The dismantlement of the sophisticated system of contrasting choruses, symbolic of the clash between Christianity and paganism. Already in the Prologue the Chorus of the *Nàumachi* (sea warriors), whose solemn intonation of the hymn *Ave maris stella* is interrupted by the perturbing apparition of Basiliola, is dropped. In the 'First' and 'Second Episodes' a whole series of choral sections were amputated. In the 'First Episode' the chorus of the faithful coming 'from the Basilica, from the Catecumenio (the area for the novices), [and] from the Oratories' and the simultaneous 'opposing laud that the women of Basiliola sing' to Diona were cut. D'Annunzio had conceived this polychoral episode as a symphony of the sounds of nature, with diverse sacred songs and the moans of the dying prisoners finished off by Basiliola's arrows. Similarly, in the 'Second Episode' the opening exchange between Christian and pagan choruses, based on the antiphonal dialogue, with the conflagration between the names of Mary and Diona, was dropped. Tito decided that the clash between civilizations was insufficiently interesting in an opera house.

c) A further consequence of (b): the anti-archaizing, anti-Pizzetti aesthetic choice that deliberately ignored D'Annunzio's original musical conception of these episodes, which abound in quotations from medieval Christian and pagan hymnology. Many of Tito's cuts seek to establish a modern melodramatic structure focussed on the main protagonists.

d) The relegation of secondary characters in order to foreground Basiliola and Marco Gràtico (soprano and tenor) as the only protagonists of the opera, with a scenic and vocal weight much superior to the other roles. A corollary of extraordinary importance was that even though he substantially retained the plethoric male cast, Tito eliminated the only other, indispensable female character: Ema, mother of the Gràtici. The consequences were important: many fundamental disputes and every reference to the sacrilegious matricide impending over the Gràtici disappeared. The perverse Basiliola, 'a super female, half Salome and half Elektra,'[1]

---

[1] Adriana Guarnieri Corazzol, *Musica e letteratura in Italia tra Ottocento e Novecento* (Milan: Sansoni, 2000), 278.

was deprived of a contrast with a perfectly antithetic antagonist, and confined to the loneliness that she shares with another *femme fatale*: Fiora in *L'Amore dei tre re*.

e) Without Ema, the physiognomy of Basiliola is transformed, for she is no longer involved in disputes with characters of a high moral stature. Her clash with the hermit Traba in the 'First Episode' was drastically cut. Moreover, the important reference to the woman's madness is completely concealed. Most of all, the demoniac connotations of the Faledra are stripped away and the character's immorality is flattened down into a generic nymphomania tinged with sadism: something that Tito took care to make more acceptable, by eliminating the more daring cues and stage directions, along with the whole of Traba's very violent invective before Basiliola when she strips. Thus the libretto reproduces the image of the perverse seducer like *Salome*, known to Italian drama since the late nineteenth century.

f) The final notable alteration is the change in the finale. Basiliola, in the tragedy, dies the death she chooses, with a final jump of self-determination that confirms her indomitable character:

> *The sailors advance, lifting and joining their large rectangular shields. Standing, in spite of the servile restraint, erect with all the tyranny of her beauty, the Faledra tosses her mane [...] Behind her, the expiatory fire burns on the altar of the sea warriors. At her first word, every din, every clamour ceases. A*

> *fateful pause hangs over the people.*
>
> *Basiliola: Gràtico, hear me. Just as I didn't belong to others / but only to those I wanted to give myself to, / so − for the august altar and for the two / wings of the great Archangel! − I don't belong / to any death but which I choose. / [...] / Hear me, hero, for the seven Pleiades! / If I couldn't mint my face / in the gold of Rome, well, watch, / I imprint it in the fire.*
>
> *She suddenly turns, throws herself on the altar, with mouth stretched out so as to drink the flame; she is similar, in the happiness of her action, to the thirsty man who plunges all his body in the pool to take a longer draught. The flame sets fire to her hair, which blazes in a second like a bundle of stubble, with a bright flash.*[1]

Tito chose a different finale, not less spectacular, but easier to realize: the 'beautiful death' that Marco Gràtico had originally imagined for Basiliola. The speech quoted above was dropped, and the stage direction was reformulated:

> *The people take the Faledra, violently drag her to the Ship, raise her to the still unadorned bow and nail her there ...*

From the autograph score it appears that Montemezzi planned to supplement Tito's stage directions with inserts derived from the tragedy, but there is no longer any sign of them in the

---

[1] *La Nave* (Milan: Treves, 1908), 244–45.

printed score.

All in all, Tito Ricordi's operation resulted in a marked reduction of the ideological power of the tragedy, through the defusing of the plentiful historical references and of the religious and cultural conflicts underlying the narrative. The drama is thus reduced to a hedonistic horizon, to an irrational immanence that exploits the decadent potential of D'Annunzio's writing. The 'Second Episode' is exemplary in this respect, for there the clash between civilizations is brought back to the individualistic dimension of early twentieth century opera. With its foolish patriotic ambitions and erudite apparatus muted or invisible, the tragedy that D'Annunzio had 'moulded with the slime of the lagoon and with the gold of Byzantium, and with the breath of my most ardent Italic passion'[1] reached the opera stage reduced to a 'theatre of violence,' dominated by mysterious forces and a wild humanity. Italy's most important music publisher deemed this formula more desirable for a La Scala audience in 1918.

3. Colours and voices in Montemezzi's music

In navigating the imposing melodrama (*drammone*), Montemezzi made some fundamental choices. First of all, he relied even more strongly on an approach already revealed in *L'Amore dei tre re*: the extraordinary variety and mobility of conflicting attitudes and situations, the marked penchant for the transition from one atmosphere to another diametrically opposed, keeping the spectator's attention enthralled through mechanisms based on contrast and surprise. Thus Montemezzi juxtaposed sequences with heterogeneous dramatic hues, trusting to this technique to maintain a continuous tension in the score. Consider, as an example, the important instrumental interlude

---

[1] 'Il secondo amante di Lucrezia Buti' in D'Annunzio, *Prose di ricerca, di lotta, di comando [...]* 2 (Milan: Mondadori, 1950), 395.

that prepares, after an agonizing wait, for the appearance of Basiliola. This moment is fundamental for the action, and also for the character, as she becomes aware of the blinding of her brothers (Prologue, n. 29): Basiliola 'looks around, hesitating and anxious. She stops before the miserable pile. She drops her father's hand. The horror turns her pale. But her strength, after an atrocious pause, prevails over her trembling.' Not without subtleties, the orchestra makes itself responsible for the stirring of contrasting feelings – emotion, fear, anger, pride – in the character of Basiliola, by attacking with a terrifying *fortissimo* played by the full orchestra, that soon leaves space for the more transparent voices of solo violas and basses (in *fortepiano*), immediately chased closely, however, by a *crescendo* of the tympani that leads to the exposition of an homophonic theme played by upper strings and woodwinds over *fortissimo* brass chords.

Generally, there is a prevalence of an attitude that is often grandiose: it is a magniloquence that is innate to the D'Annunzian tragedy, despite the interventions by Ricordi. In the 'Third Episode,' in the dialogue between Marco Gràtico, some secondary characters and the People, who are applauding the launch of the ship, the *Sostenuto* in *fortissimo* acquires more agitation while various characters volunteer to be part of the crew, arousing the enthusiastic reaction of the chorus. While preserving a *fortissimo* dynamics, the passage becomes increasingly animated and then acquires a more composed solemnity for the selection of the final sailors, under the auspices of the eternal name of Rome, culminating in the people's blessing when the six part chorus enters loudly, shouting 'Glory to the chosen!,' a textual insert introduced by Montemezzi to crown the episode. The voice sings long notes, the full orchestra plays, the tympani roll, while on stage eight *buccine* join in to double the vocal melody.

However, the focus on patriotism does not silence the other voice in the score, perhaps that of greatest value: the triumph of *decadence*. To this end, Montemezzi displays the talent of an expert orchestrator, capable of endless refinements and with an intelligently pursued strategy. Often the clangour of the late-romantic orchestra disappears in very transparent writing, as happens, programmatically, even before the curtain is raised. Indeed, the orchestral prelude to the Prologue proposes a wavy pattern with sextuplets in the first violins playing *piano*, that leaves strings, winds and harp in the background. When the curtain is raised, the sextuplet figuration continues, with harp and celesta to add some colour, while the Voice of the Boatswain is sustained by a discreet little choir of woodwinds. The terrible tragedy of the Gràtici appears therefore immersed in a glaucous, luminescent landscape, an evocation of the waves of the Adriatic from which the action emerges. And all this is independent of any scenic indication: D'Annunzio, by contrast, had opened his drama by emphasizing the brisk industriousness of a shipyard in a completely urbanized landscape. Is it possible that Montemezzi recalled another opera opened by a similar movement of liquid sextuplets symbolizing the waters from which the story emerges? Anyway, the contiguity, whether intentional or accidental, with the motive of the waves from the prelude to *Das Rheingold* reveals in Montemezzi a tendency to plan that is capable of expressing itself independently from the illustrious text, and seeks to characterize each dramatic situation musically. The colour of the beginning is symmetrically proposed again at the opening of the final episode, that takes up those substantially identical initial eight bars of the Prologue that suggested the Adriatic = Rhine equation, starting a delicate symphonic-choral scene with an auroral timbre, where the orchestra replies *alternatim* to the Catechumens' (novices') morning hymn sung by an *a cappella* four voice choir. In the first numbers of the score, the orchestral intervention at n. 2 is especially suggestive (strings, woodwinds, horns, harp, celesta and a small bell offstage), and has as its phonic contrast the choral strophe 'Ut pio Regis pariter canentis' with full orchestra (n. 3), that gives way to a trembling and gentle orchestration (n. 4). The stage direction 'The warning is lost in the whitening sky,' evocative of the lyrical atmosphere of the collection of poems *Alcyone*, finds a consistent *pendant* in Montemezzi's orchestration and is a perfect comment on the musical scene that acts as a frame to the episode of the launch of the Ship.

It is in such shoals, which are not rare, where the martial uproar of the score dissolves, that the most authentic merits in Montemezzi's writing should probably be identified, in line with that lyrical vocation expressed in *L'Amore dei tre re* (for example, in the Flora-Avito duet at the heart of the Second Act). In *La Nave*, Basiliola's scene of seduction in the 'Third Episode' is exemplary: coming immediately after the heroic tone that prevails in the passage where the crew is selected, the audience is suddenly exposed to this irruption from the Faledra, who is desperate, yet determined to claim her own dignity: 'O Gratico, remember me. / Bound to this altar!' Starting from the *captatio benevolentiae*[1] used by the poet in 'By my kiss / of love and hatred' (n. 19), Montemezzi's orchestra begins a noticeable *rallentando molto* (slowing down), accompanying the long monologue of the protagonist always with a *dolce, espressiva, dolcissima* (*sweet, expressive, very sweet*) intention.

These are subtleties of the orchestrator that exalt the effective lyricism of the singing line; this quality never fails Basiliola, who is clever at taking advantage of Marco Gràtico's memory of a conflictual and charming erotic relationship, as well as his greed for glory and power (numbers 20–26). Her seduction will work, even more so, when coupled with important scenic gestures, as happens in conjunction with the acme of sensuality in the drama when, in the 'First Episode,' Basiliola drops her tunic and remains bare breasted, in an attitude of challenge to the Traba monk and of seduction to Marco Gràtico. Introduced by the

---

[1] An attempt to win goodwill – a term used in rhetoric (ed.).

elated laughter of the 'temptress,' and characterized by a remarkable phonic violence, that gesture is followed by an episode with a very different tone: while Basiliola 'takes off her refulgent belt and starts to bend down' (n. 24), the orchestra embroiders a very delicate page, entrusted to a *solo* violin, *dolce espressivo*, then to a viola, accompanied only by the strings.

The orchestration is therefore one of the strong points of a score where opportunities for independent symphonic pages are rare, and largely restricted to the preludes to each episode (Verdi would have appreciated this loyalty to the tradition of nineteenth-century Italian opera). Apart from these there are only concise symphonic interludes, like those accompanying the entry of Orso Faledro and Basiliola in the Prologue (numbers 19 and 29). The long instrumental page that precedes the landing of the Gràtici is more noteworthy (Prologue, n. 41). Towards the end of this interlude, eight *buccine* resound from behind the scenes; they have a strong presence in the final episode, and are the most eccentric aspect of the orchestration, characterizing the magniloquent aspect of the score, just as the cello represents, especially in the 'First Episode,' its lyrical soul, and is entrusted with the exposition of the themes of greater moment: for example in the symphonic prelude to the 'First Episode' where the cellos propose an *espressivo e forte* melody. It is the theme of seduction, which will prove critical in the whole episode (for example, during the very long duet between Marco Gràtico and Basiliola at n. 36). A few pages later, the cello will follow Basiliola's intervention like her shadow (n. 6); finally, a cello *solo* will accompany the final prayer of the Survivor that the Faledra run him through (n. 17), and it will be heard again when Basiliola has fulfilled the dying man's wish (n. 19).

On the other hand, Montemezzi does not disregard the use of a thematic planning, even if this aspect of the score remains relatively undeveloped. The motive 'of the seduction' expounded by the cellos is the key thematic signature tune of the whole opera, the musical symbol of the Faledra. Expounded by her father, Orso Faledro, in the Prologue (n. 24), it consists of: 1) two starting notes, 2) a large leap onto a long sustained note, 3) the descent to a lower grade. Its pattern corresponds to the intonation of the name 'Ba-si-liò-la'; it conforms to the name of the seducer as the symbol of her identity; it synthetically records her unbounded ambition, her irresistible charm and her uncontrolled irrational tension; finally, it comes to identify itself with the name 'Aquileia,' the fatal homeland of Basiliola. It is no accident that she will shout its name, in the last bars of the 'Second Episode,' right over the notes of this unmistakable melodic gesture. On the lips of the Faledra, as well as on those of the other characters, stated in several versions, it returns at every dramatic junction of capital importance: played by the cellos at the opening of the 'First Episode'; thrown down with scorn, like a gauntlet, by Basiliola to the Traba Monk ('First Episode,' 'Come over here, if you dare, man of God,' n. 23), employed obsessively in the course of the dramatic duet between Basiliola and Marco Gràtico in the 'Third Episode,' when it is used both by the Faledra to induce her lover to take her on the Ship, and by Gràtico himself, who is almost infected by it (numbers 21–24). The passionate lyricism of this leading motive contrasts with the overall orientation of the vocal style of *La Nave*, which has an undoubtedly opposite tendency. Indeed, there dominates a vocal style, of verist derivation, that goes in the direction of an omnipresent *declamato*, sometimes flaring up in lyrical fervour, sometimes bowing down in modest tones.

Within the variety of these tones, Montemezzi reaffirmed his commitment to a dramaturgic-musical project realized 'with an extraordinary passion,' worthy of critical attention and revival today, almost a century after the first launch of *La Nave*.

Montemerri

Gabriele d'Annunzio

www.ingramcontent.com/pod-product-compliance
Lightning Source LLC
Chambersburg PA
CBHW032100090426
42743CB00007B/180